SURUCHI MO... an award ...
high tech and business news f...
D... Group Publications throughou...
appeared in numerous magazines inc...
Music is her first work of fiction.

Suruchi holds an M.S. in Journalism and
San Jose State University. She earned her .... music from
Bhatkhande Sangeet Mahavidyalaya, in Lucknow, and her M.A. in
English from Lucknow University. She lives in Northern California
with her family.

How to Order

This book is also available on special quantity discounts.from the publisher
Orient Paperbacks, 5A/8 First Floor, Ansari Road, Darya Ganj, New Delhi-110 002
Tel: +91-11-2327 8877, Fax: +91-11-2327 8879 email: books@orientpaperbacks.com

DIVINE MUSIC
SURUCHI MOHAN

A NOVEL

Orient
Publishing

DELHI | MUMBAI | HYDERABAD

In Memory of
My father, who taught me to
carry my 'own head on {my} shoulders'

To
my mother, who pointed out numerous ways
society slights its women

www.orientpublishing.com

ISBN 13: 978-81-222-0472-8
ISBN 10: 81-222-0472-4

1st Published in Orient Publishing 2010

Divine Music

© 2009 Suruchi Mohan

Cover Design by Arati Devasher
www.aratidevasher.com

Published in arrangement with
Bayeux Arts Inc., Canada

Published by
Orient Publishing
(A division of Vision Books Pvt. Ltd.)
5A/8 Ansari Road, New Delhi-110 002

Printed in India at
Saurabh Printers Pvt. Ltd., Noida

Cover Printed at
Ravindra Printing Press, Delhi-110 006

To my readers

Indian scale: *sa re ga ma pa dha ni*
Western scale: *do re me fa sol la ti*

In India, often when an artist composes a raga or a melody or a piece of poetry, she asks the audience for permission to present. I have tried to create the beauty of North Indian or Hindustani classical music through words. In thus expressing the inexpressible I have used, in addition to my own imagination, stories that have come down to me from my gurus and some that swirled around the music world, often turning an idiosyncrasy into legend.

Lucknow, however, is not a legend. It is the capital of Uttar Pradesh, a large, populous state in North India. It is historical in significance and was, until recently, a great cultural center, where poets and writers and musicians gathered to perform to large audiences, often in the bitter cold of the winter months. The language didn't matter: Hindi worked as well as Urdu, dance portrayed emotion as well as song, prose interspersed with poetry. I have used this Lucknow as the setting for my novel.

The music college stands even today. The tomb of Asaf-ud-daulah, Begum Hazrat Mahal Park, Hazratganj with its upscale shops still fill me with nostalgia.

That's where reality ends. My characters are not people I know or have ever met. If in reading you feel a character resembles a person you know, all I can say is that I am honoured you think I have breathed life into fiction.

Now I ask your permission to present.

Acknowledgements

Shenly Glen, Sheila Klein, Teresa Hager, without your patience and encouragement, this book would not have been possible. You read my drafts again and again. You held my hand, when the going got rough. I could not have hoped for a better writers' group.

Sudha Kaul, Andre Neu, for reading early chapters of the novel and listening to me talk endlessly about my ideas.

Dipak Malik, for showing me the idealism of the Indian socialist.

Sukumar da, for taking me inside the world of customs and excise.

Arti and Satya, for reading for accuracy of the businessman's life.

Neeru jiji, Dolly jiji, and Prabhat for urging me to continue on the path without self doubt.

Prologue

The sun slipped momentarily behind the deep grey clouds. Rain seemed a certainty. One could feel it on the arms, from the way the oppressive heat prickled the skin with hundreds of points. The heat was so beastly and the moisture so heavy that clothes and hair clung to sweaty bodies like bark to tree. Not a leaf stirred in the stillness. All of Lucknow waited for the first shower of the monsoon season.

The front lawn of the music school — with its dry and clumpy grass that revealed large patches of cracked light brown mud, occasional colonies of ants, stray yellow wasps buzzing listlessly — was lined with chairs across from a small wooden platform with a white sheet. About a hundred people milled around, waiting. A few mosquitoes hovered over those who styled their hair with scented oils. The mosquitoes would arrive in humming swarms with the rain, forming enormous funnels over oiled heads.

The principal and two teachers stood in readiness. As soon as a white ambassador car came to a screeching halt outside the college gates, they stepped forward and opened the rear door. Together they walked to the lawn and offered their guest a seat in the front row. Sarika remained standing, then, realizing that the principal waited for her to take her seat, sat down unassumingly. The crowd took their seats and a young girl in a white saree came onto the platform with a tanpura and began to sing a prayer. Sarika looked at the large framed picture of Kirana sahib on the makeshift stage. It must have been taken recently, for he had aged from the time she had last seen him, all those years ago when humankind appeared so different to her. Her musical career then had teetered on the verge of death. And now she was invited as a guest of honour, the most prominent living student of the college, to sing at the memorial service of the man who launched her and also caused her near-crash.

So many times she had sat on the grass of this lawn and listened to the chatter of the girls around her as she waited for her rickshawman to come and take her home. That was twenty or so years ago when she had believed that the spiritual and the sensuous were distinct, the divine and the carnal had no common ground, the world was black and white, good and evil, pure and sullied. Where some rose and others fell. And maybe that was still so, but she had begun to understand that in art the boundaries were blurred, that the one could rarely exist without the other. For what made a day whole was both sunlight and darkness.

DIVINE MUSIC

1

Sarika stepped close to the block of ice, her grandma's bed in death. Still dressed in the white petticoat and pink ankle-length housecoat she had worn the night before when Sarika had wished her goodnight, Lakshmi lay so serenely, her baby pink scalp clearly visible through the sparse white hair, her diamond nose stud catching the light of the morning sun, that Sarika softly called out her name. But it caught in a sob at the base of Sarika's throat. A fly hovered around Lakshmi's body, then settled on her nose with audacity. Sarika shooed it away with an angry wave of her arm. It flew away and came right back. Sarika waved it away again and stepped back. A trickle of water flowed from the ice block toward the door that opened onto the verandah.

The mystery of death exerted a powerful force over Sarika. Lakshmi had been so sick for so long that Sarika had accepted her diminished state as normal. But death seemed inconceivable. Even last night when Lakshmi took a turn for the worse, Sarika didn't suspect that the end was so close. Sarika's shoulders shook as she covered her face with her hands and wept. In the distance, she heard the roar of an Indian Airlines aeroplane.

Mr. and Mrs. Sharma from next door arrived. Sarika's father, Ashwini Kumar, greeted them. They stood quietly for a minute, then left their chappals in the verandah and came into the room.

'She has been delivered from her suffering,' said Mr. Sharma, taking Ashwini's right hand in both his own. 'She suffered a lot and bravely. You did what you could, but in the end He,' he said pointing toward the ceiling, 'decides what happens to each of us.'

'She was brave,' said Ashwini. 'She never complained.'

'Will you cremate right away?' asked Mr. Sharma.

'We will take her to the cremation ground around five or six o' clock, after my brother arrives from Bombay,' he said. 'He had gone there on business. He's already on his way.'

Mr. Sharma nodded. He and his wife sat down on a *dhurrie* and started chanting verses in Sanskrit from memory.

Just as a man casts off his worn out clothes and puts on new ones, so also the embodied self casts out its worn out bodies and enters new ones.

Sarika felt an arm around her. Slowly, she dried her eyes with the back of her hand and snuggled closer to her father. His arm tightened around her.

'Her soul has already entered another body,' Ashwini said quietly. 'She was a good lady; her soul will inhabit a good body.'

Sarika listened attentively, letting Ashwini's words sink in. She imagined a baby growing up to be like Lakshmi and wondered where her own soul had been before. Ashwini moved away from Sarika as the Guptas came in. Mr. Gupta took Ashwini's hand and held it. All three stood quietly for a minute.

Weapons cleave It not, fire burns It not, water moistens It not, wind dries It not.

Mr. Gupta sat down, cross legged, straight backed, next to Mr. Sharma, picked up a Gita from the *dhurrie* and joined in the chanting.

Indeed, certain is death for the born and certain is birth for the dead; do not grieve over the inevitable.

As people glided in, Sarika felt self-conscious in her nightdress and disappeared into her room. The chanting continued, filling the air with the sounds of death.

People streamed into the house throughout the day. The house cast a quiet doleful shadow on the street so that even the unaware knew they were entering an area of sadness. By the time they reached the verandah, leaving their leather sandals on the steps, their faces had assumed the demeanour of death. They slipped quietly into the living room and sat where they could find a place — men on one side of the room and women on the other. Kanta, Ashwini's cousin from old Lucknow, had already received word and she came in an old, faded cotton saree, passed through the gate quietly, hurriedly, and threw off her blue bathroom rubber chappals so one fell on the gravel and one on the verandah step, and ran inside. On seeing Nirmala, Sarika's mother, sitting quietly on a *dhurrie*, she rushed over and hugged her, letting out a loud wail. The chanting continued. Nirmala, who had been sitting composed, burst into tears. The two women cried for a few seconds in each other's arms, then freeing themselves from the other's embrace, sniffled and dabbed their eyes. They sat pensively, following the chanting from the *Gita* that lay open before them. As the day warmed, more flies buzzed into the room, finding an easy target in Lakshmi's body. The ice block sent out to the door heavier trickles that soon assumed the volume of little streams. Ramu stood with a giant wooden T-rod, shooing away the flies and trying to mop each stream with an old bath towel.

As Sarika watched, sober thoughts flapped through her mind. What left a human lifeless, as if the electricity had been turned off and the light bulb hung unilluminated? Sarika remembered Lakshmi, their conversations, their moments of closeness. Music and the increasingly powerful feeling of isolation it fostered in Sarika had brought her closer to her grandma. Non-judgmental, Lakshmi accepted Sarika's thoughts about the grownups in the world outside her home as unquestioningly as the cycles of Nature. Lakshmi's keenness took Sarika by surprise. By acknowledging Sarika's growth into womanhood, she had allowed Sarika to see life. She longed for her grandma.

Later, shadows of little plants looked like tall palm trees when Ashwini, his two brothers, and his nephew Pradeep carried Lakshmi out of the house. Lakshmi's daughters-in-law had taken off her clothes and jewelry, dabbed her body with water and prepared her for cremation. Her farewell would be simple since she was a widow. No *shringar*. No vermilion in her hair. No bindi on her forehead. No glass bangles on her forearms. No toerings. Nirmala and her sisters-in-law had draped her in a simple white saree that covered her head. That was all she would get. The block of ice, her bed for almost ten hours, was all but gone. She was ready, laid out on the bamboo stretcher. One by one, the families of the daughters-in-law — not just the wives of Lakshmi's sons but those of her nephews as well — placed a white shawl over the body. A loud male voice rang out *Ram nam satya hai*, shattering the air, already rent with sobs. Other males from the family joined in, producing a haunting, echoing effect that broke all dams of emotion. The pallbearers hoisted the stretcher to their shoulders. Flowers and petals rained on the tethered corpse. The women cried hysterically and ran behind the body. Nirmala let out a low, guttural growl and sat heavily on the driveway. The traffic in the little lane outside the house stopped. Horns and bells stopped honking and chiming as motorists and rickshawmen stood silently, then slowly wended their way past the waiting hearse, the cars, and the funeral party. Lakshmi and her sons were now in the hearse. The men — uncles, cousins, nephews, neighbours — piled into the cars. The women stood by the gate weeping till the tail lights of the last car disappeared. The neighbours then gently led the family members inside.

The men would come home after midnight when the body had burned completely, returning the next day to collect the ashes and disperse them in the Ganga fifty miles away. The quiet living room felt desolate. The servants had removed what remained of the ice, but despite all the mopping, water oozed from the mosaic floor, strewn with flowers and petals. A stray leather sandal had made its way into the room from the verandah. On the wall, the pictures of London-by-the-Thames looked incongruous.

Kanta set the daughters-in-law to work cleaning, telling them to use an old rag to sweep up the flowers and keep them carefully in a plate or a bowl near a picture of Lakshmi. Sarika stood forlornly, then moved to join the women.

'No,' said Kanta, showing her great, protuberant teeth. 'You can't do this.'

'Why?' asked Sarika.

'It is not for girls,' said Kanta, taken aback at being questioned. 'Only the daughters-in-law do it.'

'Who makes these rules?' asked Sarika, ire rising through the grief. 'Shouldn't it be about feeling rather than custom?'

'Children these days question everything,' said Kanta.

Before Sarika could say anything further, Kirana sahib entered the verandah and stuck his head through the living room door. Sarika rushed to him.

'Are you okay, Sarika?' he asked with a smile.

She nodded.

'Where is Behanji?' he asked, flitting his eyes around the room. 'Ah, there she is,' he said going up to Nirmala, who sat with her back against the wall, sadness writ large on her face. Kirana sat down next to her, mumbling his condolences — he had come just to visit, he sensed the quietness of death at the gate, what a brave lady Lakshmi was, Nirmala

14

and Ashwini had taken such good care of her. They were blessed in getting a chance to take care of a sick person. Nirmala mumbled something in response. They sat silently for several minutes, tracing the pattern of the *dhurrie* with their eyes.

'Kirana sahib,' Nirmala said remembering something. 'We are doing the *shanti path* in three days from today to pray for peace for the soul of the departed. We are not doing the traditional Hindu thirteenth day ceremony because the relatives can't stay that long. I would very much like you to attend and sing some bhajans after the *havan* is over. Amma ji loved your voice,' she said tearing up.

'I will be happy to, Behanji,' he said. 'What time is the *shanti path* and the prayer ceremony?'

'Eleven o' clock.'

'I will see you then,' said Kirana, getting up to leave.

'Sarika, walk master sahib to the gate,' said Nirmala, turning to her daughter. 'Are the lights on outside?' she asked, bending forward to look out of the window. 'How short the days have become.'

On the verandah, Kirana slid on his sandals and headed for his scooter. Sarika followed him down to the gravel driveway. The *harshringar* tree sent forth a beautiful fragrance from its small white flowers with their bright orange stalks. It was dark outside, except for the one bulb that gave out a jaundiced glimmer and the light that filtered out through the living room windows. The neighbours' house on the side of the driveway was dark, too. As she came up to Kirana's scooter, she crossed her arms and watched him, expecting him to leave right away. But he stood by his scooter and searched her face for several seconds. Surprised, she nevertheless returned his gaze, then suddenly shy, lowered her eyes.

'You will have to sing a bhajan at the prayer ceremony,' said Kirana as he took the scooter off its stand.

'Not at this time. Please, master sahib. I can't.'

'Alright,' he said smiling. 'This time I will listen to you because of your Dadiji. But when your guru tells you to sing, you have to sing.'

Sarika wiggled a big toe. He showed no urgency to leave. She felt his eyes on her.

'Will you come to college before the *shanti path*?' he asked, sitting on the driver's seat of the scooter.

'No.' After a pause. 'Will you miss me in class?'

'What do you think?' His voice trembled.

Her heart pounded crazily. Later, when she tried to recall her thoughts at this moment, she wondered at her mind's vacancy when her heart spoke so much.

'I will see you in three days, then,' he said, then dropped his voice. 'It will seem so much longer. I think about you every waking moment. Your face is before my eyes twenty-three hours out of the twenty four.' Giving the scooter a gentle push with his feet, he rolled toward the gate without starting the motor. Once through the wide-open gate, he kick-started his scooter and rode away without looking back.

Sarika remained standing at her spot. She shook slightly, from emotion or the mild chill of the October evening air. A light came on in the neighbour's window and cast its glow on the driveway. Sarika dawdled toward the house, Kirana sahib's words turning in her mind.

～

Lakshmi had been dead three days and family, friends, and priest had gathered to pray for peace for her departed soul. The living room was filling with the first few wisps of smoke from the sacred fire burning in a brazier in the center of the room. The pundit sat cross-legged, close to the fire, on a crème woolen Kashmiri prayer mat with stems and flowers embroidered with bright green and blue and pink yarn, dressed in a white dhoti and a natural-coloured silk kurta, a small red tika in the center of his forehead, a tonsured head that sported a thick *choti*, oiled and tied neatly into a knot. He worked busily with prayer objects with his bejewelled fingers, stoked the fire in the brazier, took a few flowers from a large steel plate that held all the season's crop — marigolds, red roses, jasmine, *harshringar* — and put them into another steel plate that contained a steel pot with sacred water, *roli*, rice, and sacred thread. A large garlanded picture in a gold frame showing Lakshmi in her healthy days stood close to the fire. Ashwini and Nirmala also sat on prayer mats, across from the pundit, ahead of an assortment of family and friends.

Sarika caught Kirana sahib's eye through the space between her parents. He had slipped unnoticed into the corner farthest from the fire and now sat passively, handsome in a starched white pajama and a handmade white silk kurta with an embroidered button placket, held together with gold buttons, linked with a gold chain. As he continued to gaze at her, she lowered her eyes, ashamed that he might read her feelings for him. What would Nirmala say? When Nirmala studied music, did she have such feelings? Kirana sahib shifted his gaze from Sarika and his confession that she was in his thoughts all the time jumped into her mind. She had replayed that scene at his scooter over and over until his expression, the surroundings, her own feelings were etched in memory.

The fire crackled as the pieces of coal on the bottom settled deeper into the brazier and fresh ones fell into the center from the sides; a bird flew in through the open door, circled around the room crazily in its momentary captivity, unable to find the entrance that had attracted it, stumbled upon the open door and flew out; the servants noisily moved pots and pans in the kitchen.

The pundit began chanting the *gayatri mantra*. 'Every time I say "*svaha*," you take a little *samagri* in your hand and a spoonful of ghee and put it in the fire,' he told Ashwini and Nirmala, as he continued chanting. They nodded. Each handful of the herbs and roots and the clarified butter made the fire smokier and a caliginous cloud hung over the room.

A few neighbours stood up, coughing and wiping their eyes. The family remained seated, tears from grief or smoke streaming down their cheeks. Gradually, people began to move out of the living room in ones and twos, taking deep breaths of clear air as they stepped into the verandah. Nirmala wiped her eyes with her saree every few seconds; Ashwini stared stoically at the flames, then turned his head, shut his eyes very tight, and turned back to look at the fire. Savitri, Ashwini's sister, stood up and waved her arms over the fire to train the smoke out of the window. But it remained there, hanging low like bad news.

All the *samagri* and ghee were now in the fire. The pundit had begun the *shanti path*, praying for peace in the universe — the earth, air, sky, vegetation, forces of nature, people. 'We pray for peace,' he said. 'Psychological peace within ourselves, peace from the physical forces that surround us, and peace from manmade problems. We pray for peace in all aspects of life that affect us.' The fire had almost burnt out. The smoke became thicker.

Sarika stood up and coughed. The smoke settled in the base of her throat, which had to be saved for the fifth-year music finals, less than two months away. Deliberately avoiding Kirana sahib, she wended her way through the knees of her relatives. Once in her room, she shut the door, cleared her throat again, and sat down at her desk. Why did he keep staring at her? She liked it. She liked his seeking her out in a crowd. But her own feelings confused her. She loved him, but how? She had known him before she'd ever been aware of any feelings for the opposite sex. And he was so much older. Her teacher. But what else could her feelings mean now that she was fifteen and a half?

The door opened softly. She swung around.

'Master sahib? Is the ceremony over already?'

'No, there's too much smoke there.' Kirana shut the door carefully behind him. 'I saw you leave, and I thought I'd get away, too.'

'Oh,' she said. 'Oh yes, that smoke irritates the throat.'

He stepped closer. 'Sarika, I think of you all the time.'

She could think of no response.

'I don't know why,' he said.

She stood still. He took another step forward, moving quickly to get past that voice that always nagged him when he stood at the crossroads. She was almost as young as his daughter. Countered the other voice, she was his student and he was giving her his all: body, mind, and soul. He took a quick step toward her.

'Oh Sarika. I love you.'

He said it so simply. She held the desk behind her and tried to look steadily at him, but lowered her eyes under his gaze. She did not know how long they stood thus or what they said, if anything. As desire clutched her, she clung harder to her desk. Gradually, her hands relaxed and left the table behind her. He kissed her and then he was gone. She still felt the pressure of his lips, the brush of his moustache. She tried to calm herself, hands on her heart, then on her cheeks in disbelief, fear, ecstasy. She sat down on her chair. Her lips responded to his, didn't they? His mouth had been so sure, hers so tentative. She laughed out loud. What a wonderful feeling! She felt giddy.

Several minutes later, she had composed herself enough to go into the living room. The *havan* ceremony was over, the brazier dull, and the smoke had lifted away, leaving behind a mild fragrance. People were settling somberly around the room. Kirana sahib played a few notes on the harmonium and launched into the devotionals that Lakshmi had so loved.

2

The penumbra of sundown bestowed a stateliness on the buildings surrounding the college and the tomb of Asaf-ud-daulah with its dome and slender minarets, partially under the shadow of approaching darkness, imparted a quiet sombreness to the scene so much at variance with the disquiet in Sarika's mind. It was her first day back at the college after her grandma's death. Sarika paid her rickshawman with exact change and as she walked through the college gates, footsteps quick with excitement, musical notes floated out through the open windows and tickled her senses. A burst of sitar, violins, drums, and ankle bells provided harmonic accompaniment to the melody of voice in an unintended symphony.

Barely aware of her surroundings, she ran upstairs to Kirana's class. She stopped suddenly at the sound of low voices, glanced at her watch and saw there were still a few minutes before class. Stepping back, books in hand, she strained her ears to decipher the hum that came to her through the open door. The small opening between the door jamb and the curtain afforded her a glimpse of Kirana sahib and Mrs. Sinha, who sat close to her teacher, one leg crossed over the other, clutch purse tucked under her armpit, clingy chiffon saree thrown carelessly over the left shoulder, boldly showing not only a low-cut, round necked blouse but also the lacy bra underneath. She spoke breathlessly to Kirana sahib, through a mouthful of betel, gesticulating profusely. He kept his eyes fixed on his small teacher's desk that stood on the platform and responded to Mrs. Sinha with an occasional nod. His lips made Sarika's heart race. She felt once again their pressure on hers. The sensation was strange, unmatched in its novelty, heightening the intensity of her feeling to the extent that it partially dulled the sadness of Lakshmi's demise. And the realization that the feeling was mutual threw her into a state of frenzied joyousness. She laughed out loud, then self consciously surveyed the corridor. Sarika moved to the railing in the verandah. The sun had sunk even lower and the tomb of Asaf-ud-Daulah across the patch of green assumed a haunting loneliness. Sarika waited until it was time for the class, then went inside.

Kirana sahib's face lit up at the sight of his young student. Mrs. Sinha noted the change of expression on his face, midsentence, and followed his gaze open mouthed. Sarika greeted them, then took off her chappals and sat down on the platform, covered characteristically with a *dhurrie* and coarse white sheet.

'How is Amma?' he asked.

'It's been affecting her more since the relatives left. Suddenly, the house is big and empty. The last two years or so, Amma did nothing except take care of my grandma.'

'Is that why you were absent from class all of last week?' asked Mrs. Sinha. Sarika nodded. Mrs. Sinha took off her sandals, and as she tried to climb up onto the platform, her saree slipped from her shoulder. 'Oh, Baba!' she exclaimed, putting her hand over her blouse as if in shame at being exposed, but in no hurry to return her errant saree to its rightful place. Kirana blushed and lowered his eyes. Sarika watched with amusement.

'Master sahib missed you,' said Mrs. Sinha, flipping her saree over her shoulder.

'What?' asked Sarika.

'Master sahib missed you when you were away last week,' she repeated. 'His favourite *shishya* wasn't around. The class didn't quite feel the same.'

Sarika ignored the remark and opened her notebook to a clean page.

'So, today is your first day back? Is that why you came early to class?' asked Mrs. Sinha in a honey voice.

'Is that why *you* came early?' asked Sarika, unable to keep the anger out of her voice. 'Did you want some time alone with master sahib?'

Mrs. Sinha flushed. Kirana sahib smiled at Sarika. Encouraged, Sarika continued. 'And do you have eyes at the back of your head? How do you know that I came early? You had your back toward the door.'

'You were the first to come into class,' Mrs. Sinha said. Other students were taking their seats.

'Actually, you were here before me.'

'She is so smart, isn't she?' Mrs. Sinha cooed to Kirana sahib. 'Your favourite *shishya*.'

Kirana looked up at her sharply. He drew a deep breath, as if to say something, then opened his desk, took out his roster, and turned to the month of October. 'Let us begin,' he said. '*Sa.*'

The class sang the tonic note in unison. *Sa-aa.*

Sarika felt Kirana sahib's tension throughout the class and tried to catch his eye to let him know that she understood, that she would be there if the world misunderstood him, to comfort him with words, with a touch. She knew he seethed, but regard for Mrs. Sinha's age kept him quiet.

He left the room immediately after class. Mrs. Sinha slipped on her sandals and, without waiting to buckle them, ran after him. The group dawdled out of class and headed toward the staircase. By the time they reached the main gate, Sarika was alone with the flour-tin lady. The two checked to see if their rickshawmen had come, then seeing no one, stepped back and stood silently against the black metal fence that separated the pavement from the lawn.

'You have to be very careful with older men,' said the flour-tin lady to the air in front of her. 'Especially when you are so young and pretty and talented.'

Sarika searched her face in the dim light for any clues to her thoughts. What had she noticed in class? Sarika ran through everything she had said or done in class that day.

'When I was a student of literature, I was moved by powerful love stories,' continued the flour-tin lady. 'I searched for that kind of love in the lives of those around me. But I came to realize that most of us do not enjoy idealized love, like that between a Laila and Majnu. It is only a fantasy. An older man, especially a married man, can make you feel that he's taking you on an adventure, because he knows things about a domain that you are just waking up to. But most of the time he's after only one thing. You are too young to see that just now.'

Sarika raised an eyebrow. 'If you mean master sahib, he's like a father to me.' Had this lady seen her trying to catch Kirana sahib's eye? Sarika wondered.

'Remember this for life,' the flour-tin lady said quietly. 'No one is your father except your own and no one is your brother either. Especially in music. That is how they work their way into your favour. They disarm you with their caring and then disrobe you. Once they have used you, they throw you away like a fly that has accidentally fallen into a glass of milk. The fire of social condemnation burns the woman while the man goes scot-free. Our society is very harsh to its women,' she added with a sigh.

'But, Aunty...' protested Sarika, groping for words that would convince her classmate that her relationship with Kirana sahib was untainted by lust. Kirana sahib would never cast her off. But she found no words, and her hands went cold. She took a deep, rasping breath.

The flour-tin lady's rickshawman arrived, producing a loud, continuous ring with his bell, which was soon joined by a merry tinkle from Sarika's rickshawman.

'Don't take what I said "otherwise",' the flour-tin lady said, taking Sarika's icy hands in her own. 'You are younger than my daughter and I speak to you as the mother of one.'

Sarika nodded and got on to her rickshaw.

Mrs. Sinha's needling troubled Kirana's fine sensibility and cutting his last class short by about ten minutes, he drove down to Sarika's house, hoping to catch her before the family sat down to dinner at eight-thirty. Luck was on his side. Sarika came out into the drawing room for her lesson while the family ate. Kirana spoke little and coached Sarika for her fifth-year finals. As she warmed up and rose to every challenge he threw at her, his body began to relax. The tension lifted from his shoulders and his clenched jaw loosened itself as his thoughts shifted from Mrs. Sinha's comments to the music he taught. By the end of the lesson, he had begun to sway to the beat of the tabla.

As he rose to put on his sandals, still talking to Sarika about the nature of the raga they had been singing, he tapped her foot with his. Surprised, Sarika saw the playful smile hidden under his moustache, and tapped his foot in return. Soon they were holding each other at arm's length, laughing hysterically, trying to avoid being tapped. Sarika, younger, was more agile.

Hearing them, Nirmala came out into the living room. Amazed at first, she soon joined them in the laughter. 'You fight like children,' she said. 'Sarika, careful. You will hurt master sahib.'

'Amma, he tapped me first,' said Sarika, keeping a close eye on her teacher's manoeuvres so as not to lose her edge. 'I am only defending myself,' she said, partially between her teeth, concentrating hard. She made a quick movement to avoid a tap and deal one of her own.

Kirana looked at her earnest face and a wave of warmth for her swept over him. He stopped. Her child-like desire to win touched him tenderly. It was this quality, this doggedness, that made him certain he could propel her career as far as his talent and hers would allow. He put

22

on his sandals and patted her on the head. She smiled an open, honest smile and stood by her mother. A minute later, he took leave of Nirmala and left for home.

3

Tiny seeds of rivalry had been sown during the second-year vocal music exams eons ago. Mrs. Sinha stood in the corridor of the music college and students went past briskly. Having finished the practical part of her second-year exam, she hoped to catch someone to whom she could talk, who would reassure her that her exam went well, that she would pass in the first division. But people went by unmindfully. From the other classrooms she heard the tremulous voice of an examinee following instructions delivered by the examiner in a booming voice or the resonance of the sympathetic strings of the sitar. The doors to all these rooms were shut and curious classmates stood outside to hear the exam in progress. The fluorescent lights in the hallway flickered into life, as darkness fell.

Mildly frustrated, Mrs. Sinha jaunted to the tuning room and nabbed Gajendra, the tabla accompanist who was tuning up with another candidate.

'You sang very well, Hemalata ji,' Gajendra said. 'See, the examiner asked you everything you had prepared.'

'Yes, I am happy. You helped me a lot,' she said, referring to the accompaniment Gajendra had provided her at home, which helped her rhythm immensely. Like all accompanists, Gajendra had a passing knowledge of ragas, which he had used to good effect when accompanying Mrs. Sinha, never letting her stray from the theme. 'Where is Kirana sahib?'

'I just saw him. He heard your exam.'

'But I haven't seen him since. I want to know what he thinks.'

'What will he think,' said Gajendra in his easy-going way. 'Your exam went well. That's all he'll think. You're lucky to have had him in second year. Next year, he won't be teaching second year.'

'Truly?'

'New principal, new rules. But why should you worry. Your second year is over. Go home, relax. Your exam is over. Is Sinha sahib in town?'

Mrs. Sinha nodded.

'Go to the movies with him.'

Mrs. Sinha laughed. 'You know how he is. He is not the moviegoing type. Music is what moves his soul.'

'And that's why you are learning music,' said Gajendra, giving her a beaming, betel-stained smile. 'Oh, there goes Kirana sahib,' he said as a figure went by the door in haste.

Mrs. Sinha rushed toward the door. Just as she poked her head into the corridor, she saw Kirana disappear into a large tear-shaped crowd that had formed outside the door to one of the classrooms. She wove her way toward him. He reemerged, waved smartly to her, told her that her exam had gone off well, and marched away. In a moment he returned with the principal, and together the two men entered the tear-drop again. Mrs. Sinha stood on her toes to look beyond the crowd. Kirana parted the curtain, held it up for a split second to let the principal in, and followed him into the room. A snatch of music drifted out before the tightly shut door muffled all sound. Mrs. Sinha tapped a young man on the shoulder.

'What's happening in there?'

'An exam.'

'Obviously. But why is there such a crowd?'

'Because she's singing so well.'

'Who is? What's her name?'

'I don't know,' said the man, shaking his head. 'Some girl in second year.'

'Oh.' Mrs. Sinha moved around to get closer to the door, but the crowd resisted her. Her curiosity much aroused, she wondered who in her class sang so well that not only had Kirana sahib gone in to hear, but dragged the principal in, too. Unless it was someone in the other second-year class. A little irritated that her exam had already been forgotten, she popped in again into the tuning room to catch Gajendra, but he had gone. Mrs. Sinha retraced her steps to the crowd. She hadn't been there more than a few minutes, when the door opened again and several teachers and the principal tumbled out, chewing betel and laughing. She noted each face. The crowd dissipated and Mrs. Sinha moved to the side. Kirana sahib came out smiling and just as Mrs. Sinha took a step forward to go up to him, Sarika, tanpura tucked under her arm, followed.

Mrs. Sinha quickly appraised her small frame, light skin, hazel eyes, prominent jaw line, and her long, thick brown hair braided into a single plait. She looked so childlike in her checked skirt, white socks, and black Bata shoes that Mrs. Sinha couldn't resist saying, 'Good exam, Sarika.'

'Thank you,' Sarika said in a daze, barely comprehending, as she walked toward the tuning room to unload her instrument. 'Sarika,' said a deep voice. She turned to look at the speaker. 'Brilliant exam,' said Kirana. 'Put your tanpura away and come back here.'

'Kirana sahib,' said Mrs. Sinha. 'The examiner tried to confuse me by making me sing *Marwa* right after *Yaman*. Did I sing alright?'

'Yes, of course. I've already told you that your exam went well. I am very pleased. You worked hard and you will get a good result. Oh, Sarika, there you are,' he said turning to the girl. 'I was thinking...' He moved away from Mrs. Sinha.

Mrs. Sinha's face fell. She was Kirana sahib's student; Sarika was in the other class, yet he evinced more interest in her exam and in *her*. 'Of course he'd ask her,' she mumbled, tucking a wad of prepared betel leaves into her left cheek.

'What?' asked Gajendra, who came from behind and stood by her.

'Of course he'd ask her,' she repeated. 'She's the home secretary's daughter. He's not going to ask me!'

Gajendra laughed. 'She is also young and can bring him fame,' he said in his teasing voice, edging toward the spittoon outside the principal's office. 'Is she really the home secretary's daughter?' he asked, striding back.

Mrs. Sinha ignored him and turned her attention to Kirana and Sarika. As soon as they had finished talking, she ran after her teacher and whispered in his ear.

4
~

The evening of his wife's exam, Sinha finished work at the factory at the usual time, swung by his petrol pump in the middle of town to check on his men there, and then instructed his chauffeur to drive him to manager Yadav's house. Yadav lived quite far from the petrol pump, about a couple of miles, and Sinha listened to his favourite cassette as the car crawled through sleepy traffic on narrow roads. The sun had long dropped below the horizon and the pale yellow lights along the streets did little to illuminate the dark streets, which appeared darker from the tinted windows of his car. As soon as his car reached the manager's house, Yadav and his wife stepped out of the verandah of their modest house and welcomed Sinha with joined hands. He tumbled out of his white Chevrolet Impala and nodded to the couple.

'Bhabhiji?' said Yadav, looking into the back seat of the car to see if Mrs. Sinha was perhaps hidden there.

Sinha shook his head. 'Exhausted after her exam.'

'I hope nothing serious,' said Yadav.

'No,' said Sinha, shaking his head. 'Nothing serious.'

'Come in. Please come in,' said Yadav, bowing to welcome his boss into the house. 'It is a big honour.' Yadav and his wife led Sinha sahib into the courtyard. In the center, Yadav had erected a makeshift stage, covered with red carpet and decorated with two potted palms on the two corners. Across from the stage, he had laid out *dhurries* in perfect order so that not a square inch of ground showed. 'We just had our courtyard cemented, since we had a good year at the business,' Yadav said, smiling self deprecatingly. 'It looks so much cleaner. Oi, boy,' he said, turning to a little boy who emerged from the kitchen with a trayful of drinks. The boy came up to him. 'Sir,' he said bowing to Sinha.

Sinha looked at the selection and shook his head.

'I will get some appetizers,' said Mrs. Yadav, leaving the two men. As soon as she moved away, Yadav stepped closer to Sinha. 'Some?' he asked, indicating a shot glass with his hand. He laughed and waited.

Sinha tilted his head slightly.

'Whisky, Sir?'

Sinha nodded.

'On the rocks, Sir?'

'Yes.'

'Sir, please sit down,' he said, leading Sinha close to the stage and indicating a small area on the *dhurries* that had been marked out for distinction with a few big floor cushions. 'Sir, please make yourself comfortable.' Yadav helped Sinha sahib down on to the largest, softest cushion and hurried off. Mrs. Yadav emerged from the kitchen with a plate of sizzling hot potato tikias for Sinha sahib.

'Sir?' she said, extending the plate to Sinha.

'All of them?' he asked, raising his eyebrows.

Mrs. Yadav laughed. 'I brought them for you. I will set them down here. Ah, your drink is here,' she said as Yadav appeared. Mrs. Yadav left and mingled with the other guests.

'So, you are having some kind of a program today, Yadav?' said Sinha.

'Yes, Sir. I thought we'd do a variety program. We were too busy during the festival season to do anything, but any time is good.'

'Good. Good.'

'And I thought we'd thank God for the good year we've had, Sir.'

'Yes. Our factory did well this year. Sooner than we expected. Before we know it, the tax people will be after us.'

'That's true, Sir. Success always brings out the tax folks. I hear the income tax commissioner has conducted a few raids here lately. Some people were caught.'

'And then let go, after they took care of all the government officers. As if we put in all this labour so we can give away all our money to the government in taxes. Bloody fools. Why should we give anything to them? They are a bunch of thieves.' He popped a tikia into his mouth and took a deep draft of the whisky. 'You know,' he continued philosophically, 'the thing with these government officials is that they want your money to go not to the government but into their own pockets. So in a way, they are beggars.' He let out an angry breath. 'But they don't behave like beggars. They will try to act tough, try to hold a club over your head as they tickle your palm for some money. What respect.' He took another swig.

Yadav laughed.

'But they are the easy ones to deal with,' Sinha continued. 'The greedy ones are easy. The tough ones are the honest ones. You must have heard that Ashwini Kumar just recently became the home secretary. He's a tough, honest man.'

'We don't have to worry about pleasing him, Sir. He doesn't head up income tax or excise. Right now, the commissioners in both those departments can be bought.'

'True,' he said. 'But when such a big officer is honest, everyone becomes a little subdued.' He held out his empty glass to Yadav.

'Yes, but he will be too busy working on his department to have the time to interfere with the others.' Yadav took the glass and went inside to refill. When he came back, he did not sit down next to Sinha. 'Sir, give me leave for a few minutes. I think our artists have arrived. Let's start the program, then I'll join you.'

Sinha nodded and took a sip. 'Good whisky, Yadav,' he said to his manager's retreating back. Yadav swung around and bowed, then carried on toward the back door. Sinha continued to enjoy his drink, popping an occasional tikia into his mouth.

Soon, Kartar the dagger eater was on the stage. He looked tall and imposing in his pajama-kurta. Stepping to the front of the stage, he pulled out three daggers from the sash he wore over his kurta and held them out to the audience. Slowly, his accompanist, who sat in one corner of the stage, began to beat out a rhythm on the dholak. Following his beat, Kartar juggled the daggers. The dholak gained momentum. Faster and faster went the dholak player. Faster and faster juggled Kartar, his daggers occasionally catching a glint of light from the lamps in the courtyard as they flew up into the air and came back with precision into the juggler's hands, until accompanist and artist reached a climax and then began to slow down. Kartar pulled each dagger from the air and quickly slipped it into his sash. The dholak stopped beating and in the silence Kartar took a few deep breaths and tilted his head back. Slowly, he took a dagger and put it down his throat. His head jerked involuntarily. His hand groped for the second dagger and then the third. When the last was smugly ensconced in his throat, he threw up his hands and looked at the starry sky. The audience clapped. One by one, he took the daggers out and looked straight ahead. His eyes teared. The audience applauded again.

'Where did you find him?' Sinha asked Yadav, who had slipped next to his boss as Kartar juggled. 'He's very good.'

'The brother of my wife knows him. Another drink, Sir?'

Sinha gestured no. 'What else is coming up?'

'We have a young woman here,' said Yadav. 'She's a student at the music college, but she teaches my wife at home. She needs the money, my wife likes to learn a little bit here and there, so it works out very well.'

'Will the young woman sing?'

'Yes. That's what I'd started to tell you. She has a beautiful voice. In Assam…'

'Assam?'

'She's from Assam. Over there, they used to call her the koyal of Assam.'

'Truly, the cuckoo bird?'

'Yes, sir.'

'Why is she here, then?'

'She came to Lucknow on scholarship to study music further.'

'Will she sing now?' asked Sinha.

'There she is,' said Yadav, pointing at the stage with his chin, where the young woman had clambered on. 'That's her.'

'What's her name?'

'Swati.'

Swati settled down with her harmonium and played a quick succession of notes. The murmuring audience fell silent. Swati cleared her throat. Instead of the preliminary slow alap, she burst out with speed, and her voice rippled out like a playful brooklet. With a quick, short exposition, she started a bhajan devoted to Lord Rama. The tabla player joined her and so catchy was the beat that many in the audience began to tap. Swati felt the music intensely in her body and without effort she rocked to her own singing.

'You were right,' whispered Sinha to his host.

'I told you.'

'Introduce me to her after the program.'

'Certainly. She'll finish soon. I will ask her to join us.'

At the end of her second devotional, Swati switched to a different beat, which indicated to the audience that they could join in the refrain. And they did with enthusiasm, clapping in time to the music.

'We have two or three other items and then we have Sunaina Devi, whom you like, Sir,' Yadav said, when Swati had finished.

'Sunaina Devi. The one who sings ghazals. What an evening — bhajan, ghazal, *geet*.' Sinha relaxed further into his cushion.

Sinha prided himself on feeling the soul of music and the depth of its lyrics. 'Bring me a singer and I will tell you what lies in her soul,' he

29

had once bragged to Yadav, who giggled with awe. Sinha's knowledge of Urdu allowed him to probe words for their hidden meanings. Unlike his wife, who devoted herself to classical music but sometimes sang lighter compositions to please her husband, his preference lay in listening to semi-classical pieces, into which he immersed himself with abandon. His white Chevrolet Impala was equipped with a tape player, perhaps the only one in all of Lucknow. And he kept an 'imported' two-in-one radio and tape recorder under lock and key in his office at the steel factory. Music soothed Sinha and he let it glide over him like a balm to take away the stress of long hours at work. 'So, Sunaina Devi,' he said with anticipation.

'Sir, we asked her to come because you like her so much,' said Yadav. 'You probably don't want to miss her recital. Why don't you come and have dinner?'

Sinha looked at his watch. 'It is dinner time.'

'I can get you your plate here, Sir, if you want.'

'No, I will come and get one myself. And listen, send a plate of food over for the driver.'

'No problem, Sir. Swati ji,' Yadav called out to Swati, struggling with the harmonium across the courtyard. 'You could have left the instrument on the stage, Swati ji. I would have asked someone to take it inside. Here,' he said, going up to her. 'Let me take it from you.' Yadav put it back on the stage. 'Swati ji,' he said, walking back to Sinha. 'Meet Sinha sahib, my mentor, boss. Whatever I say about him is too little. Everything I am today is because of him.'

'Namaste,' said Swati, bowing slightly.

'You have a very sweet throat,' said Sinha, as he absently joined his hands together in greeting. 'One doesn't hear voices like these often.'

Swati flushed with pleasure.

'You do sing beautifully, Swati ji,' said Yadav. 'That thing you did at the end where everyone joined in was so enjoyable.'

'Have you been at the music college long?' asked Sinha.

'It's my first year here. I came here this year in sixth year.'

'Mrs. Sinha is also at the music college,' said Yadav.

'She's in the second year, I think,' said Sinha. 'You wouldn't know her.'

30

'I'm sure I'd know her if I saw her,' said Swati. 'Who is her teacher?'

'One Kirana sahib,' said Sinha.

'Ah, yes. He's a very good teacher.'

'I was taking Sinha sahib to the table to get a plate,' said Yadav. 'Come with us and get something to eat.'

'A little later. You carry on.'

'Not hungry?' asked Yadav.

'Not right after a performance.'

Sunaina Devi had moved her audience to tears and now it was time to go home. The Yadavs stood on the verandah and bade their guests farewell.

'You are leaving, too, Sir,' said Yadav, hurrying up to Sinha who stood at the edge of the verandah.

'It's late.'

'I will go tell your driver to bring the car around,' he said. 'Oh, he's seen you. He's coming up himself.'

'This was very nice,' said Sinha.

'Listen,' said Yadav to his wife, deep in conversation with Swati. 'Sinha sahib is going.'

'Okay,' said Mrs. Yadav. Left standing alone, Swati followed slowly.

'So, when can I hear Swati ji again?' Sinha asked in general.

The Yadavs looked at each other; Swati blushed.

'I don't know if she sings in public very much,' volunteered Yadav. 'She comes to teach my Mrs. twice a week. You could...'

'Yes, yes,' said Mrs. Yadav. 'I'm sure Swati ji won't mind if you come hear the lessons. I'll have to practice really hard if I have such a keen listener.' She laughed. 'Will you mind, Swati ji, if Sinha sahib comes and hears our lessons sometimes? He is quite a connoisseur.'

Swati mumbled incoherently.

'We'll figure something out so you can hear Swati ji's beautiful voice again,' said Yadav.

'Are you going back to the college now?' Sinha addressed Swati.

She nodded.

'I can drop you there, if you like. It's not much of a detour for me.'

'Yes, yes,' said Yadav.

Swati tensed and did not move.

'I think it will be better if we drop her,' said Mrs. Yadav. 'It is late and it is best if I go with her.'

'Alright,' said Sinha. He descended the verandah steps and got into his car. The driver closed the door carefully after him and ran around to the other side. Sinha gave a quick, sharp wave and looked straight ahead as the car drove off into the darkness.

~

Mrs. Sinha went home after her exam. That morning her children, Achala and Vineet, had come home from New Delhi, where they were both in college. After picking them up from the railway station, she had retired to her room to think about her music finals. Now she wanted to be home with them.

'Papa is quite determined that you will join the business,' Mrs. Sinha said as they sat down to dinner. 'And marriage is the logical first step.'

'Why marriage so soon? And isn't Achala supposed to get married before me since she is a girl?'

'Don't worry about Achala. We'll find someone for her soon enough.'

'You won't have to,' said Vineet knowingly. Achala squirmed.

'What do you mean?' asked Mrs. Sinha, with her mouth full.

'Nothing,' said Vineet. Achala gave him a dirty look.

'No, something is up. What is it?' Mrs. Sinha looked at her daughter and then at her son.

'Nothing,' said Vineet again. 'I was just teasing her because one of her friends is having an affair with one of the two male teachers at her college. It's quite the talk of the town. Ever since then, I've been telling her she'd better stay away from the other one, else you and Papa will go crazy.'

'Really,' said Mrs. Sinha laughing and relaxing a little. Achala slumped into her chair in relief. 'Vineet is right. You'd better not do something stupid like that. We will not be able to show our faces anywhere. Just this morning it was the judge's daughter. About five o' clock the guard wakes me up to tell me that the judge's daughter has eloped. That too with the son of the judge's clerk!'

32

'Oh,' said Achala drily. 'Hope the chap's worth it.'

Mrs. Sinha glared at her.

'When does Papa get home?' asked Achala. 'I expected to see him at lunch today.'

'He was planning to,' said Mrs. Sinha quickly. 'I know he wanted to come, but work must have kept him. While you are here,' she said turning to Vineet, 'you should help Papa with his business. It's all together too much for him to handle alone.'

5

That moonless night, the wind carried a soft shower on its back. It rustled in a high-pitched murmur through the rows of papaya trees with their broad leaves and drummed a dull, insistent tap on the window. The two cousins lay curled in the dark room, barely aware of nature outside as drapes drawn decisively over shut windows and doors kept even the tiniest breath of air from entering the room. But keeping the wind outdoors did nothing to dispel the cold air that hung heavy with the dampness of the chilly December night. The girls rolled first to one side and then to the other until the sides of their cotton-velvet quilts were tucked tightly under their bodies. As their body heat permeated their quilts and warmed them in turn, they slowly uncurled themselves and faced each other across the one foot of coldness that separated their beds.

'How was your journey down here?' Sarika asked.

'Good,' said cousin Nisha.

'Why didn't Pradeep come?' asked Sarika, referring to Nisha's brother. 'He said he'd come.'

'Some business kept him away. He's too involved in politics for his own good.'

'Why politics? It's full of corrupt people.'

'He thinks he can make a difference. Change the world.'

'Oh.'

'More important, how was your music exam?' asked Nisha.

'Alright. The examiner asked me so many questions that principal sahib asked him why. The examiner said he squeezed only the juicy lemon.'

33

'What an analogy,' chuckled Nisha.

'I know. Principal sahib and all the other teachers in the room thought it was funny, too. Anyway, the examiner blessed me to become a great artist when the exam was over.'

'Really?'

'When I went into the room, the examiner looked so bored. He just sat there looking out of the window. I started my choice raga and he slowly sat up and turned his head toward me. That's when I knew it was going well for me and then, of course, teachers from other classes started coming in.'

'Imagine having to listen to so many students, most of them bad, sing the same thing.'

'Other people said I sang very well, but I can think of many small things that I didn't do and should have.'

'You should believe your teachers.'

'There is this teacher, Kirana sahib…' Sarika said.

'Is he good looking?'

'I don't know. I've never noticed his looks. Anyway, we were all standing in the corridor after my exam when he came to me and asked if I would join his class next year in third year. He's teaching third year from January.'

'Is he a good teacher?'

'Supposed to be. *Gharanedar*, learned from a maestro, lived at his guru's house while he was learning. He's such a good artist. He sings for the radio too. I can't believe he asked me!'

'Intelligent chap. He knows which student can bring him fame.'

'But you know,' continued Sarika, 'there was this lady, who I think is in the other second-year class which this Kirana chap teaches, who stood watching him very closely as he spoke to me. She gave me the creeps. As soon as he was done, she glared at me. I was so taken aback.'

'What's her name?'

'Mrs. Sinha, Saxena, something like that. I'm not sure. Mrs. Sinha maybe. I've seen her around the college. Anyway, after glaring at me she ran off to whisper something in his ear.'

'What did she say to him?'

'How am I to know. She whispered in his ear.'

34

'Oh, maybe she wants to be his favourite *shishya*.'

'Maybe. She's most welcome. I don't even know him.' Silence fell and the two cousins plunged into their own thoughts. Sarika's thoughts flitted from object to object and finally settled on a movie theater she had passed on her way to the college. She looked at her cousin's silhouette in the darkness. A thin beam of light came in through the partially open bathroom door, cutting the darkness of the room with laser sharpness. Her voice changed. 'I saw the most shameful hoarding at Liberty Cinema.'

'What?' asked Nisha immediately interested.

'They had a larger-than-life cutout of some actress — I don't know who — in see-through clothes that left nothing to the imagination. At another end of the hoarding, they showed a man pulling her clothes off and another one holding a gun to her head.'

'It's only a movie,' said Nisha.

'I know, but still. How do these actresses do these scenes?'

'They have to or no one will come to see them.'

'But still,' said Sarika, 'how do they do them? I mean, how do they take their clothes off in front of everyone? Someone told me once that they just wear skin-coloured clothes; they don't actually take off their clothes.'

'I don't know,' said Nisha, 'but I don't think so. How can they wear skin-coloured clothes?'

'You mean they actually take off their clothes?'

'Yes, I think so. Whom do you ask?'

'Do you talk to your ma about it?' asked Sarika.

'No,' said Nisha. 'I don't know what Mummy would say. Do you?'

'Not a chance,' said Sarika. 'I am afraid to ask her. I think she'd be angry with me for even noticing such a thing,' she said.

'Well, you can't help noticing,' said Nisha.

They heard the muffled rattling of a truck as it went by their house, causing all the stray dogs on the street to bark in unison. Sarika's tense body began to relax as she gradually let go of the events of that day. A cloud of sleep descended on her tired body.

'Do you ever think of marriage?' Nisha asked. Sarika emerged from her cloud.

'Hmm?'

'Marriage.'

'Who's getting married?' asked Sarika.

'No one's getting married, you goose. I'm asking you if you ever think about marriage.'

'No. Do you?' asked Sarika.

'Sometimes,' said Nisha. 'I'll get married before you, you know; I'm fifteen. Two and a half years older than you. I have to clear the way for you.'

'True. What about marriage? What do you think?'

'This and that.'

Sarika closed her eyes again and started drifting into sleep.

'Elizabeth and Mr. Darcy.'

'What?' asked Sarika sleepily.

'I want a romance like Elizabeth and Mr. Darcy's,' said Nisha emphatically.

'But they're characters in a novel!'

'It doesn't mean it can't happen in real life. I wonder if I'll ever meet a man like Mr. Darcy.'

Sarika glanced at her cousin in the dark and fell asleep.

6

It was a small victory for Sinha, but he showed no exuberance, as he led Swati confidently down the street to the café. Swati walked a few steps behind him. The town center was busy in the early afternoon and women, uniformed children, betel-chewing clerks from neighbouring banks and insurance companies, and beggars crammed the sidewalks, littered with sticks from ice cream bars, plates and bowls made from dry leaves, and bits of newspaper that had served as containers for all kinds of savoury snacks. Sinha turned a couple of times to see if Swati was following him. As he reached the café, he stopped and waited for her to catch up.

'Here it is,' he said, dawdling up the steps and walking right in. 'What would you like to have?' Sinha asked Swati, as he settled into a chair, without waiting to be shown to a table.

Swati took a chair across from him, picked up her menu, and lowered her head into it.

'Coffee, tea, a pastry?' he asked, as the waiter came up and stood with his notepad held in readiness.

'Tea.'

'Nothing to eat?'

Swati shook her head.

'Sure?'

Swati nodded.

'One tea, one coffee, and a plate of pastries,' Sinha told the waiter. He settled comfortably into his chair after the waiter had left and looked at her from across the deep grey sunmica table with chipped sides. The fluorescent lights in the restaurant shone on the table, bringing out a fine web of scratches on the surface. The pale yellow walls of the café showed areas of darkness above chair backs, where shoulders and heads had rested. 'Have you been to Lazeez Café before?' he asked Swati.

'No,' she shook her head.

'Do you like it?'

'Yes.'

'How is everything in Assam? Your parents, brothers and sisters?'

'Very well.'

'What does your father do?'

'Both my parents are government-school teachers.'

Barely managing by, then, he noted mentally. 'Do you have brothers and sisters?'

'Yes, I am the oldest.'

Sent out to earn. 'Did you go to see them during the winter holidays?'

'Yes. Right after the exams.'

'Did you get your result yet?'

'Yes.'

'And?'

'I will continue to receive a scholarship.'

'Excellent.'

Silence ensued, during which Swati kept her eyes on the table. Sinha thought of something to say. 'My wife did well in her exams.'

'I am sure.'

'Do you know Kirana sahib?'

'A little. I sometimes go to him with some difficulties. He has a good knowledge of ragas.'

'Here, have a pastry,' he said, holding the plate out to her. Swati took a small chocolate one. As she reached out to pick up a pastry, Sinha saw that her arms were bare under the thin wool shawl that she had wrapped around herself. 'What do you think of Mrs. Yadav's singing?'

Swati smiled.

'Not much of a singer, is she?' he opined.

'She tries and she loves music. Her interest in music is touching.'

'Yadav also likes music,' he said. Yadav had told Sinha that Swati came to teach his wife in the late morning. This morning, like on many other occasions, he had dropped by casually at the Yadavs. He listened with much interest as Swati coached Mrs. Yadav, praising both teacher and student at appropriate times. At the end of the lesson, he gallantly offered to drop Swati at the music college in his car, so she wouldn't have to brave the cold winds. His connection to the music college through his wife and his frequent visits to the Yadav residence in the two months that had elapsed since their first meeting had weakened Swati's resistance to his offer. For the first time today, she accepted a ride in his car.

'I think Mrs. Yadav started learning at her husband's insistence,' Swati said. 'She was always interested, but was simply a listener. Mr. Yadav wants to make her a singer.'

Sinha laughed. He noticed how quickly Swati ate her pastry and drank her tea, lacking the upper class ease to linger over her snack.

'Would you like to have another cup of tea?' he asked.

'No.' Swati shifted in her chair.

'Should I drop you back at the hostel then?'

'Yes,' she said and stood up. Sinha led the way to the car. 'Drop me at the crossing closest to the college,' she said after a moment's pause.

Swati ambled to the college and let herself in through the small gate. The hostel rooms were quiet — the women were all at lunch. Not that she had discovery to fear, since they all knew she had gone to tutor and would have been seen walking to the hostel by even the most inquisitive. She unlocked the door to her room, flipped on the light switch, hung her cotton bag on a peg, slipped off her chappals, and slid under the quilt on her bed, her back resting against the wall. She rubbed her bare feet against each other for warmth. Her north-facing room with its one small window and concrete floor was frigid even though outside it had begun to warm up. Carefully, she took her diary out from under her pillow and her pen from her blouse and began to write.

Swati's diary was her confessional. She wrote home every week, about the college, her tuitions, her preparations for this or that concert or audition, painting a picture of a smooth life. But it was into her diary that she poured her heart — the people she met who defied classification and who might arouse her parents' disapproval; her struggles with poverty, for the scholarship and the few tuitions were not enough; her own longings to try different things and pull out of poverty and become a great musician. 'Everyone says I have a beautiful voice,' she wrote once when all her money had finished by the third week of the month, 'but what good is that if no one can hear it! How do I break out of this?'

7

The class listened in stupefied silence to Shyam Sunder Kirana's melodious voice flowing out to them over the drone of the tanpura. Sweet and mellow, it felt like honey pouring over the ears, leaving them mesmerized, yet yearning for more.

Sarika felt a strange feeling of calm go down her spine as she sat on the wooden platform covered with a thin white cotton sheet over a thin cotton *dhurrie*. The gourd base of the tanpura rested comfortably in her lap as she strummed the strings on the long neck of the instrument. Her teacher's voice washing over her ears produced almost a physical sensation, akin to sitting in the lotus position on a hot summer's day and pouring a mug of cool, soothing water down the back. Startling at first and giving rise to goosebumps, it washes away the heat from the body, leaving a residue of calming coolness. As his voice connected notes effortlessly like pearls on a string, Sarika marked how he elaborated a small raga, weaving an intricate design with just the five notes of the theme.

39

'*Bhoopali* is a very sweet evening raga,' said Kirana over the sound of the tanpura. 'You have to try to show the yearning of the beloved for her lover.'

The ten women around him, ranging in age from almost-thirteen to forty five, nodded, the oldest ones the hardest.

'The alap should make the raga very clear,' he continued. 'So much so that when you are done, listeners should be able to see the raga in front of them like the figure of a beautiful woman,' he said, cutting the air with his hands to show his meaning.

Sarika giggled at his description of the exposition of the theme. Kirana raised an eyebrow at her; she blushed and buried her eyes in her notebook.

It was the beginning of February, the first day of class in third year. Their upstairs classroom felt cozy within the closed doors and windows and the warmth of so many bodies on the wooden platform. On this platform sat the teacher's desk, no more than two feet high. Kirana sat cross-legged behind the desk, close to the wall, resting his back against it from time to time, his students around him in a semicircle. Scattered in the room were a couple of wood chairs with cane seat and back and in two corners of the room stood two large wood and glass cupboards for the tanpuras — one for women and one for men, with thicker strings meant for deep male voices. The tablas went on two little shelves behind the tanpuras.

'The two pillars of Indian classical music are rhythm and melody,' continued Kirana. 'If either of those two pillars is shaky, you cannot build the beautiful structure of a raga or embellish it with all the little ornamentational devices that you have at your command. And not everyone can have a great operatic voice, but any voice can be made malleable with practice. Sincere practice. Every single day. You will reach a point where if you don't pick up your tanpura to sing, you will writhe with the agony of a starving man.'

Awed silence greeted his words. Kirana had transported everyone to a completely different plane.

'Let us begin,' Kirana said. '*Sa*.'

The class joined in the tonic note. Sarika sang mechanically as she strummed the instrument and looked through the windows that overlooked Begum Hazrat Mahal Park. Kirana's class had no windows into the corridor, just one door, draped with an orange and green and yellow curtain, that he kept closed during lessons to keep out the inquisitive. He was teaching the *bandish* now and Sarika withdrew her eyes and thoughts from the window and looked at him.

'I will hear this composition from each of you tomorrow,' he said winding up the class. 'No books allowed in class. All compositions must be memorized.'

The women nodded and murmured as Kirana left the room. Slowly, they got up from the platform.

'What a difference from second year,' commented Geeta, a few years older than Sarika. 'Even on the first day it seems more advanced.'

'When Kirana sahib sang today, I felt as if I had left the earth with all its pettiness and problems and soared to heavenly heights,' said Mrs. Sinha. 'It is so rare to feel that kind of pathos in somebody's voice.'

'I felt,' said another lady, 'I felt like an apsara in the court of Indra — listening to the gods sing. I was a student of Hindi literature before marriage.' Sarika noted she said 'marriz' and smiled. 'I got married at sixteen and had my daughter at 17, but I finished my M.A. after marriage. But today as he sang, I thought about my literature classes. This is how art is supposed to affect you,' she continued. Sarika looked at her oily black hair, parted neatly in the center to reveal a thick line of vermilion.

'How old is your daughter now?' asked Mrs. Sinha.

'Sixteen.'

'Are you going to marry her off?'

'No,' she said. 'I want her to study. Once you get married, your family and in-laws take up all your time. I always practice in the kitchen while cooking. The top of the tin canister of flour is a permanent place for my music book and as I cut the vegetables and season the lentils and roll the dough, I take a quick peek at my book to look up a forgotten note or word in a composition. It makes my cooking seem less like a chore, especially in the heat of the summer.'

Sarika looked at the woman's notebook, newly purchased for the school year and meticulously covered with brown paper, a white label in the center for her name and address. Soon the telltale floury fingerprints would appear. Her story had earned her the nickname of the flour-tin lady the year before.

'I wonder from where he gets all that pathos in his voice,' said Mrs. Sinha to the group. All eyes turned to her.

41

'What do you mean?' asked the flour-tin lady.

'Oh, people in the college say things,' said Mrs. Sinha, wrapping her delicately embroidered Pashmina shawl smugly around her.

'What things?'

'All kinds of things. About his family, his wife's family. How ordinary his wife and her family are compared to his.'

'How do they know? Has he told them his story?' persisted the flour-tin lady.

'I've never asked them that.'

'Even if she is ordinary, it doesn't mean Kirana master sahib is unhappy.'

'I'm just saying what I've heard.'

'A hundred mouths, a hundred stories,' said the flour-tin lady icily.

After a few seconds of hostile silence between the two women, the group made its way slowly out of the classroom near the head of the stairs and descended the grand mosaic staircase with its wrought-iron banister. It was eight o' clock and the college was beginning to show the signs of desertion. As they reached downstairs, Sarika spotted Ahmed, the college servant, sitting on a wooden bench, immediately across from the principal's office. Ahmed was a clean-shaven, gaunt old man dressed in a white pajama and a white kurta with a Nehru collar. 'Did you start *Bhoopali* today, *bitiya*?' he asked Sarika.

'Yes, Ahmed ji. How do you know?'

'I stood outside your class and listened,' said Ahmed laughing.

'And you recognized it?' she asked amazed.

'Yes. I have been hearing these ragas since I was 10 and my father worked for the founder,' said Ahmed. 'Those were the good days. But then the college ran out of money and the government took over and it is not the same now. But *bitiya* you are lucky. Kirana sahib is a good teacher.'

'Yes.' She stood, not knowing what else to say, then smiling, descended three steps into the portico and walked to the gate where her rickshawman was waiting to take her home. Sarika jumped in and wrapped her shawl tightly around herself. As the cycle-rickshaw picked up speed, the ends of the shawl began to flap in the wind and for several amusing seconds Sarika battled to bring the errant garment under control.

They approached the Kaiserbagh crossing with its great Asoka pillar balancing the four lions that looked out into the four directions. Sarika tensed and held on tightly to the sides of the rickshaw; this part of her ride home always frightened her as she watched her rickshaw merge into the chaos of the circus that led into six different directions. The expanse of old Muslim-style butter-yellow buildings, broken by roads, looked a sickly blue-yellow in the fluorescent light. Trucks, buses, cars, tongas, rickshaws, hand-pulled carts, bullock carts, bicycles, rushed to the center, no one waiting for the other, each pushing ahead, seemingly headed for collision yet miraculously missing the other by mere inches. Despite the cold, peanut and guava vendors with pushcarts and hawkers selling oranges and apples out of small wicker baskets coming apart at the edges still plied the streets bare-footed in a thin dhoti and threadbare shirt, their day's earnings tightly wrapped in a rag and tied securely around the waist. Hoping to make quick sales before turning in for the night, they illuminated their produce with the smallest of kerosene lamps that gave off a thin stream of thick black smoke that mingled seamlessly into the haze created by slum dwellers burning tires for warmth. Sarika noticed them as she did the passing landscape. As her rickshaw cleared the circus, her one thought was on reaching home and practising the new raga.

8

Kirana rolled his scooter under the narrow circular staircase and pulled it up over its stand with a loud clang. He took off his gloves and scarf and put them in the side compartment, locked it and ran up the steps to his house. Before he could knock, the door opened and Surya came out smiling with baby Kalavati in her arms.

'I heard the scooter stand on the cement; it does make a loud noise,' his wife said, moving aside to let him in.

Kirana smiled and stretched his arms for the baby, already making cooing sounds at the sight of her father.

'How is your new third-year class?' Surya asked.

'Good. They seem to have good voices, but I'll find out more tomorrow when I make them sing individually. Where are Sonali and Lalit?'

'They should be back soon. They ate and went out into the alley to play for a little while.'

'Alone, in the dark? I'll go and get them.'

'They will be fine.'

'Don't let Sonali go alone. She is growing up.'

'She has always played with the children in the alley. It's safe here,' Surya said, surprised at her husband's concern.

'Times are very bad. There is no government. I read in the paper at college today that a group of schoolgirls and teachers was going to Agra on a train. A group of boys forced their way into their compartment and raped them.'

'Oh, baba. Did the police catch them?'

'Yes. One of them was the son of the deputy inspector general of police. He was let go.'

'Let go?'

'He should have been given the harshest punishment to set an example, but no. I'm afraid. We are ordinary people. If anything were to happen to any one of us, there's nowhere for people like us to go.'

'Nothing will happen. Don't worry so much. Look, here they come.'

They heard quick footsteps coming up the staircase. Kirana let them in, and shut the door decisively behind them. 'Did you do your *riyaz* today?' he asked his son, pretending to be calm.

'Yes,' said Lalit. 'I practised for an hour.'

'Sonali? Did you sing?'

'No,' said the 12-year-old, shaking her pig tails.

'Come, have dinner,' came Surya's voice from the kitchen. Kirana handed the baby to Sonali and sat down at the small table where his wife had laid out his dinner. Surya brought a hot paratha from the kitchen and put it on his plate. When she had stacked a few on another plate, she sat down next to him and began to eat as well.

'There is a very young girl in my class,' Kirana said. 'Sarika.'

'How old is she?'

'About our Sonali's age. Maybe a year or two older. No more.'

'Does she sing well?'

'She has a very beautiful voice. I listened to her exam in December.' He paused for a moment. 'She has a lot of potential, so I asked her if she'd join my third-year class. If I can get one or two good students like her, it will be good for my career. It is so hard to find anyone with dedication these days.'

'You don't know how dedicated she'll be. She may be like our Sonali, never wanting to practice.'

'You remember I told you about Mrs. Sinha?' Kirana asked through a mouthful.

'Is she in your class now?'

'Yes.'

'And you'd been hoping to be rid of her in third year.'

'She always takes me by surprise when she comes running to me — a married lady like her. I don't expect this from her. Tomorrow somebody might say something about me and her. What would that do to my reputation? It takes a man years to build a reputation. It can be destroyed in a flash. Just like that.' He snapped his fingers.

'She has a reputation in college,' he continued. 'She is the only one who drives herself to college in a brand new car. No one else has a car. Certainly no other woman drives. We have the wives of some senior government officers, but they come in chauffeur-driven cars.'

'Why did she want to be in your class again?'

He patted Surya gently on her arm. 'I don't like her, you know that. And her wealth doesn't impress me.'

'But *she* likes you.'

They ate in silence.

'I try,' she said after awhile. 'But sometimes it's hard to have your husband surrounded by women of all types all the time.'

'Surya, there has never been anyone except you in my life. In my profession, particularly, it is so common to have affairs, but for me you are everything. When a man has given a woman everything he has, there is no room for anyone else.'

His wife nodded. 'The world is, of course, built on trust, but I am human and I see these women pursuing what I had to give up. Pursuing it with my husband.'

45

'Try to sing a little every day when the children are in school,' he said gently.

'With the baby?'

They had finished their meal. Sonali brought her little sister and put her in her mother's arms.

'When will you hear from All India Radio?' Surya asked her husband.

'I don't know.' He reached out and tickled baby Kalavati's chin; the baby gurgled. 'It will be good to become an A-grade artist. A little more money, maybe a few more chances to sing.'

'Some extra money will be nice,' said Surya sighing. 'The children are growing like reeds. Lalit needs new shoes for school. The milkman raised the price of milk again and sugar is becoming almost unaffordable. I have cut out Sonali's milk, but I want Lalit to have milk since he's a boy and the baby definitely needs it. How to make ends meet?'

'I will look for some tuitions.'

'They take time away from your own *riyaz*.'

'Now that I've auditioned for the A grade, I can perhaps ease off on my practice and take on some students privately.'

Surya stood up with the baby, put her husband's plate on her own and went into the kitchen to clean up.

9

'No, no. You have to have some more today. Before we know it, you'll be gone to Assam. How can you just have tea?' Sinha insisted. They sat at a corner table at the Lazeez Café. It was a hazy day and from the window Sinha could see the wind whipping up pieces of newspaper and dried leaves and dashing them against the glass pane. Occasionally, a big, brown leaf made a scraping noise against the window and blew on. 'You have to eat something,' he said.

'I don't feel like having anything. And we'll soon have lunch at the hostel,' said Swati.

'Surely the food here is better than hostel food.'

'It is,' Swati said, laughing hesitantly.

'Let me order some potato cutlets and some pastries. And how about some ice cream?'

'No, no ice cream. My throat is very sensitive.'

'Okay. Waiter,' Sinha called out and ordered when the man arrived in his white pants and shirt, grey from frequent washing in the river. 'You have to take care of your throat all the time?' he asked Swati, when the waiter had left.

'I have a concert coming up at the college.'

'Oh?' He raised an eyebrow.

'And then…,' she paused, as if to decide whether she should tell him everything.

'And then?'

'Oh, I am planning to audition for All India Radio's B-grade, so I have to practice very hard.'

'Ah, the cuckoo bird. If you qualify for All India Radio's B-grade, that will be a big thing. Artists twice your age are not able to make it.'

'I want to be A-grade soon, but I have to start at the bottom.'

'Of course. How was your performance at the governor's house?'

'It went well. Mrs. Sinha was there.'

'Yes,' he said. 'She likes to go to these things.'

'There is one girl in her class — Sarika. Does she know her?'

'I don't know. Why?'

'I hear she's brilliant.'

There was a long silence, during which Swati noticed that Sinha sahib dressed expensively. He wore a navy blue blazer with plain brass buttons, a red and navy silk tie, heavyweight grey trousers, black socks and shiny black leather shoes with rubber soles. Sinha was a dark, heavy set man, with no features of any distinction, and greying hair that was curly despite its shortness. That curliness gave him a little-boy look. He wore a large gold ring with three diamonds on his right ring finger.

The waiter was back with the food. 'Before we begin,' he said as soon as the waiter had gone, 'let me wish you a very happy birthday.' From his briefcase, Sinha took out a box wrapped with red paper and watched Swati closely as he slid the gift toward her.

'What's this?' she asked, taken by surprise. 'And how do you know it's my birthday?'

47

'I make it my business to know these things. Open and see.' Gift giving was something Sinha did seriously. Over the years, he had gauged the power of gifts and used it at will.

'I can't...'

'Go on. Open the gift and see for yourself.'

Swati undid the ribbon and delicately unwrapped the gift, careful not to tear the beautiful paper, as she wiggled her finger under the transparent tape to tease it open. With the tips of her fingers, she parted the folds of the wrapping paper and saw a white cardboard box printed with the name of a famous saree store in Lucknow. Her eyes widened in disbelief. With trembling hands, she undid yet another string that tied the box and removed the cover and the tissue paper. She gasped. Folded professionally into a rectangle was a deep yellow silk saree embroidered all over with tiny gold medallions. She ran a finger over the saree to feel the softness of the silk, then moved her hand away. Closing the box quickly, she slid it to the center of the table.

'I cannot take a gift from you. Least of all, such an expensive one.'

'It is a small thing,' he said, observing her carefully. She lifted her cup with a quivering hand and took a sip of tea. As she put her cup down to eat a piece of the pastry, she stole a glance at the saree box. Sinha picked up his cup and took a sip of the coffee. 'It is a small thing,' he said again.

Swati ate her pastry hastily. 'I can't,' she said with lowered eyes.

'You cannot refuse a birthday gift. I had no obligation to give you a present. I am giving you one because I want to. Come on, you can't refuse me this little pleasure.' He slid the box toward her.

'It's too expensive. I can't,' she said, keeping her eyes on the box for a brief moment.

'It is nothing. Unless you don't like it?' he said shrewdly.

'Oh no, no. Please don't think that. I like it very much. It is...it's gorgeous.'

'Then I suggest you keep it,' he said, reaching over and putting the box in her hands.

'I could never give you something similar on your birthday,' she said, putting the box back on the table, but keeping her hands on it.

'You don't have to.'

'Then I'll always be in debt.'

'No, we'll find a way to make sure that doesn't happen,' he said, smiling pleasantly at her. 'Instead of always meeting me at Mrs. Yadav's, you can sometimes meet me like this and sing for me.'

She blushed.

'And this is just a small token from an admirer,' he said.

10

The buzz in the audience died as Swati came on to the stage in a yellow silk saree with gold medallions. Putting her tanpura down carefully, she sat on the center of the stage, covered her toes with the gold border of her saree, adjusted the microphone to her height, and nodded to the tabla player. Clearing her throat, she began a semi-classical piece that celebrated Krishna romping around with the cowgirls, spraying coloured water over them.

All of Kirana's third-year women sat together in the concert hall. Sarika listened carefully, noting how Swati negotiated the high notes, her handling of the rhythm, her improvisation. Swati had the best voice in college and Sarika admired this young woman in seventh year, set to go on to a career. Swati's manoeuverings within the raga impressed Sarika, a third-year student just waking up to the depth of Hindustani classical music.

'I'll go and talk to her,' said Mrs. Sinha, as soon as Swati had finished and left the stage.

'Oh?' said the flour-tin lady.

'I'll tell her how good she was,' she said. 'I know all the girls in the hostel. I can go talk to them anytime.'

'Of course,' said the flour-tin lady.

Sarika watched Mrs. Sinha leave the hall in a great hurry, as if some monumental task awaited her, marvelling at the number of people she knew. How did she talk to everyone with such ease? Even with the teachers, she held forth on any topic with great comfort. Mrs. Sinha was back with the same quickness.

'Did you talk to her?' asked Sarika.

'Yes. I ran from there after a few minutes.'

'Why?'

'Everyone else had begun to crowd around her as if she were a great artist. But, of course, she took a couple of minutes to talk to me. It's different with me,' Mrs. Sinha said, tucking a wad of betel in her mouth. Since the college flautist had started playing, Mrs. Sinha had to sit down. Almost before the intermission was announced, she was up again. 'Come on,' she said to her classmates. 'Let's go out.' Slowly, the group followed her out into the open.

It was the first week in March and the air already had the budding warmth of summer. Holi, the festival of colour, celebrating the wheat harvest and the coming of spring, was early that year. It was a good time, not too hot and not too cold, when the leaves still looked bright and new and flower shows in the botanical gardens and the governor's residence and sundry upper-class homes gave the city an added dash of colour before the hot summer winds singed their way through orchards and streets and gardens. The new principal loved flowers and large pots of colour adorned the open areas. Sarika, Geeta, and the flour-tin lady admired the flowers, gazed into space, and talked about trivial things.

'Oh look!' exclaimed Mrs. Sinha, who stood at some small distance from them, as Kirana burst on to the scene, followed by an entourage of male students. Kirana's third-year class looked but did not move. 'I'm going to find out what's happening.' Mrs. Sinha followed the last man with a sense of purpose. The group went back into the hall, as others did. A few minutes later, a subdued Mrs. Sinha came back and joined the group.

'What's going on backstage?' Sarika asked.

'Oh, Kirana sahib is singing and Naushad is playing the violin.'

'Naushad.' Sarika tried to recollect. 'Oh, the son of Ustad Mulayam Hasan?'

'Yes. He was passing through Lucknow and principal sahib asked him to perform. He graciously agreed to.' As Mrs. Sinha gave out this information, Sarika noticed that she seemed to be pulling out of whatever had pushed her down. 'I had a quick word with Naushad. He remembered me from the time I had met his father, many years ago.'

Sarika trained her eyes on the stage, where Kirana sahib was settling in to sing with two tanpura accompanists and a tabla and a harmonium player. Mrs. Sinha dashed out in search of a spittoon, then dashed back in and sat down with her group.

'Amazing lady,' said Kirana to his wife late that night. 'I wish you had come to the college function.'

'Mrs. Sinha? What did Mrs. Sinha do?'

'She wanted to accompany me on the tanpura today.'

'And?'

'I told her that I was asking two people from the gents class. I didn't want a lady accompanying me.'

'What did she say?'

' "Oh, then I'll accompany Naushad sahib," she said.' Kirana looked at his wife, still in disbelief. Surya burst out laughing. 'What did you tell her?'

'I said "you go relax, listen in peace to all of us perform. Why would you want to sit upright on stage and get hot under the lights." That's all I could say. I had to have a gent play with Naushad, too.'

'Who else performed?'

'Swati sang.'

'Is anything wrong?' Surya asked noting the suddenly serious look on her husband's face.

'I don't know.'

Surya waited for him to continue.

'There's something different about her,' Kirana said. 'I don't know what it is. She doesn't come to me as much in college for help. Maybe…'

'Maybe she doesn't need as much help. Last year was different because it was her first year here from Assam. She was new and unsure of herself. It's probably changed now.'

'Could be. But I'm sure that's not it. And then, the saree she wore this evening for her performance was so expensive. For a poor girl like her.'

'What are you saying?'

'I don't know.'

'Everyone has at least one good saree in her box, no matter how poor. That must be her only one.'

'True. That's probably what it is. What a long, tiring day,' he said yawning and stretching himself. 'Tomorrow morning I won't go anywhere.'

'Good,' said Surya. 'We'll have the house to ourselves then, while baby sleeps.'

11

Sinha instructed his chauffeur to park in the shade, buy some samosas, rasgullas, and tea, bring them up, and then wait for him by the car. He wouldn't be too long. Slowly, Sinha carried his bulk up a flight of stairs and let himself in through the front door and onto the verandah of the small flat. Panting, he wiped the sweat off his forehead with a large, white handkerchief embroidered with his initials — SKS — and looked down the quiet street of the compound that housed a hundred of these identical units. Swati wasn't there yet.

He turned around and went into the sparsely furnished drawing-cum-dining room and as his derriere sank into the divan, he saw little wisps of dust escape the deep brown seat. He dusted the cushion with his bare hand and reaching out turned on the small crème ceiling fan, watching as it slowly gained speed, each blade black with dust, moving faster and faster until it became a blur of crème and black. Sitting back, he looked around to reacquaint himself with his surroundings. Despite the hot, dry weather, the room had a damp, musty smell to it. The small windows — little holes in the wall — were tightly shut and their panes almost opaque from grime collected over many years. The plain concrete floor of the room was covered with a thick layer of dust and Sinha saw the imprints of his feet where he had come into the room. He would have to ask Yadav to send someone to clean the place. It was the first time he had come here this season, after his acquaintance, a member of the legislative assembly, had gone home to his village and sublet Sinha his flat. The call bell rang and he went to the door.

'Back already?' he said to his chauffeur. 'Come in and put the stuff on the table in the dining room.'

'The rasgullas didn't look fresh, sahib, so I bought some milk pudding,' said the chauffeur, putting everything carefully on the table covered with a plastic table cover. 'The milk pudding looked very fresh. They made it just this morning.'

'Good.' The door bell rang again. 'Go and wait for me by the car,' said Sinha, following him to the door. 'Swati ji, come in,' he said, smiling at the young woman. 'I was watching the road for you.'

Swati entered and stood in the verandah.

'Did you have any trouble finding this place?'

'No, the rickshawman knew.'

'Good. It is so hot, it would have pained me to see you go around in the heat looking for this place. But why are you standing here. Come in. Please come in,' he said, pointing the way to the drawing room. 'Please sit down,' he said to Swati, who stood awkwardly, clutching her canvas bag hard. 'May I offer you a cup of tea? You came at the perfect time. As you saw, the driver just brought this stuff upstairs.' He held out a mug of tea. 'I am not offering you a snack, because you have to sing for me and if you eat now you'll make an excuse and escape singing for me today.' He smiled at her.

Swati put her bag on the divan and took the mug from Sinha sahib's hand. 'Please sit down. Why are you standing?' Swati sat down next to her bag.

'This tea is not very hot,' he said, sitting down next to her and letting his hand brush against her arm. She did not move away from him. A few weeks ago in the car he had let his hand fall accidentally into her lap and on her hand and she had moved away from him as if a bee had stung her. He had looked at her, surprised, unable to understand the fuss or unaware that his errant hand had slipped away from him. Then, as she jerked her hand away, he pretended to see his on her lap for the first time and put it on the car seat in between them. The next time he had brought her a bottle of Intimate in apology, saying that he was so preoccupied with work that at times he didn't know what he did. Certainly insulting her in any way had not been his intention. She had refused the gift. He said it meant that she had not forgiven him. She had slipped it silently into her canvas bag. The next time they met, Swati wore the Intimate. 'No matter how hard you try, when you get the tea from outside, it always gets cold,' he said.

'It is fine,' she said, taking a sip. 'It is a hot day.'

'You never take a cold drink.'

She smiled.

'What will you sing for me today?' he asked, patting her on her shoulder.

'Whatever you want,' she said, not moving away, but not relaxed either.

'What does your heart want?'

'I will sing what your heart wants. A *geet*, a bhajan. I don't have my instrument here, but I will do my best.'

'There is a harmonium here. But your throat is so melodious, you don't need an instrument.'

'Yes?' she said, smiling at him.

'Yes,' he said, trying to hold her gaze.

When Swati left after an hour or so, Sinha locked up the apartment and directed his chauffeur to take him to the factory. He knew Swati would succumb; it was just a matter of time. As a businessman who believed in accumulation and paying out as little as possible, he observed the subjects around him very well. Swati was poor and though Sinha had little regard for the morals of the lower classes, he knew that her parents' profession as teachers would have shaped her moral outlook. Had she belonged to just the poor, she would have been his by now. But he was in no hurry. It was part of good business to cultivate relationships, to give full attention to the object present, make a note of key traits, wait for the right opportunity, and then focus on the next problem at hand. By the time he reached the factory and turned on the two-in-one in his office, Swati no longer occupied any space in his conscious memory.

~

'So college will close in a week and then you'll be gone to Assam,' he said a few weeks later. 'It closes on 10th May, yes?'

'Hm,' she said.

'You look worried.'

She looked at her hands.

'What is the matter?' he asked.

'I am not going to Assam.'

He raised his eyebrows.

'I had rented a room in Kali Bari so I could stay in Lucknow in the summer. Many students from the hostel stay there, because we can't go home every time the college closes. I have my tuitions, my AIR (All India Radio) audition, so I thought I'd just stay here and practice and teach. Everything was finalized. Then yesterday, the landlord told me that he gave the room to someone else.'

'Why?'

'He could pay him twenty rupees more than I could.'

'So now you don't have a place to stay?'

She nodded.

'Have you looked anywhere else?'

'The rents are very high everywhere. I can't spend everything I earn on rent.'

'What will you do then?'

'I don't know. I can't go to Assam.'

'No.'

Sinha regarded her benevolently. Swati was a simple girl. A diffident mercenary. Lacking pride, she accepted his gifts with humility and showed an almost childlike appreciation of them, once she had gone through the obligatory refusals. As long as he could dazzle her eyes with his wealth and throw her a few odds and ends, she would be loyal to him and might even nurture some little affection for him somewhere in her heart. She was no different from the government officers and clerks that he routinely bribed. The difference lay in their attitude. Like old people accepting help but not admitting to taking it for fear of seeming dependent on their children, the file movers of the government liked to be made to feel that they were the lords. Sinha had to pay tribute to their Egos. He pandered shamelessly, flattering them, yet observing them, noting their weaknesses to be used to advantage at a later time. In Swati's acceptance of his simple demands in return for gifts he found something vaguely touching. He sensed in her a strong obligation to repay him with her talents for the material knick-knacks he threw at her. As long as she did not foolishly harbour any unrealistic expectations of him, he felt his little arrangement with her would work well.

'I can help you,' he said softly, leaning toward her.

She looked up immediately.

'This flat is mine for a few months,' he said, peering into her eyes. 'If you like, you can stay here until college reopens in early July.' Sinha had rented the flat for the past two years and sometimes he would let his relatives or friends use it during a wedding when space was tight.

Swati groped for words.

'You don't have to worry about anything or think too much about it. You can treat it as your own for the time you're here. Other people have stayed here in the past. Yadav put his guests here last year when his sister's daughter got married. Sunaina Devi has also used it.'

'Oh.'

Sinha shrugged.

'No rent?' she asked.

'No. You stay here as my guest. I've already told you that other people have stayed here. If you don't need it, I'll give it to whoever else wants it.'

Swati gulped.

'Think about it. It is just a matter of two months.'

Sinha relaxed into the divan and rested his back against the wall, keeping his eyes fixed on Swati. He could almost see the wheels of thought turning in her head, as if replaying the events from the past six months or so that had led her to this flat and into this situation. If she had believed in the purity of his intention at first or had thought that his interest in her was simply related to her beautiful voice, she now understood that his journey had led all along to this destination. Her mouth twitched ever so slightly as she comprehended the terms of the rental agreement.

He would come here often and she could never refuse his demands. The image of her family flashed through her mind. What could she do — she had to fend for herself. For a few seconds, as she looked straight ahead at the wall, she appeared to weigh her options. So far, his demands hadn't been too hard to fulfil. His expectation now would be the hardest, yet not unusual to the realm in which she operated. And after awhile, she would get used to him. Drawing her lips tightly together, she turned to him.

'And what will you want in return?' she asked. Her eyes met his playfully.

In reply, he held her by the shoulders from behind and pulled her to himself.

She turned sideways and briefly met his gaze.

12

Ravi woke up with a start. The Westclox alarm clock on his desk showed 7:45 and he had to report to his department at 8:00 a.m. He jumped out of bed, grabbed his shaving mug with his shaving brush, razor, toothbrush, toothpaste, and shaving cream, and charged to the bathroom. Why couldn't he remember getting up and turning off the alarm clock? He drew a blank. The bathrooms were wet and quiet since those who had to work that morning had already left and the others were still fast asleep. Ravi speeded through his shave. Damn, he said, as blood trickled down his chin. He held his towel to his cut for a few seconds, then rushed through toilet and bath, ran back to his room, held a Dettol-soaked cotton swab to his chin as he picked up his stethoscope, blood pressure instrument, and percussion hammer, let the cotton fall to the ground as he padlocked his room, and ran out of his hostel, all in a record time of twenty minutes.

It was his second day as an intern in the gynaecology rotation, one he didn't care for except that it fed into his obsession to be a great doctor, and he did not want to be late. He speed walked through the banana-skin littered streets of Old Lucknow from his hostel to Queen Mary's Hospital. He ran up the stairs and into the duty room. The senior resident was talking to her team of doctors and looked at her watch as Ravi tried to glide unnoticed into the group. Ravi lowered his eyes and listened carefully to her explanation of a particularly serious case that had come in the night before. The junior resident added some details from that morning.

'So whom do we have here?' asked the senior resident, walking into the first-stage room wherein lay a young woman.

'This is Swati,' said the junior resident. 'She came in this morning. Wants an MTP.'

The senior resident raised an eyebrow and unclipped the young woman's case sheet from the headrest. 'We don't have her complete history yet.'

'She just came in,' said the junior resident. 'Looks a little fishy.'

'Ravi,' said the senior resident.

'Yes, ma'am.'

'Take her case history. We'll come back to this one.' She began to walk away, then turned toward Swati again. 'She's over eighteen?' she murmured.

'Yes,' said the junior resident. 'We don't need permission from her guardians.'

Ravi watched their retreating backs for a second, then took the case sheet and stood next to the woman. He fumbled in his apron pocket for a pen, avoiding her. She was there with another woman of her age — no mother, no older person arounsd her — just a young attendant, only mildly interested. She did not wear the marks of a married woman.

'Name Swati Borah,' he said, glancing at her. She gave the barest nod. 'Age?'

She met his eyes for the briefest moment, then cast hers down.

'Twenty two,' said the attendant.

'Husband's name?'

Swati kept her eyes lowered.

Ravi held first one woman and then the other in his gaze. 'Is your husband here?' he asked Swati.

Swati turned her head away from him.

'What is your name?' Ravi asked the attendant.

'Mandira.'

'Where is her husband?'

'She is unmarried,' said Mandira.

'Are your parents here?' Ravi asked Swati again.

She shook her head.

'Where do your parents live?'

Swati tilted her head toward her attendant.

'Assam,' said the attendant.

'Are you all alone then?' he asked kindly.

'Yes,' said Mandira.

'Where do you live?'

'In the hostel,' said Mandira after a long pause.

'What hostel?' asked Ravi frowning in concentration.

'The music college.'

'Oh,' said Ravi. 'You're a student at the music college?' Do you know my sister, Sarika? The words almost spilled out of his mouth, but he checked himself.

Swati nodded.

A dagger pierced his heart. She looked so young and vulnerable. After several seconds, Ravi spoke, not sure whether he should ask the question. 'Did someone at the college do this to you?'

Swati shook her head. Relieved, Ravi asked gently,

'Does the father know? Have you asked him to marry you?'

Mandira stood still; Swati remained silent. Ravi ran his eyes over the woman's young body draped in a cheap nylon saree, at her thin hairless arms, hands that had seen hard work, at her bare feet with the chipped nail polish, and came back to her face again. Her fine, yellowish skin, high cheekbones, and black eyes bespoke a North-eastern ancestry. She had parted her jet black hair in the middle and wore it in two braids that came down to her hips. Aware of Ravi's appraising look, Swati turned her head away and Ravi saw tears rolling down her cheeks, even as the features on her face remained so remarkably still.

'What do you want us to do?' he asked.

'Cleaning,' Swati said, barely audible.

'Date of last period.'

'August.'

'Don't remember the date?'

Swati shook her head.

'Two months, then,' he said, more to himself than to her. Under the subheading Clinical diagnosis, he put down 'Early pregnancy for medical termination of pregnancy.'

'Do you know the man?'

Swati nodded.

'Did he…force you…rape?'

She turned her head away from him and cried; her shoulders shook as the tears gushed out.

'Swati,' he said gently. 'You must tell me. If not now, then a little later. If it was a rape, we have to tell the police.'

'It was not a rape,' said Mandira in a flat, toneless voice.

Ravi studied the young woman's face. How did she get herself into this situation? Appearing so innocent. There was something movingly decent about her: He was not willing to believe that she would sell her body for money. Did someone use a moment of weakness to his advantage? Yet, how could a respectable young woman get herself into this predicament? After all, poor women abounded, but not all got themselves into this mess. Wasn't the victim at least a little responsible for her fate in a circumstance like this? Maybe, then, his sympathy was misplaced. Maybe he should be careful around her, for who knew what she might say to clear herself?

'Can you walk?' he asked Swati.

She wiped her tears with the end of her saree and nodded.

'We will go to the septic labour room. That's where you'll be cleaned. Come, I will show you where it is.'

Swati looked at Mandira.

'Mandira will have to stay outside. She can't come in with you,' he said as they reached the room used for unbooked cases of pregnancy on the same floor. 'You will have to wait here,' he said to Mandira.

Fear leapt into Swati's eyes.

'Mandira will be here when you come out,' said Ravi, as they went in. Ravi steered Swati toward an empty table. 'Lie down here in your petticoat. Doc' sa'ab will be here soon.'

'Do you have everything ready?' the senior resident asked everyone in general as she swept into the room.

'Yes, Doc' sahib,' said the junior resident.

As the doctors came around the table, Swati sought out Ravi and he saw terror in the young woman's eyes. He noted the light skin and the prominent external jugular vein. The doctors talked routinely about her. She lay silently, listening, and clenched the sides of the delivery table.

13

The murmuring ceased as Nagde sahib walked slowly into the class, measuring each step with his walking stick. Putting all his weight on his cane, he sat on the chair and faced his five seventh-year students who faced him. 'We were doing Raga *Rageshri*. Swati, start the alap and the *vilambit khayal*.'

Swati strummed the tanpura for several seconds, but her voice froze in her throat. Tears streamed down her pale face.

'What's the matter, *beta*?' Nagde sahib asked. 'Start singing.'

Swati lay her tanpura down and broke into sobs.

'Are you not feeling well?' he asked with concern.

Swati continued to sob.

'You can all go,' he said to the class and the tabla accompanist. 'I will listen to you tomorrow; you must know all the compositions by heart, otherwise I will make you stay after class and sing till you know them.'

The class rose slowly and left, staring openly at Swati as they dragged their chappals out of the room. After the last person had exited, Nagde sahib slowly rose from his chair and sitting down next to Swati said very gently, 'Go to your room, *beta*. Everyone has now left.'

Swati wept hysterically now.

'What is the matter?' Nagde sahib asked.

'I am ruined, master sahib,' she said after several minutes.

Nagde sahib slowly raised his stiff, arthritic arm and put his hand on her shoulder.

'I have had an abortion.' It came out quickly, as if she were scared that she might change her mind about making the confession. 'I had planned not to tell anyone after I came back from the hospital, but I feel so weak that I can barely sit up. I don't know what to do or where to go. What will I tell my parents? How will I show my face to society? All the girls in the hostel know. Soon it will be all over the college. Everyone will point at me and smile.'

Nagde sahib nodded slowly. In his fifty-year career in music, this was not the first time he had heard of an unwanted pregnancy. 'Who is the father?' he asked very softly.

Swati doodled a design with her index finger on the white sheet on the wooden platform.

'Is he at the college?'

She shook her head.

'Go back to your room and rest,' he said. 'Don't come to class until you feel strong enough. Another year and you can go back to your parents.

61

No one in Assam will know any of this. If you want, I can talk to the principal and we can take the matter to the higher authorities, but you'll have to tell me who the father is.'

'Master sahib,' she said, trying to keep her voice steady. 'What will I do? What will people say? I am ruined. No one will ever marry me. If my parents find out,' she said in a fresh flood of tears, 'they will kill me. They will call me *charitraheen*. People will call me *charitraheen*.'

'Why are only *you* the characterless one?' Nagde sahib smiled at her incredulous face. 'The father should share half the responsibility, too,' he said. 'Now go to your room and rest.'

~

The following week, Mrs. Sinha came rushing into the group, breathless from the exertion of climbing the flight of stairs from the ground floor to the first floor. The circle of students waiting outside Kirana's class opened a little to let the newcomer in. 'Did you hear?' she asked.

Mrs. Sinha put her hand on her heaving chest and moved her head up and down to indicate that she wanted to catch her breath. The group looked intently at her. As she stood panting, she took out from her handbag a silver box with a circle of fine filigree work in the center of the lid, opened it carefully and gingerly took out two prepared betel leaves, then closed the box, and put it back in her big black leather handbag. Preparing betel leaves was a ritual Mrs. Sinha observed with great rigour every morning. She sat on the verandah in her rattan chair and spread her paraphernalia on the previous day's newspaper that lay on the elegant crème rattan table with a red stripe. Meticulously, she picked a leaf, spread some lime and *kattha* — a narcotic vegetable extract — that turned the lime red, and set it on the newspaper. When she had thus prepared ten leaves, she cut some betel nuts with a *sarota* — a scissor-like implement — and scattered them on the leaves. Then she folded each leaf three times into an imperfect triangle and put it on a moist rag. When all the leaves were on the rag, she wrapped them up and put them in her silver betel box. She looked around and made her way to the iron railing of the verandah where her classmates stood and tucked her betel leaves into her mouth. The group re-formed around her.

'A big *kand* happened here the other day,' she said softly, leaning back against the railing.

The girls moved close together, shoulders touching.

'Oh, it was a big scene,' said Mrs. Sinha, moving her neck back for emphasis. She chewed her betel leaves with deep concentration, then turned to see if anyone stood on the side lawn below. Seeing no one in danger of receiving a cascade, she spat out a stream of betel juice. Turning again, she wiped the edges of her mouth delicately with a corner of her embroidered lace handkerchief, tucked her handkerchief into her bra strap, and began to narrate her version of Swati's story.

'Do you think one of the college teachers here did?' Mrs. Sinha completed her sentence by moving her head in a circle. 'I wonder who it could be... Mishra ji or Sharma ji...'

Sarika blushed as she suddenly understood Mrs. Sinha's implication. Casting her eyes around quickly to see if anyone had noticed her reaction, she was glad to note that they were all busy listening to Mrs. Sinha. Sarika tried to appear calm like the others.

'How do you know this story in such detail when you were not there?' Geeta interrupted.

'What don't I know?' said Mrs. Sinha smugly. 'I know everything that happens in the college. People tell me everything.'

'You mean Swati told you this story?' Sarika asked in disbelief.

'No,' said Mrs. Sinha petulantly, 'but one of the girls in the hostel did and she's in Swati's class, so she should know.'

'Then maybe that girl should know who the father is. How do you know one of the teachers at the college has done this?' asked the flourtin lady. 'How can you start thinking of each teacher that way?'

'I'm not saying anything, baba,' said Mrs. Sinha, taken aback. 'I'm very careful in what I say. You know that.' The group looked at her steadfastly. 'I'm just saying that that is what people *can* think. And people can say all sorts of things when something like this happens. But, of course, in Swati's case we do know ...' Mrs. Sinha stopped midsentence and the group followed her gaze to the top of the stairs.

Sarika, a little slower than the others in following signs, soon saw the cause for Mrs. Sinha's silence. Swati and Mandira walked by and for the briefest moment Sarika caught Swati's eye. Swati appeared to notice the sudden silence and everyone's gaze; she hung her head and quickened her step. A wave of sympathy swept over Sarika. Nevertheless, she tried to discern lust in Swati's face. Her eyes, bashful as ever, reflected a feeling of only a tenuous hold on her environment. Eyes as reflections of the soul meant nothing; Swati looked guileless as ever. Hard as it was for Sarika to comprehend the carnal, she understood that Swati's illegitimate relationship could lead to ruin. Despite her talent, people at the college would think about Swati's slip before giving her credit for her music. Her abortion had branded her on the forehead. There was no escaping the memory of the deed as long as she remained at the college.

Kirana sahib called them from inside. It was time for class.

~

'This rain will not stop any time soon,' said the principal, peering out into the darkness from the portico of the college building. It was after eight in the evening and apart from a few teachers, everyone had gone home. The rain had been falling in sheets all afternoon and evening, accompanied by strong winds, and few students had come to the college that day. 'The gods have something in mind.'

'Some sin,' said Gajendra, who stood with his umbrella in readiness.

'How will you bike home in this rain?' asked the principal with some concern.

'Oh, principal sahib, if I have to fall on the road and die today, I will. Not everything is planned by us alone.'

'True,' said Kirana, patting Gajendra on the shoulder. The three men stood in a row and watched the burst of raindrops on the tar driveway. The lights on the college gates appeared blurred from even the few yards that separated the men from the gate.

'Does anyone know what is happening to Swati?' the principal asked suddenly.

'Why do you ask?' asked Gajendra.

'Just like that.'

'Still. There must be a reason.'

'I go to the girls' hostel once in a while to see how everyone is doing and on talking to Swati found out that she was preparing for the All India Radio audition.' He glanced around. 'And then the warden told me...' he said in a conspiratorial tone.

'You mean you didn't know?' asked Gajendra unabashedly.

'And how would I know?' asked the principal sharply. 'At any rate, she wants help as she prepares for the audition. Who can help her?'

'You could,' said Gajendra with a laugh, inviting a hostile glare from the principal.

'Kirana sahib?' asked the principal.

Kirana stiffened.

'Would you consider teaching a poor girl?' the principal added after some thought. 'She needs to find her feet.'

'Kirana sahib has helped her in the past,' said Gajendra through a mouthful of tobacco. 'Haven't you, Kirana sahib?'

Kirana took a deep breath. He had built his reputation as a helpful person, but that idea did not stretch to cover a woman who had slipped morally in the eyes of his acquaintances. His image had always to be protected.

'Have you, Kirana sahib?' asked the principal.

'So she's planning an AIR audition, is she? I didn't know,' said Kirana.

Rain continued to fall loudly on the tar driveway in front of the men.

'When is her audition?' asked Kirana.

'Soon, I think,' said the principal.

'Don't know when this rain will stop,' said Kirana, as lightening flashed in the distance.

'So, Kirana sahib,' said the principal, turning toward him, 'have you taught Swati in the past?'

'Informally.'

'Meaning?'

'I asked her to come to my room before my first class if she had any difficulties. My doors are always open to any student who wants to learn from me. She came a few times...'

'*Phir kya baat hai.* Then what's the problem! You can teach her again, can't you?' the principal persisted.

What was a man to answer, wondered Kirana. If he agreed, he would be going against his better judgment which dictated to him to stay away from the girl. What if one day his name became linked with hers? Yet, how could he deny the principal this not-quite-request? In the dark, he felt principal sahib's eyes on himself. 'I suppose,' he said softly. 'If she came to me.' He could always wiggle out of it later — somehow strike the balance between keeping principal sahib happy and not opening his reputation to questioning. As Kirana contemplated ways of unbinding himself, the principal was distracted by the sound of shuffling footsteps. He looked up, just as it seemed that Nagde sahib would miss a step on the three that led down to the portico. With one quick movement he took the old teacher's arm. Kirana quickly took his other, glad to be out of focus. A circle formed around Nagde sahib.

'The spirit is still strong,' said Nagde sahib, leaning on his cane.

'How's Swati, Nagde sahib?' asked the principal. 'She's in your class, is she not?'

'Colourful behind lowered eyes,' said Gajendra.

'As well as a woman can be, who has in one day lost both her unborn child and possibly its father,' said Nagde sahib.

14

The room filled with the sound of the tonic note rendered in a deep voice. Sarika listened intently as Kirana improvised the alap, a detailed exposition that quickly went into intricate note combinations, showing her paths never tread before, depths never before plumbed.

'You can sometimes use a little voice to create a big ornament, like an artist etches a landscape on a grain of rice,' he said. 'Little strokes, great effect.' He demonstrated his meaning. 'And every time you sing, devise a new way of reaching perfection.'

Sarika looked at her teacher in awe, at this her first private lesson after having learnt from him in college for a year and a half. They sat cross legged, facing each other in the center of the living room, from where Sarika had moved the coffee table when she had heard Kirana sahib's scooter pull into the driveway in the late morning. Leaving their sandals at a respectable distance from the learning area, the two were now settled comfortably on the soft cotton rug. Nirmala observed the proceedings from her vantage point on the chair with a mirrorwork pillow. Nirmala wanted to spend the first few lessons during Sarika's summer vacation observing Kirana for she belonged to the old school that had never dissociated musicians from the sphere of courtesans. The stakes were high for lessons from a man meant entrusting her daughter's chastity to a class of colourful humanity.

Kirana had approached Sarika just before the beginning of the summer holidays to tell her that he wanted to teach her at home during the summer. Flabbergasted, she asked her mother, who reluctantly assented, not willing to see in her daughter the artistic potential her teacher saw. Nirmala belonged to a high-bred family of bureaucrats for whom the only professions worth following were those that put one in a high social class. None of the arts qualified. She watched closely as Kirana taught.

'Always treat your notes delicately,' he said. 'Like a lover treats his beloved.'

Sarika giggled. Nirmala glared at her. Sarika bit her lip.

'Each note has a nature,' he continued. 'When you sing a note, think of the emotion it should evoke, both in you and in the listener. Think of *dha* as standing all alone. It is a lonely note; he has no one in the world. Think of him as standing alone in a desert. Feel his pain. And as you feel his pain, you will be able to sing in a way that brings out that pain.' He sang and showed her. Sarika felt the goosebumps rise.

'And take a gentler approach to *ni*,' he continued. 'Like *dha* making a request to *ni*. And as you approach *taar sa*, keep going around it, never quite touching it until the audience writhes in restlessness for the note. Then when you sing the high *sa*, your audience will sense a release.'

The sounds and smells of the kitchen floated out to the room, mingled with music, and hung below the ceiling like gas balloons. Ramu had begun lunch preparations and the insistent whistle of the Hawkins pressure cooker, the dropping of a steel pot into the stone sink, the clatter of steel plates, the smell of asafoetida and whole red chili peppers heated and dropped into a pot of cooked lentils, the piercing smell of seasoning a vegetable, drifted through the air, lending a further homeyness to the dark, sleepy room.

The sun was already high in the sky and the shades were drawn over the windows to keep out heat and glare. The ventilators with their dark cloth covers, right near the high ceiling, were closed, the ceiling fan worked furiously, the cooler in the window blasted air and moisture into the dry air of the room. All provided a low-pitched accompaniment to the drone from Sarika's tanpura. Sarika looked eagerly at Kirana sahib as she finished a piece of improvisation.

'Sing slowly at first to make sure every note is right. Speed will come automatically when you have mastered a combination.'

As the summer holidays progressed, every lesson strengthened the base of Sarika's knowledge of music. The very *palte* she had sung since new first year — *sa re ga, re ga ma, ga ma pa, ma pa dha, pa dha ni, dha ni sa* and then the descent — took on a whole new complexion as he taught her different ways of singing these same exercises.

'Remember, these *palte* form the foundation of the *taans* you will improvise as you go into the more senior classes. Later this year, I will stop dictating *taans* and you will have to create your own. Take any one *palta* or two *palte*, combine them and see how many different note combinations you can make. Take *sa re ga, ga re sa* — the ascent and descent in three notes and see what you can do with them,' he said and started singing. 'So with just three notes you can make so many combinations. With all the seven notes, you can make hundreds.'

Sarika practised hard so she could sing for her teacher when he came two days later. She listened for the sounds of his arrival — the gate creaking open, the crunch of the gravel under the wheels of the scooter, the passage of a few moments, the clang of the closing gate. But that day, the excitement of seeing Kirana sahib was dampened when she had to turn away a friend from the door as Kirana sahib sat waiting for her on the living room rug. As she drifted away from childhood friends, Sarika searched for a reason. 'I never know what to do when people ask me to sing,' she said, addressing her mother and Kirana sahib in the darkened living room. 'I can't just start singing classical music. I need my instrument, I need accompaniment. No one understands.'

Kirana laughed.

Sarika continued. 'They tell me "what do you learn in the music college every day if you can't even sing for us?" I don't know what to tell them.'

'Tell them you're learning classical music,' said Nirmala, who had learned vocal music herself in her younger days and now displayed her talent only at social gatherings, where she always obliged those who asked her for a song with a beautifully rendered bhajan or devotional. 'It is not like light music that can be sung anywhere or at any time, without instruments or accompaniment. You need a certain atmosphere for it.'

'I tell them, but they don't understand,' said Sarika. 'They are used to seeing people singing film songs on stage at weddings, at Holi or

Janmashtami functions, and wonder why I can't do that. Why I can't sing a film song. I tell them I don't know any.'

'Tell them that no matter what you sing, you will sing four *taans* at the end,' said Kirana smiling. 'But seriously,' he continued, directing his remarks at Nirmala. 'What Sarika is saying is true. That is the irony of a classical singer's life. Even today, after all these years, I don't have a good answer for those who ask me to sing. And they say, "how can you *teach* singing if you can't sing *yourself*?" I let it slide.'

'Doesn't it bother you?' asked Sarika. 'It would, me. What bothers me more is that my friends whom I have known all my life say that. The funny thing is if I tell them I can't sing, they say why don't you play your instrument for us? I have to tell them you can't play a tune on the tanpura; it's just drone. They think it's a sitar. Anyway, they are not my friends any more.'

'Why?' asked Kirana.

'Because we have nothing to say to one another. They are still interested in film stars and I'm not.'

'You don't see movies any more?' asked Kirana.

'Of course I do,' said Sarika. 'How should I say it? But actors and their lives don't interest me the way they used to. I am more interested in the lives of great classical musicians. My friends couldn't care less. It irritates me.'

'An artist has to be sensitive to produce beauty, it is true, but he can't let other people's ignorant comments bother him too much,' said Kirana. 'If he did, he wouldn't be able to concentrate on his art. He would only be thinking of their comments.'

'But why do they say such things?' asked Sarika.

'Because they don't understand the change that is coming about in you,' said Kirana. 'The more advanced you become in your music, the less people will understand and you will find yourself going farther and farther away from those who do not inhabit your artistic field.'

'Artists are social outcasts,' said Nirmala; 'the greater the genius, the more the isolation. That is the tragedy of their lives. They work doggedly in anonymity in their youth. If they are lucky, their contemporaries may recognize them, but they are still a lonely breed. You see, adulation is not enough. They want understanding, communication with an equal, empathy, which is denied them, for few can enter their domain. We

69

cannot conceptualize their artistic experiences, and we ridicule what we can't understand.'

'But why should the world be so cruel to artists?' asked Sarika, not from a need to learn further, for her mother had already captured the essence, but from a desire to keep the conversation going such that she remained the aggrieved party in a world largely insensitive to her type. These conversations made her feel close to her teacher. It was an environment she shared with him.

'They aren't deliberately cruel; they just don't understand,' said Kirana, in the tone of an elder speaking to a child.

Sarika was struck with Kirana sahib's sensitivity, which seemed to be drawing Nirmala out of her aloofness. Sarika noticed those old hawk eyes becoming gentler and a little more relaxed. Nirmala didn't look ready to pounce all the time, settling instead into a sort of happy, matronly state where Kirana sahib was welcomed into the house as a friend and well wisher. Sarika, for her part, was surprised at how quickly her mother had warmed up to Kirana sahib, after her initial resistance to having a music teacher come to the house. As Kirana sahib occupied a larger portion of her mind, Sarika took it on herself to ensure that Kirana sahib stayed in her mother's good graces. She tried not to give in to her adolescent moodiness, for Kirana sahib had told her to be happy at all times. Nirmala noticed the change and told Ashwini that Kirana sahib was a positive influence on their daughter.

～

'I must tell you about a family I know,' said Mrs. Sharma, the neighbour. 'The daughter had a severe problem with constipation, so they started her on yoga. They didn't know the teacher at all, just followed somebody's recommendation. I don't know what that teacher did, Mrs. Kumar, but that girl put on so much weight that now it is hard for her parents to find a boy for her. She is of marriageable age, but they can't find anyone. She is such a good girl, I tell you Mrs. Kumar, so talented, so sweet natured, but what to do about the weight? It is so sad.' Mrs. Sharma paused and shook her head. 'They are willing to give a good dowry, but …It is a big problem. You see, that is why I am very scared to suggest anyone.'

Nirmala nodded sympathetically as the two women talked across the hedge that separated their houses. 'I've heard these stories about yoga, too, that if you stop doing it you put on a lot of weight. But I don't know what to do. Sarika's music teacher has told me to find a yoga class for her to increase the capacity of her lungs through the breathing exercises and to make her voice more steady. He has even told her to hold a burning candle in front of her mouth to see if the flame flickers.'

'And does it flicker?'

'Yes. So you see, she needs to make her lungs stronger.'

'But ask Gupta ji on the other side of my house. He, I think, does yoga every morning. Mrs. Gupta was telling me he has high blood pressure and he has been doing yoga for that every day for two years.'

'And has it helped him?' asked Nirmala.

'Mrs. Gupta says it has. And he's learned from someone in Lucknow itself.'

'I will ask,' Nirmala said.

But the Guptas held no more insights into yoga than the Sharmas. At dinner time, Nirmala tried to bring up the yoga issue, but as the family sat around the formica table for six, Sarika talked ceaselessly to her father and it became hard to focus on a serious issue.

'I'm switching to arts after high school,' said Sarika. 'I can offer music as one of my five subjects — might as well since I spend so much time on it.'

'I would rather you studied science, but with your music, arts may be better,' said Ashwini to his daughter.

'Papa,' said Sarika. 'There is this lady in my class who was saying the college doesn't attract as much talent as it used to after it went over to the government. Is that true?'

'I don't know,' said Ashwini. 'The teachers are paid much better than they've ever been. But it's probably true, because any time the government takes over, fairness goes out the window and everyone tries to bring in their own. How was the music lesson today?' Ashwini asked his daughter. 'Did Kirana sahib come to the house?'

'Kirana sahib says she should learn yoga,' said Nirmala. 'Her lungs don't have enough strength. She has to be able to hold her breath longer.'

'At least for a minute,' said Sarika.

'Send her to a yoga class if that's what Kirana sahib says,' Ashwini said to his wife.

71

'Why are you always getting after her?' Lakshmi asked her daughter-in-law. 'She's such a little girl; you are always asking her to do more than she is doing. Let her enjoy her childhood.'

Nirmala sighed and began to remove the spoons from the dishes in preparation for the servant's clearing up. She had learned ever since Lakshmi had started living with them that her mother-in-law liked to have the last word. It irritated her, but she kept quiet. Whatever the differences between herself and her mother-in-law, peace had to be maintained at all times, for Lakshmi was older and came to live with her son by right. Nirmala knew Ashwini would agree with her, but he would never speak up for her in his mother's presence.

A week later Sarika had a yoga class to go to. Her father had asked his stenographer to find out who could teach yoga to his daughter. The stenographer asked around until someone made a recommendation.

~

It was on her way home from a yoga lesson early one morning that Sarika caught a quick glimpse of Swati with a man whose face she couldn't see. Surprised to see her accompanied at that time of day, she thought about her abortion, then reprimanded herself for thinking like Mrs. Sinha. Swati's fall had jumped immediately to mind. She felt ashamed of herself for thinking so. Possibly Swati's father was visiting from Assam.

'I saw Swati this morning,' Sarika said to Kirana sahib. 'Mrs. Sinha, the gossip queen, hasn't said anything to us about her lately and I just wondered how she was faring in college. I hardly ever see her since her class is at a different time and she doesn't seem to come out of her room until class time.'

'She fell into bad company,' Kirana said to Nirmala. 'She was a nice girl when she came to the college on scholarship in sixth year, but very poor.'

'Does she learn from anyone privately?' asked Nirmala.

'No,' said Kirana.

'Will no one take her because she's too poor?' asked Sarika with a note of righteousness.

'She has a beautiful voice, but she's not very intelligent, when it comes to learning,' said Kirana, a hint of irritation in his voice. 'Your voice will take you only so far.'

'Oh.'

'When she first came to the college, I told her I could help her and a few times she came to me before the start of class. I taught her for several months but gave up, because she does not have the calibre to pick up what I tried to tell her. She can work wonders with her voice, but when I tried to get her to think of different paths to a raga, she was very slow. The arrangement petered out as she became busy with her tuitions.' Silence ensued and Kirana shifted uncomfortably in his seat as he thought of the principal's question to him about his availability for Swati preparing for her AIR audition. If she hadn't created a mess for herself, he would have had no objection to coaching her, her slowness notwithstanding. He saw no point in telling Sarika and her mother that he had not encouraged her too much after her unfortunate affair had come to light. Indeed, his attitude had been such that none but the most tenacious could have continued to learn from him. But again, the principal's request could not be denied.

'Yet she continues to receive her scholarship,' said Sarika.

'She can do a limited number of things very well,' he said, trying to get his thoughts back on track. 'And she has the gift of a beautiful voice. It is rare to have a voice like hers.'

Sarika felt a pang at this praise of another that took her by surprise. A comment about Swati's character rose immediately to her lips in retaliation, but she held herself back for she wanted Kirana sahib to always see her at her best. They sat silently for a few minutes, each wrapped in thought.

'What a lady she is,' said Kirana, shaking his head in disbelief. 'She has the dirt on everyone.'

'Mrs. Sinha?' asked Sarika, divining his thought.

Kirana nodded. 'She lives in a very big house. Sinha sahib must be a very successful businessman.'

'What kind of business does he own?' Nirmala asked.

'I don't know. Something to do with cars, tyres, I am not sure. Anyway, I went to her house: I have never seen anything like it. Imported furniture, Persian carpets, a Philips stereo system. Behanji,' he said turning to Nirmala, 'your husband is such a senior government officer and you live so simply.' He said it with unaffected awe. Mrs. Sinha, with all her money and her affluent lifestyle that put her in a different orbit from the ordinary, was so much easier to understand than Nirmala, the wife of the powerful home secretary, who could have chosen a lifestyle commensurate with her husband's official status. So many wives did, in effect becoming more conscious of rank than their husbands. But Nirmala's unassuming ways were disarming. When it came to orbits, Nirmala was definitely the sun; Mrs. Sinha's path never even came close to hers. 'Mrs. Sinha displays her wealth shamelessly,' he said.

'Successful business people always live well,' said Nirmala smiling. Sarika had lost interest in the conversation. When she thought about Kirana sahib after he left, what remained was the caressing tone of voice he used with her; what he said to her about himself, about her; the confidences he shared about the people she knew at the college — the principal and his power play, Kirana's disagreements with some of the other teachers, affairs; she ran through her mind all her conversations with him, going over and over a particular phrase or sentence that showed that she was special to him. But the nature of the exchange changed when her mother was around and it bored her. She fidgeted.

'Let us begin,' said Kirana, noting her restlessness. Sarika picked up the tanpura and began to play. '*Sa*,' he said.

15

Kirana's fifth year class paused and collectively cleared its throat. 'Yes,' said the teacher with a merry laugh, 'this raga asks how much *riyaz* you have done. You can fool others, but not your throat. Begin again.'

Already hoarse, only half the class sang, unwilling or unable to make one more foray into the *taar saptak*. It was the beginning of fifth year for Sarika, and her class was trying to master Basant, a raga that celebrated trees bursting with new foliage after the winter, flowers just beginning to bloom, earth rejoicing in rebirth. The raga favoured the high notes and as Sarika nudged her voice into the higher octave, she felt her throat was stretched over a rack. By the time the few who had ventured to sing came back to the theme phrase, their voices had shrunk to a squeak.

'Rest your throats for a few seconds,' said Kirana, resting his back against the wall.

'What a difficult raga, Kirana sahib,' said Mrs. Sinha. 'The throat feels as if one's been singing all day.'

'Yes,' he said absently. 'Sarika,' he said after a short pause. 'Prepare to sing a raga in Saraswati Hall for the Holi program.'

'What?!' said Sarika in bewilderment.

'A raga for the Holi program.'

Saraswati Hall was the college auditorium. Its floor was divided into three sections, like three giant steps. The audience sat on the floor covered with *dhurries* and white cotton sheets, teachers in the front and everyone else in the back. Sometimes as a student performed on stage, the principal would teach him from the floor, singing a note combination and urging the performer to try his own theme a little differently. The audience watched enthralled as the student, honoured that the principal considered him worthy of being taught, tried to reproduce accurately the intricacy of the combination.

'A solo?' asked Mrs. Sinha.

'Yes,' said Kirana.

'I'm quite ill prepared,' Sarika said.

'This is a good reason to prepare. It will also help you get over stage fright. Choose any evening raga you like,' he said. 'If you come to college fifteen minutes before class tomorrow, I will listen to you.'

'Let us resume *Basant*,' said Kirana.

They cleared their throats and sang the compositions through to the end. After class, Sarika sought out Geeta. 'I can't do it,' she said.

'It will be alright, if master sahib thinks so,' said Geeta. 'He wouldn't ask you if he didn't think you could do it.'

They had descended the mosaic staircase and reached the entrance to the building by the principal's office. Sarika was gripped with an awful feeling in the pit of her belly. She shivered in her light wool shawl. She stopped and said, 'You carry on.'

Geeta smiled and squeezed her hand. 'You'll be fine,' she said.

'I am dying of fright,' said Sarika. 'I am going to tell master sahib that I'm not ready to sing on stage yet.'

'Don't do that. He'll feel insulted.'

'Insulted?'

'These music teacher types want complete obedience. He's your guru; if he tells you to do something, you have to.'

'Oh.' Sarika paused. 'I hadn't realized that,' she added softly. 'I think I'll go talk to him.' She ran up, two steps at a time, mentally noting the shaking third step in the second landing, barged into the room and stopped short. Mrs. Sinha was on the platform, shawl thrown carelessly over one shoulder, revealing a thick gold chain, saree bunched up across her chest, showing a lace bra under a thin blouse. She cried softly, keeping her lace handkerchief across her nose. Behind his little desk, back to the wall, Kirana sahib slowly marked attendance for the just completed class.

'I'm sorry. I will come back,' said Sarika.

Mrs. Sinha looked up. 'No, no, why should *you* go away?' she said, wiping her tears quickly. 'You talk all you want to master sahib. I will go away.' She picked up her purse from the floor and marched out.

'I'm glad you came when you did,' said Kirana. 'I can't handle women's tears.'

'Why was she crying? She seemed okay just now in class,' Sarika said, forgetting her fear.

'She wanted to know why she couldn't sing on Holi. After all, she is the most senior person in the class. I told her that her voice didn't carry, even with a microphone. She then asked me if you and she could sing together. I refused because your voice would completely drown hers out. In a duet, both parties should have equal weight. That upset her. She said I liked you more because you were younger.' Kirana sahib shook his head. 'A full-grown woman like her!'

'What did you say?'

'Her voice,' he continued, obviously upset, 'is weightless. It evaporates even in the closed space of a small room before it has had a chance to press itself against anyone's ear. Technically, she gets everything right, it is true, but her voice is like a shapeless mist. What do you notice when she sings?'

'The tabla accompanist,' Sarika said giggling. 'He has a very good hand.'

'Exactly,' said Kirana sahib. 'No one notices her music. They pay attention to other things.'

'What did you say to her?'

76

'What does it matter what I said? Does it ever matter what anyone says? People will always believe what they want to, especially if it can explain away someone else's talent or success. But let's forget her.' His voice became gentler as he asked her, 'What brought you back here?'

'Oh, I'm just nervous about singing in Saraswati Hall. I'm not ready,' said Sarika timidly.

'What raga do you want to sing?'

'I don't know.'

'Think about it. Maybe you can choose the raga you sang in your fourth year finals. You already know that very well. A little practice and you'll be ready to go. Let me know tomorrow what you decide.'

~

And now here she was, in the middle of her Holi holidays, dreading each day that brought her closer to her stage concert. She had practised hard that morning and was now in her grandmother's room, trying to feed her porridge.

'Just a little more, Dadiji,' said Sarika. 'How will you build up the energy to fight the horrible effects of the chemotherapy if you don't eat?'

Lakshmi shook her head.

'Okay. Maybe a little later. Do you want to lie down?'

Sarika lowered her grandma's head on to her pillow and covered her with a heavy blanket. Sarika herself was hot. Holi was already here; summer would soon be upon them.

Lakshmi lay very still under her covers. The cancer was back and she was going through another round of chemotherapy; this time the fight was gone from her. She opened her eyes for a brief second and looked at her granddaughter. Sarika slipped her hand under the quilt, found Lakshmi's and gave it a squeeze.

When Lakshmi started feeling weak again a month ago, relationships in the household began to change. Though no one told her, Lakshmi knew the end was near. She stopped trying to get the last word in with Nirmala, who in turn suddenly became more tolerant of her. Seeing the easing of tension between her mother and grandmother, Sarika felt a deep sympathy for the dying woman. She wanted to reach out to her, hug her, to hold her close, to let her know that she was there and would not let

77

her feel alone, as so many times her grandmother had. She had come out every morning to the gate as Sarika left for her yoga class. In little things — waiting for her at the gate when it was time for her to return from the music college, sitting with her after dinner while she struggled with her food and Nirmala left the table to give instructions to the servants, putting a tika on her forehead before every test, making her favourite *nankhatai* biscuits — she had shown Sarika how much she cared. Sarika had been slow to respond. Not just her mother's, but her life, too, had been affected when her grandmother came to stay after she was diagnosed with cancer. She had spent all of her life in her own house in Moradabad, a town west of Lucknow, where she had lived with her son Ashok until her husband's death. But after the death, Ashwini had brought his mother home to Lucknow for a change of scene. When cancer struck, she stayed on. Life took on a different hue. Sarika, used to her nuclear family, had been slow to respond to her grandmother's affectionate gestures. Now that she had loosened that curtain of reserve that had kept her from her grandma, a new kind of emotion had begun to well in her heart.

Sarika studied her grandma's face — the large eyes, closed from feeling so sick; the proud nose with its sparkling half-karat diamond; the beautiful lips, now parched and cracked. For someone her age, her face was remarkably smooth. A few wrinkles around the eyes and a deep line that went from the sides of the nose to the corners of the mouth were the only signs that her skin was losing it tautness. Sarika ran her eyes quickly over her body weighed down by the covers. So petite. And she had given birth to six children!

The doorbell rang. 'Sarika,' said Nirmala, who had just walked in. 'The door.'

'Master sahib,' said Sarika, breaking into a broad smile, on seeing who stood at the door. 'What a surprise.'

'I thought you must be very nervous about your recital, so I decided to come and listen to you,' said Kirana. 'Have you decided what you'll sing?' he asked, settling down on the rug in the living room.

'*Shuddha Kalyan.*'

'Good.' As Sarika settled down with her tanpura, Kirana continued. 'You remember Ustad Mulayam Hasan, the famous violinist? His son, Naushad, will be teaching at the college from next term. You remember Naushad?'

'Yes, of course. I've heard him accompany his father and then about two years ago he played at the college on Holi.'

'It will be an interesting shift to tradition. As you know, the retiring professor does not come from a family of musicians.'

'Why is he coming to the college when his career has been made for him by his father?'

'Has it? Naushad has never shown the talent of his father, but he is certainly better than his predecessor. And the college hasn't seen anyone of his stature after it got acquired by the government.'

'He plays well,' said Sarika, suddenly sorry for the young man. She had overheard some teachers at the college dismiss his talent as being unworthy of comment when compared to his father's. 'Yes, but why this big break from the family's tradition of keeping the art strictly within the family or the staunch loyalists?'

'Possibly to see what he can do on his own. He is going to try out the college for a year or two.'

'How old is Naushad?'

'Twenties.'

'I like Ustad Mulayam Hasan,' said Sarika. 'He makes the violin sing.'

'That is the beauty of his music. It takes a certain soul to play like that. Let us begin. *Sa.*'

16

The circle was tight around Mrs. Sinha when Sarika barged in. 'Where's master sahib?' asked Sarika, oblivious of the air of anticipation she had so rudely stirred.

'He's in the principal's office. I think they're holding a meeting for the Holi program,' replied Mrs. Sinha irritatedly.

'She's telling us about Kirana sahib and his wife,' whispered Geeta as Sarika sat down.

'A love marriage?' said the flour-tin lady, unable to suppress the smile brought on by the thought that Kirana had loved his wife before marriage.

'His wife and he met while learning music in the Punjab and have been together since,' Mrs. Sinha said.

'Did they elope?'

'People say they ran away, but I think she must have trapped him. He is so handsome and she is so ordinary. Why would he have chosen her? You know how smart these Punjabi girls are. You know how if a man is guileless they can make him drink water from a leaf.'

'You mean he allowed himself to be led by the nose by his wife?'

'I decided to ask him one day,' continued Mrs. Sinha, looking around the room for approbation and ignoring the comment. She hated interruptions because they broke the rhythm of the story. Nine pairs of awed eyes watched her. 'He comes to my house to teach me sometimes because of his special regard for me. Anyway, I asked him one day. I said, "Kirana sahib, there is this big rumour about you and Mrs. Kirana. Everyone at the college says you and she eloped. Is that true?" He said he had heard that rumour, too, and that it wasn't true. He said the families knew each other from before. It was not even a love marriage, which would have been shameful. His father, who was a freedom fighter and a big idealist, chose Mrs. Kirana for his son, because he knew the girl's father, who was his friend and who would never be able to marry his daughter, having fallen on hard times. I don't know how much of his story to believe. How can there be the rumour in college, if there's no truth to it?'

'Rumours are, by their very nature, not true,' said Geeta.

'There is no smoke without fire,' retorted Mrs. Sinha. 'I am not a loose talker. I am saying this because I have reason to believe this is true.'

'And what could that reason be, except to besmirch somebody's name and reputation, which you seem to love doing?'

'You can keep your idealistic notions to yourself. The truth is the truth.'

'And you don't know what that is.'

'You don't want to accept what that is.'

Geeta glared at her.

The class fell silent, pondering the gossip. Sarika thought about Mrs. Kirana, whom she had seen a few times at the college concerts — overweight, big eyes, an aquiline nose, and sensuous lips painted lavishly with red lipstick. She wore her thick black hair in a single braid that ended with a black nylon ribbon and two short locks that she tucked behind her ears as a fashion statement. By themselves, her strands were a variation on those worn by film actresses, tresses that hung in front of their ears like the tendrils of an opu plant, but her hair always looked so uncombed that these locks mingled with the general confusion that reigned about her head. She wouldn't be bad looking if she lost some weight, concluded Sarika. But one thing that even Sarika with her critical teenage eye had noticed was the expression of pleasantness on Mrs. Kirana's face: approachable, good natured.

The women began whispering around Mrs. Sinha, who tucked a wad of betel leaf into her cheek with studied nonchalance. Sarika ran through the story in her mind, uncertain of its credibility, yet somehow drawn into and bothered by the picture that Mrs. Sinha had painted for them. Ahmed the college servant came into the class. 'Kirana sahib has said that he will not be able to teach today. He is still in a meeting with principal sahib about the Holi program. Go home. Come to do your class tomorrow.'

They went down the stairs and out onto the front lawn where they settled again into a little circle. Mrs. Sinha started a story about the head of the dance department. One by one the girls trickled out to the gate to catch their rides home.

Suddenly, Kirana emerged from the principal's office and stood talking to a couple of teachers in the portico. Seeing his group on the lawn, he came toward them smiling. 'You all are still here?'

'Some of us are waiting for our rickshawmen, master sahib,' said Geeta, standing up.

'I couldn't teach you today. Our meeting with the principal ran over. Tomorrow we'll have class as usual.'

He turned around and started walking toward the gate. Mrs. Sinha ran after him and said something. Apparently unable to hear, he stopped and bent his head toward her. Sarika watched closely from the lawn. Her mind still dwelled on Mrs. Sinha's story about him and his wife and she paid keen attention to his interaction with another woman. Mrs. Sinha was no longer the confident, boastful woman of a minute ago; she was like a little girl, standing on tiptoe to whisper something into Kirana sahib's ear. She stepped back and giggled as she finished whispering. Kirana looked at her and nodded. The smile was gone. Mrs. Sinha smiled, touched her chignon, and walked away. Kirana resumed walking, then turned around suddenly, as if he had just remembered something. He came up to Sarika's circle on the lawn.

'Sarika,' he said. 'Have you decided what raga you will sing in Saraswati Hall?'

'Yes,' she said a little perplexed. Hadn't they already gone over that at home two days ago?

Kirana glanced quickly at the girls in the circle, then said, 'Do you have some time now? Come up to class and I will hear you. Go upstairs. I will join you after I've had some tea,' he added. 'Come on time tomorrow,' he said to the other girls. 'I will hear those of you who haven't sung *Basant* for me and then I will start a new raga.' He turned and walked toward the gate.

Sarika picked up her books from the grass and went to wait for her teacher in the empty classroom. She started the drone.

Kirana joined her shortly.

'I will come tonight to your house to hear you,' he said to her. 'I did not want to say this to you in front of the girls from the class, that's why I asked you to come up.'

Sarika played the tanpura softly.

'What is the matter?' asked Kirana softly. 'You don't look your usual self. Is something bothering you?'

Sarika shook her head and kept playing the instrument. She had trouble swallowing Mrs. Sinha's story but had not the nerve to ask.

'Tell me, what's wrong?'

'Nothing.'

'Then why are you so serious?'

'No, nothing.'

'Alright, then,' said Kirana, 'I'll see you later this evening. You can leave the tanpura where it is. My next class will be here soon.'

As Sarika was getting off the platform, Mrs. Sinha walked in, panting slightly from the climb up the staircase. She took in Kirana and Sarika.

'I am sorry to interrupt,' she said sarcastically to Kirana. 'I didn't realize you were with your favourite *shishya*. I can go out.'

'No, no, you're not interrupting,' said Kirana coolly. 'What can I do for you?'

'Nothing, I just wanted to double check the time you will come tonight. Around eight?'

'I hadn't said anything about today,' he said. Sarika noticed his irritation.

'Oh,' she said. 'I thought you had.' She stared at Sarika as she spoke to him.

'No. Besides I have to go somewhere right after college,' he said firmly.

'Can you come after you have finished with the secret place you are going to?'

'No, not tonight,' he said.

She turned to Sarika. 'Want to walk out together?'

Sarika put on her *chappals* and went out with her.

'Where do you think Kirana sahib is going after college?' asked Mrs. Sinha. 'Do you think he teaches other students at home? He says he doesn't take on too many tuitions.'

Sarika tensed. 'I really don't know,' she said. 'I don't keep myself informed of his schedule.'

'What do you think his wife says when he comes home so late?'

'I haven't ever talked to his wife. Maybe she doesn't mind.'

'Which wife wouldn't mind her husband coming home at eleven o' clock? After all, she might want to go out in the evening. He's never there.'

They walked in silence. They were near the entrance gate. Mrs. Sinha stopped suddenly and faced Sarika, who had continued to walk ahead. Realizing that Mrs. Sinha was not with her, Sarika stopped and turned toward her.

'Does Kirana sahib teach you at home?' Mrs. Sinha asked Sarika.

Taken aback, Sarika peered through the fading light to see if her rickshawman had come. As if to aid her in her search, the lights on the college gates came on. She became aware of Mrs. Sinha's unrelenting eyes on her. Not wanting to lie, yet unwilling to tell the truth, she averted her gaze, then realizing the inappropriateness of her response to such a woman, met her eyes.

'Why?' Sarika asked. 'Why do you want to know?'

'No, nothing. I just asked,' said Mrs. Sinha, looking intently at her. 'But why?'

Mrs. Sinha laughed and walked away. Too late, Sarika realized she had already given this meddlesome woman the answer she sought. A firm denial would have satisfied her curiosity better than responding to her question with a question. She heard her rickshawman's bell and tried to think of one last thing to say to Mrs. Sinha. But nothing came to her. She stepped angrily onto her rickshaw and headed home as darkness fell.

17

It was a hot May day, a couple of months after Sarika sang in Saraswati Hall, and she was riding home from school in a rickshaw. It had been a good performance, and overall, after Kirana had dealt with Mrs. Sinha's tears and Sarika's nervousness, the feeling all around was one of well being. Kirana felt that he had made a good choice of student in Sarika; Sarika dreamt about becoming an artist with Kirana sahib's help; and Mrs. Sinha tried hard to find a place for herself between those two. Sarika, now fifteen, accepted continuous thoughts about Kirana sahib as part of her regular mental routine. As she grew, his image took on a larger and larger space in her mind. She saw the world through the lens she imagined he held, without which she would come directly in contact with objects and situations she felt ill-prepared to face. She wondered at times how she came to be thus, but it all seemed natural. Kirana sahib taught and nurtured her like a child and she responded to him like one. Or did he and did she? It was a thought too uncomfortable, a feeling too troubling to ponder. She felt the sun boring a hole in her head as her rickshaw came to a stop outside the gate to her house.

A loud guffaw greeted Sarika as she walked into the house through the front door. She reached Lakshmi's room with a quick step and peeking through the curtain saw several people sitting around, with Lakshmi in the center on her large double bed, propped up on pillows and covered with a single wool blanket on such a hot day. At Lakshmi's feet sat her daughter-in-law Veena, newly arrived from Moradabad.

'Chachi,' said Sarika softly, taking a couple of steps into the room. Veena, Nisha's mother, saw Sarika and broke into a smile of pleasure.

She came up to Sarika and patted her gently on the head. 'You look taller,' she said.

'Hello, Sarika,' boomed Uncle Ashok, Veena's husband.

'Sarika, hello,' said Pradeep, Nisha's brother and Veena and Ashok's son. 'My little cousin soon won't be little any more.' Pradeep sat at some distance from his parents.

'Come, *beta*. Come, sit next to me,' said Lakshmi softly. Sarika sat down next to her pile of pillows. Veena resumed massaging Lakshmi's lower legs and feet with her long, delicate hands.

'Amma won't get well like this,' her uncle's voice boomed as he wiggled his toes with their long nails curling over the ends. Ashok's arms were crossed over his expansive chest, which revealed its hairiness from under the open top two buttons of his shirt. His sweaty armpit patches came down almost to where his waist might have been in his thinner days. His bottom hung off both sides of the narrow dining room chair and his big, loose belly folded step-like over the belt of his pants. Holding his legs wide apart, he shook them hard to some unknown beat. 'Amma needs pure ghee sweets.'

Sarika studied her uncle and aunt from Moradabad, at the tubby and the gorgeous. Veena's thick black hair, parted in the center with a fine line of vermilion, came down to her waist in a single braid. Her perfectly arched eyebrows, doe eyes, fine nose, and sensitive mouth made her look like an actress in an art film. Veena massaged Lakshmi's legs with great care, pressing her shin with her thumb, all the way down to her ankles, then going up just below the knee and gently pressing her leg with both hands. Ashok chatted contentedly to everyone. They seemed so different, yet happy.

'My days for eating and drinking are over,' said Lakshmi resignedly.

'Amma, why you are talking like this?' scolded Ashok. 'This is just a temporary phase. Soon you'll be well again.'

Hearing her uncle, Sarika wondered if he believed what he said. It was hard to comprehend death, to see it as the final reality, to believe that it would actually happen. Yet Dadiji was not getting better and Nirmala and Ashwini sometimes talked in hushed tones, when they thought Sarika was not listening. Her uncle's confidence in his mother's recovery startled her — it defied everything she'd seen for the past few months. Nirmala came in, followed by the manservant, with seven cups of tea, seven plates and spoons, and snacks for everyone. Veena got up from her spot near her mother-in-law's feet and passed the tea around the room as Nirmala took her place at Lakshmi's feet. The servant put the snacks down on the bed and left the room.

'I have to see how I am going to divide my jewelry among all my children,' Lakshmi said. 'I also want to give something for each of my grandchildren.'

'Amma...' started Ashok.

'And I also have some money in my passbook. I want to give some...' said Lakshmi.

'Amma,' Ashok interrupted her, 'why are your thoughts so negative? When you get well, you can plan out how you will distribute all your things. You give everything you want with your own hands to your children and grandchildren.'

'I do not know how long I have,' said Lakshmi. 'I want to distribute everything with my own hands. Of course, after I die you can do what you like.'

'Amma ji, don't talk like that,' said Nirmala. 'Once you are well, you can take care of these things. Negative thoughts won't help you recover.'

'How is Nisha?' asked Sarika, addressing Veena. 'Why didn't she come? It's almost time for summer vacation.'

'Nisha wanted to come,' Veena said. 'She was supposed to join us in Moradabad from Delhi, but her friend is getting married today. So she stayed on in Delhi.'

'And Pradeep, how's university life treating you?' asked Sarika.

'He's still busy being a socialist,' said Ashok.

'At the university?' asked Sarika.

'Yes,' answered her uncle. 'Our son thinks we should distribute all our wealth to the poor. He is convinced we've acquired it by exploiting the poor. Misplaced idealism.'

Pradeep sat languidly in his chair and pretended to ignore his father.

'He'll grow out of it,' said Lakshmi.

'I hope he grows into sense,' said Ashok.

'I don't know how he's become involved in politics,' said Nirmala. 'Pradeep?'

'I have tried to convince him to forget politics and focus on his studies, but he accuses me of being a true capitalist, saying that I think only of generating wealth,' said Ashok. 'Of course he ignores the boring fact that he's received an excellent education because of all this generation of wealth by his father.'

'He is guilty of possessing the idealism of youth,' said Lakshmi slowly. 'He wants equality. What's wrong with that? Later, he will understand.'

'The sooner, the better,' said Ashok.

'So, Pradeep,' said Nirmala, 'what's going on at the university? What are you student leaders up to these days?'

'Not much,' said Pradeep politely.

'No? I read something in the Delhi papers the other day. Some dharna or other. Were you involved in staging the dharna?'

'Yes.'

'What was it about?' asked Nirmala.

'We were protesting the use of university property and personnel for personal use.'

'Okay?'

'It seems a lot of the senior administrators think that they can use the university car for their own personal use and the department peons can work at their homes. Sometimes we'll go to the department and there won't be anyone around because everyone has been employed to do personal tasks.'

'Why do *you* have to be involved in all this?' asked Ashok with obvious irritation. 'You are there to study. Finish your degree and get out. Let these administrators be. They are not going to change because you staged a dharna.'

'So did anything come of it?' Nirmala asked.

Pradeep shook his head.

'Of course it wouldn't,' said Ashok. 'These boys just waste their time.'

'Look at Lucknow University,' said Mrs. Gupta. 'These student leaders have not allowed exams to be held. It's May now and exams should have been finished by now. But as it stands, there is no sign of the exams ever being held.'

'You can't believe everything you read in the newspapers,' said Pradeep sitting up in his chair for the first time. 'The head of the students' union at Lucknow University is a friend of mine from Moradabad. He was saying that although the politicians give public statements about the problems in universities caused by student leaders, they later call them and tell them to get involved or seek their help in removing someone from office. How do you explain that kind of duplicity?'

'That may be,' said Ashok, 'but more often than not, students protest for all the wrong reasons. Any time the university tries to discipline a student, all hell breaks loose. A student cheats in an exam and is expelled and you students stage a dharna. There's no idealism in that.'

'So will Nisha come here in the summer to see Dadiji?' asked Sarika, quickly.

'Nisha'll come home for the summer holidays,' said Veena.

'Which friend of Nisha's is getting married?' asked Lakshmi.

'One of her college friends.'

'Getting married already?' asked Sarika. 'How old is she?

'Eighteen,' said Veena. 'Her in-laws have agreed to let her finish her B.A. after she gets married.'

'If you don't want your daughters to work, what's the point in making them sit at home? Marry them off,' said Nirmala.

'We are going to start looking for someone for Nisha,' said Ashok.

'Chacha! Nisha is less than three years older than me. I can't even think of marriage,' said Sarika.

'It's okay to start looking for a match at eighteen-nineteen,' said Nirmala.

'There is a boy in Lucknow itself,' said Ashok.

'How old is he?' asked Nirmala.

'Some twenty-three, twenty-four years old.'

'That's a good age to get married,' said Nirmala. 'The younger you are, the easier it is to adjust, especially for the girl. Her in-laws can mould her. Only then can the girl get along in the family. These days people marry their daughters late, and then they have big problems in adjusting.'

'They marry them late because they want them to have a career,' said Mrs. Gupta. 'If they do something professionally, they are easily twenty three or twenty four by the time they settle down.'

'Twenty three-twenty four is too late for girls' said Nirmala. 'They are too independent by then. I don't believe in all this. Marry your daughters off and retire in peace.'

Sarika watched the others nod in agreement. Twenty three was the right age for a woman. It was too young for a man. What if her parents decided to marry her off at eighteen or nineteen, as her Amma felt should be done? The thought was disturbing. She would be in exactly the same position as her cousin Nisha, finishing her B.A. Even if she didn't become a career woman, and she knew her mother was opposed to it, she still didn't want to be tied to someone at such a young age. For one, she wanted to spend more time on her music, despite her mother's lack of ambition for her. For Nirmala, music was a necessary refinement for a woman of culture. A career in music, still regarded by Nirmala's generation as the profession of courtesans, was not something she envisioned for her daughter. It would not pain her more than the normal thwarting of one's child's simple desires by another if after marriage Sarika's husband forbade her to sing. She would take it as a matter of course. But Sarika wanted to become a great artist with the help of Kirana sahib. Marriage at such a young age would put an end to all of that. No sense of self, however tenuous. Yet, here were these grownups deciding everyone's fate according to their own beliefs, charting out her life based on the deepest tradition. Sarika shuddered.

She picked up her bag and left to wash up. Lakshmi's eyes were now closed. Dadiji was dying and wouldn't be there to speak for her.

18

Mrs. Sinha led her daughter, Achala, to her boudoir and sat on her bed. 'Who is this boy?' Mrs. Sinha asked holding an open letter in her hand and tapping it with her finger. 'Who is this Pankaj?'

Achala glanced at the writing on the envelope and lowered her gaze. Silence hung between the two women, despite the loudness of the air conditioner that adjusted its pitch to the variations of the voltage. 'He's a friend of Vineet,' she mumbled.

'Why is he writing to you then, if he is a friend of Vineet? What friend of yours is this?' she asked Vineet, who had slunk into the bedroom, waving the letter in his face.

'He's doing his M.Com. with me,' said Vineet. 'And unlike me, he's cleared both years of the chartered accountancy exam.'

Mrs. Sinha glared at him. The atmosphere in the room stifled the three of them. 'You've been home for two months and I didn't suspect anything. And tomorrow, you would have left and I still wouldn't have known anything. What will Papa say? He's coming home for lunch today.'

'Maybe Papa will listen to me,' said Achala.

'He writes he can't wait to see you in Delhi again,' said Mrs. Sinha, ignoring her daughter's trusting remark. 'He wants to know if you have broached the subject of marriage with your parents and if...'

The doorbell rang.

'That must be Papa,' said Mrs. Sinha, getting up from her bed. Looking straight at Achala, she tore the letter into small bits and threw it into the waste paper basket.

'Are we ready for lunch?' asked Sinha striding into the room. Mrs. Sinha nodded silently. Sensing the tension, he asked, 'What's happening?'

'Let us have lunch,' said Mrs. Sinha and called out to the cook to get lunch on the table. The family washed their hands one by one at the sink in the dining room and sat down quietly. The cook brought out lunch on a large tray and set each bowl carefully on the black marble table. Mrs. Sinha picked up a stainless steel ladle and stirred the bowl of lentils. 'It's too thick,' she yelled out to the cook. 'Fix it and bring it back.'

'Are you all packed and ready for college?' Sinha asked Achala, as he helped himself to curried chicken.

She nodded absently, as she took the bowl her father passed to her.

'What is the matter?' he asked his wife.

'Maybe Achala will tell you,' said Mrs. Sinha. The cook was back with the lentils and Mrs. Sinha ladled out some in small bowls to each family member.

'Achala?' said Sinha.

Achala gulped.

'Will someone tell me what's going on?' he asked, unused to being kept waiting by his family.

'Achala wants to marry one of Vineet's friends,' said Mrs. Sinha.

'What?!'

'They've been corresponding with each other right under my nose. I just happened to open and read a letter today.'

'Where is the letter?' Sinha asked, holding out his hand.

'I tore it in a rage and threw it away,' his wife said.

Sinha slurped his lentils.

'Will you listen to what I have to say?' Achala asked him hopefully.

'What is there to hear?' rejoined Sinha. 'The question of marriage doesn't even arise. You will marry someone we choose for you.'

'But he's from a good family and...' began Achala.

'What does his father do?' Sinha asked, suggesting by his tone that no matter what his daughter said he would run her down.

Achala understood her father's tone and her heart sank. 'He is about to retire as a police subinspector in Punjab.'

'And you expect me to marry you into a home like that? Police subinspectors stand outside my door when they come to see me. I don't even let them into the office. And you expect me to accept such a man as the father-in-law of my only daughter? You expect me to embrace such a man when he comes to my house?'

'Papa...'

'No.'

'Why should his rank alone matter? After all, our grandfather...'

'*Khamosh*. Silence. You will not talk about your grandfather in that way.'

Startled by her father's words, Achala bit her trembling lip. She took a deep whistling breath. 'Papa,' she said quietly. 'Papa...'

'Maybe we should at least listen to her,' said Mrs. Sinha, melting a little now that her husband had taken such a tough stand against their daughter. Usually, it was her husband who took her daughter's side.

'Nothing, nothing doing.' Sinha ate quickly.

'Please, at least listen to me,' Achala said.

'Let's listen to her...' said Mrs. Sinha.

'No, there's nothing to hear. Didn't you know that we would never approve such a thing? How could you have become so involved? Marry the fellow. The limit!' said Sinha angrily. 'Don't you know he's after your money? Why else would he be interested in you? You have neither the brains nor the looks.'

There was stunned silence around the table. Mrs. Sinha slowly put her spoon, which had been poised to go into her mouth, down quietly on her fine bone china.

'And what will you do if I marry him anyway?' said Achala, pushing back her chair and standing up, showing her father's tough, stubborn streak on seeing all doors close upon her. 'What *can* you do?' she asked, eyes brimming with tears.

'We will disinherit you,' said Sinha without blinking, unwilling to brook opposition from one completely dependent on him. 'We will believe that we have only one child.' He stood up and went to the sink in the corner of the large dining room and rinsed out his mouth noisily. He wiped his mouth with the towel on the rack and left the house without a word.

Slowly, Achala sat down on her chair and began to sob softly as a feeling of helplessness grew about her. Certain that Sinha, an indulgent father, would at least listen to her, his unreasonableness seemed to her an act of betrayal at a time when she most needed his support.

'Why are you hung up on marrying him?' asked Mrs. Sinha in a conciliatory tone. 'Papa is right. Forget about him. We'll find someone nice for you and you'll live happily with him.'

Achala's tears fell into her lap.

'Vineet, what do you say?' Mrs. Sinha turned to her son.

'He's a nice chap,' said Vineet.

'There are many nice chaps. We can find her one. Why should she want to marry one whom we haven't chosen? What will the world say? We will be held up to ridicule. And then, if the family had been very highly placed, it would have been different. But this boy has no family background. Can you imagine a man like that leading the groom's party to our door on the day of the wedding? What will all of our associates and family think?'

'That is hardly a good enough reason,' said Vineet.

'Now you are also speaking from her side,' said Mrs. Sinha, abandoning her softer tone. 'Children these days...'

'I love him,' said Achala, desperately.

'What?!'

Achala hung her head again. Mrs. Sinha looked sharply at her. The worst kind of image arose in her mind.

'What have you done with him?' she asked Achala.

'What do you mean?'

'Don't ask me what I mean. You, who have fallen in love so shamelessly, should surely know. Tell me,' she said yelling hysterically, 'have you?'

Vineet turned red. Achala sobbed harder.

'You have, haven't you?' Mrs. Sinha walked up to her daughter, took her by the shoulders and shook her. 'Tell me, you have, haven't you?' Achala shook her head and continued to sob.

'Oh God, for what action of mine are you showing me this day?' said Mrs. Sinha, as she began to tear up herself. Vineet stood up and left the room. Mrs. Sinha turned again to her daughter and glared at her. 'Own up.'

'I haven't, Mummy, I haven't,' said Achala, sobbing uncontrollably. 'Please believe me. I haven't done anything with him.'

19

It was after eight when Kirana arrived at the Kumar residence in the warm, still evening air of July. He parked his scooter in the driveway, and as he walked toward the verandah, sliding his keys into the pocket of his trousers, he looked at a dense crowd of insects vying with one another for a spot closer to the sickly fluorescent light. In their struggle to get closer, they provided a hearty meal for the two or three geckos lurking nearby. He quickened his step to escape the swarms as he walked through the verandah to the front door and rang the doorbell and waited. In the morning the insects would all be on the floor, dead from the heat of the light they sought, their wings separated from their bodies. Their glory short lived. He saw the same thing at his house every morning as his wife swept them into a dust pan.

He felt a twinge of impatient excitement as he rang the doorbell again. What was taking so long? He had rushed from the college, even letting out class five minutes early. The head of the tabla department had wanted to go out with him for betel leaf, but he had refused, got on his scooter, and made his way here. Ramu came to the door, telltale dough on his hands, and ushered Kirana into the living room. The family were in the middle of dinner, he said.

Kirana settled comfortably into the couch. He looked around the room, noticing for the umpteenth time the simplicity of the furnishings in the house of a senior government officer. The couch, the cane chairs, the faded cushions could easily use replacement, but Ashwini Kumar valued Gandhian simplicity over everything else. His father had been a well-known freedom fighter, Nirmala had mentioned in passing one day. Ramu came back into the room, bearing a glass of cool water on a steel tray.

'Sarika bibiji is finishing dinner. She will come out in five minutes,' said Ramu, extending the tray toward Kirana.

'Tell her to take her time. I am sitting here comfortably,' said Kirana, wiping his mouth with a large grey handkerchief.

'Tea, sahib?'

'No, I just had some. No tea.'

Ramu nodded, held out the tray to receive the empty glass from Kirana and disappeared behind the drapes.

Kirana was alone with his thoughts again. He had known Sarika almost three years. He was proud to be associated with her, both for her talent and family. The principal had told him jokingly the other day that he had hit a gold mine with Sarika. When she sang, people asked who taught her. She was the most promising of all the students at the college. If she became a great artist, he would have had a big hand in shaping her career. And the family. How could anyone undermine the importance of being associated with someone so high in the bureaucracy — the home secretary! And to have such close relations with the family. It added a certain luster to his own position at the college. He could afford to smirk at the wife of the junior officer who came to the college in her hipster sarees, for her husband was much junior to Sarika's father in the strict hierarchy of officialdom. She had asked him to teach her privately, but he had said no. If he hadn't known Sarika's family, he might have thought differently. It was good for the image, for that had to be burnished constantly. And the Kumars were such a simple, idealistic, and affectionate family. Mr. Kumar, despite his position and unlike Mrs. I.A.S., treated him with great respect. With Mr. Kumar, he never felt like a class two officer talking to a senior government officer. He was always the teacher of his daughter and consequently deserving of respect. The harsh sound of the chair dragging over the mosaic floor made him smile in anticipation.

'Which raga do you want to sing?' Kirana asked, as his student came rushing into the room.

'When? What's the occasion?'

'Founder's day. Ravindralaya.'

'Master sahib!' Sarika sat down on the couch in disbelief. 'Ravindralaya! I'll die of fright.'

'You will sing very well. Where's your Amma? You must tell her the good news. Is she still having dinner?'

Sarika left the room. Kirana looked after her proudly. His student would be singing at Ravindralaya. He had asked principal sahib if Sarika could perform at founder's and he, impressed by her rendition of *Shuddha Kalyan* at Holi in Saraswati Hall, had agreed. She had grown so much in the time he had known her. She was just a child when she had first started in his class in third year. She was becoming a young woman right in front of his eyes. Beautiful. Unsullied. Fresh. Intelligent. A dream student. Nirmala walked into the room smiling, followed by Sarika, wringing her hands. Kirana stood up and joined his hands in greeting. 'Congratulations. Your daughter will be giving her first solo performance at Ravindralaya. Principal sahib thinks she's ready for it.'

'Please sit down, Kirana sahib,' Nirmala said, taking a chair across from him. Ashwini Kumar walked into the room.

'Congratulations,' said Kirana.

'It is all your hard work, Kirana sahib,' said Ashwini.

'She's your daughter,' Kirana said. Sarika's father sat down. 'There is not much time. Only six weeks, and with her day college and my evening schedule...'

They heard the sound of shuffling footsteps and turned toward the dining room door. Lakshmi had finished dinner. She held the door jamb and stood still for a minute, as if trying to orient herself with her surroundings. Sarika ran over to her and took her arm. Nirmala took her other arm. Together, they walked her slowly to a chair, as Ashwini stood by helplessly. Lakshmi lowered herself gradually and sat with a soft thud on the chair.

'Mataji,' said Kirana to Lakshmi, 'how are you feeling?'

'Quite well. The body is old and feeble; why should we grieve for that? But tell me, when does Sarika have to sing?'

'The first week of September. What raga will you sing, Sarika?' asked Kirana, turning to his student.

'Would *Bihag* be okay?'

'You will have only fifteen minutes; you have to show a little of everything. It is all about presentation.'

'But fifteen minutes are not enough. I will barely be able to finish my alap.'

'Fifteen minutes are more than enough. You should never sing so much that people go away feeling satisfied. They will then say, "She sang well" and forget about it. You should always sing just enough to whet their appetite but leave them unsatisfied. They should say at the end, "How did it end so soon?" Then they will come to you for more.'

'Do you want me to sing today? I've just had dinner,' said Sarika.

'I know you've just had dinner and can't sing now,' said Kirana enjoying her large eyes and her open, honest face. 'I'll come again. Tomorrow, maybe. Wait for me until 8:30. If I'm not here by then, have dinner.' Kirana stood up. 'Give me leave now,' he said, looking at Nirmala and Ashwini.

As he rode his scooter home over the dimly lit streets, his mind moved turbulently. Lately — he could not quite pinpoint when or how it all began — he had begun to feel the pull of Sarika and each visit with her threw his mind into chaos. Distance from her, even the formal relationship of class, settled him down, until a new meeting lathered up his emotions. When he had gone to her house that evening, his emotions had been well under control. Now. He loved Surya, of course, but how much more he had to explain to her to get a point across: Sarika understood even before he had finished his sentence. Her quick intelligence along with her teenage perception made it such a pleasure to share his thoughts. His mind flashed back to when he had merely mentioned a woman's gesture to Sarika and she had understood that the dance teacher at the college wanted him sexually. With Surya, he had had to explain so much more and then reassure her through her tears. He parked under the staircase to his house and paused.

Surya met him at the door. 'You're late today,' she said without reproach.

Kirana noticed a letter on the table addressed to his wife. He recognized the writing to be her mother's. 'Is everything alright at your mother's?' he asked, sitting down.

'It's my sister. She is having trouble with her in-laws.'

Kirana drank a sip of the buttermilk. 'Delicious,' he muttered.

'Her in-laws are giving her grief because she cannot conceive, saying it's been five years and if she can't have a baby, they should look for someone else for their son.'

'How do they know it's her and not him?'

'They went to a doctor, who said he was fine.'

'Did they do any tests?'

'I don't think so.'

'Then how do they know?'

'That's what the doctor says. Her in-laws say she didn't bring any dowry and now can't have a baby. She's a net loss. She wants to come home for some time.'

'And what does Amma ji say?'

'Amma says that she should stay with them and try to get them to change their mind about her through her exemplary behaviour.'

'Amma ji is right.'

'You think so? Even at this time when she wants to come home to be away from those people?'

'You have such a kind heart.'

'I don't know what to think.'

Kirana finished the buttermilk in his cup and let out a big breath.

'Maybe she should move,' said Surya uncertainly. 'She is beautiful and sweet natured. Why should she have to suffer?'

'That is also true. She should not have to suffer,' said Kirana.

'But Amma says her behaviour should make it impossible for them to turn her out.'

'That is also true.'

'If she can win them over, everything will be fine.'

'It is the reputation of both families, after all,' said Kirana.

'True. What is a little suffering for the reputation of the family?'

'You think like I do.'

Surya smiled.

'Before college, I went to Mrs. Sinha's house. She was very distressed today because her mother passed away.'

'What did she die of?'

'Heart failure. She went out into the courtyard after her bath to hang her towel out to dry and came back and told the servant to make some tea for her. He took the tea to her bedroom and she was dead on the bed. It was a good death, but Mrs. Sinha is very upset, naturally. She didn't get to see her at the end.'

'Naturally.'

'She feels her home is gone. She has one brother, and he has been more or less cut off from the family because his wife has never tried to feel part of the family. So, she feels that her parents' home is gone forever and life for her in her own family doesn't seem that happy either.'

'Is Achala at home with them these days?'

'She is in Delhi for her M.A. They had some unpleasantness at home before Achala went back to Delhi because Sinha doesn't want her to marry a boy she loves. Mrs. Sinha was saying that Achala has agreed to give up this boy.'

'Sinha sahib...' Kirana paused.

Surya waited with a morsel poised to go into her mouth.

'He seems such a hard fellow. I don't like Mrs. Sinha, but I can't help feeling sorry for her.'

'How can you feel sorry for someone you don't like?' she asked lightly.

Surya understood his feelings for Mrs. Sinha, but since her security rested on his dislike of the women he knew, he explained, 'As an artist, you have to try to understand the whole range of human emotions. I don't like Mrs. Sinha as a person, Surya, but I understand her pain. Her mother's death, her daughter's affair, everything has come at the same time for her. That her husband doesn't support her emotionally doesn't make it any easier for her.'

'Of course.'

'Wherever I might go during the day, Surya, I always come home to my family at night,' he said gently. A man couldn't go too far wrong if

98

he came home and slept next to his wife every night. Hadn't Surya said that to him, too, on occasions? He wasn't wrong, then, in his feelings for Sarika as long as in his deeds he was faithful to his wife.

'Sometimes when I'm alone, I think of all sorts of outrageous things,' she said in a tone of confession. 'You know that I trust you completely.'

He patted her hand.

20

'I can't believe you're going through this at such a young age,' said Sarika.

'Truth, my dear, is stranger than fiction,' said her cousin Nisha. 'I am allowing myself to be made a spectacle of, to be paraded like a heifer at a fair, while they try to judge my pedigree to determine what kind of grandsons I will bear them.'

Sarika laughed. 'But seriously, this is not funny.'

'Ninety-nine percent of girls go through this. So will I. In fact, if I didn't go through this, for whatever reason, I'd be in real trouble.'

'How can you be so indifferent? You say all this as if it didn't bother you! Yet how can it not? It bothers me so much I want to run out of the house banging every door loudly.'

'I'm not hot blooded like you,' said Nisha smiling. 'Why fight a battle in which the odds are stacked against you even before the battle lines are drawn?' She stretched and rolled onto her back. Sarika shifted, holding the edge of her bed to see how far she could go without toppling over.

'You're taking up most of the bed,' Sarika complained. They lay close to each other on the single bed in Sarika's room.

'I beg your pardon,' said Nisha, 'but I think your plait takes up half the bed. You take up the other half.'

'Well, at least they didn't put your ad in the matrimonial section of the *Hindustan Times*,' said Sarika. ' "Wanted: suitable match for fair, beautiful, homely girl, wears no spects." Spects, my dear, spects.'

'Yes, I was spared that, thank heavens. And they always put "homely" and "beautiful" in the same sentence. I wonder if they know that homely doesn't mean one who'll stay home and breed for you. The cold-blooded murder of the English tongue,' she said, feigning a British accent.

'I know. Did Veena chachi give you a set of dos and don'ts for when the boy's family comes to see you tomorrow?'

'What do you think? She wants me to go get a facial today. Get my eyebrows shaped, arms and legs waxed. She wants me to look my best. Will you come?'

'Of course. You can meet me in Hazratganj after my music class. Then we can be home before eight. Master sahib might come tonight to teach me.'

The drone of the ceiling fan created a sleepy atmosphere. The fine beam of sunlight that came in through the window drapes divided the room into two darkened halves. A lizard ran across the floor. Sarika shuddered and turned on her side. The door to her room was closed to keep out grownups. The mothers were in her Amma's room, discussing Dadiji, she guessed. Her mind drifted to Kirana sahib and suddenly she longed to be with him.

At length Sarika asked, 'Do you sometimes wish you could talk to a man about things?'

'What kind of things?' inquired Nisha.

'Things that lie close to your heart, that you can't tell anyone, but wish you could to a man.'

'Yes, I do have things like that to talk about. But I would never tell them to anyone except my husband. They are so personal that only a husband should know them.'

'Why?' asked Sarika.

'Because it would be awkward with anyone else. You don't want that kind of closeness with anyone except a husband. Why, do you wish to talk to a man?' asked Nisha after a few minutes of silence.

'Hm. Sometimes,' said Sarika.

'And?'

'And nothing,' said Sarika. 'There's no one to talk to. I mean no man to talk to. But *you* might have one soon,' she said cheerily. 'What's the name of the chap who's coming to see you?'

'Alok.'

'Alok what?'

'Alok Pradhan.'

'Have you seen his picture?'

Nisha nodded.

'What does he look like?'

'Not Mr. India, but not bad. Not bad at all,' she said smiling.

'Aanh, you like him,' said Sarika.

'I've never seen him,' said Nisha smiling.

'But you've already fallen in love,' said Sarika.

'How can I have fallen in love when I've never even seen him?'

'But you have. I can feel it in my bones,' said Sarika. 'No wonder you don't mind being paraded. You're in love with the chap's photo. What does he do?' asked Sarika.

'He's just got his first posting with the State Bank of India. Right here in Lucknow, next to his parents. Isn't that nice? To have to live with the in-laws? Although, thank God, it's not his permanent posting. He's still a trainee.'

'Hm.'

'I'm trying to stay calm till it actually happens. He can be the first and last or he can be the first in a series of chaps I see.' Her voice changed. 'What if I'm rejected?'

The ceiling fan whirred. How would it feel to go into a living room and sit in the midst of people who are trying to evaluate you? Everything would be weighed. And what if she likes him and he doesn't like her? But, he doesn't even know her, she thought angrily. How can he dislike her? 'Think positive for now,' said Sarika.

'I'll try,' said her cousin. 'Although there's not much to think positively about if you're rejected.'

'True.'

'Don't you have to go to the music college?' asked Nisha, stretching. 'I'll have the bed to myself then.'

'You mean you can actually sleep amid all this anticipation? Hats off to you. Well, I'd better go, else I'll be late.'

~

Later, that evening, after his last class at the music college, Kirana came to Sarika's house. He coached her on each alap. 'Don't present a basketful of goodies to your audience all at once. Show them a little something new each time. Like a magician who shows one trick at a time.'

Sarika tried again. Kirana stopped her.

'Simplify, simplify your alap,' he said. 'If you are singing *ga*, show the beauty of *ga*. *Ga* is a very important note in *Bihag*. Don't be all over the place. Let people appreciate a little at a time. Move from the simple to the complex. Don't start with an alap with lots of complex combinations. Ease into it...'

Sarika was tired and dozed off as Kirana talked. Nirmala, who had taken a few minutes out of her time with Veena and Ashok and the preparations for the boy's family to see Nisha, couldn't believe her eyes. She called Sarika's name to wake her up.

'Behanji,' he said. 'Let her sleep. A sleeping child looks so innocent.'

Nirmala watched. As the tanpura started slipping from Sarika's hands, she leapt out of her chair and grabbed it, preventing a fall and a break. Sarika looked in bewilderment, at Kirana and then at her mother. The lesson was over for that day.

'What a nice man he is,' said Nirmala, as the door closed behind him.

'I dozed off,' said Sarika sheepishly.

'Yes, and he told me not to wake you up. What a thoughtful, considerate man!'

'Tomorrow's Nisha's thing.'

'Yes. You can tell him when you go to the music college tomorrow that he should come on Sunday morning.'

'I'm scared to death.'

'Keep your wits about you. You'll do very well.'

～

'They'll soon be here,' said Sarika, sitting on her haunches and meticulously holding down the pleats of Nisha's chiffon saree.

'Seven o' clock,' said Nisha, adjusting the tops of the pleats one more time before tucking them into her petticoat. 'Of course, if they observe

102

Indian Stretchable Time, they'll be here a lot later, which will be good, for it will then be a shorter evening. Oh, where are my new flat-heels? The 'boy' will look shorter than me if I wear heels,' she said imitating the grownups.

Sarika laughed. 'Your nerves amaze me. Let me bring the jewelry from Amma's room.' Sarika returned a couple of minutes later bearing all the stuff the grownups wanted Nisha to wear — diamond earrings, a gold necklace, and two gold bangles on each arm. She watched as Nisha put on the bindi, eyeliner, and lipstick. The lipstick had been a debatable issue, since Veena had been against its use. But in the family hierarchy, Sarika's parents were at the top, after her grandma, and Nirmala had offered the lipstick her blessing. Nisha looked lovely, face glowing, eyebrows arched, arms and legs smooth and shiny as a waxed apple. 'You look so nice. He'll fall in love with you right away,' said Sarika.

'Ha. We'll see about that.' The doorbell rang. 'Heavens, they're here,' said Nisha.

'I'll go take a peek,' said Sarika.

Nisha stood in front of the full-length mirror on Sarika's dressing table and scrutinized herself, turned first one way and then another to see if the length of her saree was even throughout. She smacked her lips to even out the lipstick, took a deep breath and sank onto Sarika's bed.

'He's quite handsome,' whispered Sarika excitedly as she came back into the room and stood in front of her cousin.

'Who all are there?'

'His sister and his parents. His mother seems very nice. No wicked mother-in-law for you.'

'Have our family descended on the drawing room yet?'

'Yes, they're there in full force.'

Nisha sighed, suddenly exhausted from the emotional strain of the event. 'O God,' she said suddenly, crossing her arms in front of her belly.

'You can't slump now,' said Sarika. 'You have to be at your best.'

'You won't believe this,' said Nisha, standing up. 'I think I've got an upset tummy.'

'No!'

'Yes.'

'It must be anxiety.'

'Or the kababs I ate yesterday. I am in deep trouble now,' Nisha said, throwing off her saree and running into the bathroom.

'Why did you take off your saree?' asked Sarika, shaking her head in disbelief.

'I don't know,' came her cousin's voice from the bathroom. 'Seemed like the thing to do. Wouldn't it get crushed?'

'Nisha,' said Veena, bursting into the room. 'Nisha, *beta*. The boy is here. He's very handsome. Where's Nisha?' she asked Sarika.

'She's in the bathroom.'

Veena looked at the saree on the bed and an alarmed look came on her face. 'She hasn't even put on her saree yet? I thought she had put on her jewelry and everything.'

'She had.'

'Then…'

'What are they doing?' asked Nisha, coming into the room.

'They're having cold drinks,' said her mother. 'Why aren't you ready?'

'I'm coming. Why don't you carry on?'

'I'm going to help you with your saree,' said Veena.

'You don't need to,' said Nisha.

Sarika slipped out of the room in the midst of the mother-daughter exchange and made her way to the medicine cabinet in her mother's room. Rummaging through the stacks of physicians' samples her brother brought home, she came across a package of anti-diarrhoeal, took a tablet and headed back to her own room. Veena was on her haunches, holding down the pleats, with her back to the door, when Sarika entered. Nisha looked up momentarily and Sarika quickly held up the tablet. Nisha tucked her pleats in and was ready to go.

'Come on,' said Veena, exasperated.

'A drink of water,' said Nisha.

Sarika ran out again and came back with a glass of water, slipping Nisha the tablet as she handed her the glass. 'Let's hope your stomach holds,' she said between her teeth.

'We're in deep trouble,' Nisha said aloud.

'Why?' asked Veena.

'Just because the "boy" and all are here,' said Nisha, emphasizing the word boy.'

'Hurry up,' said Veena.

Nisha stepped away from the mirror and stood by her mother, who led her out of Sarika's room. Sarika followed.

All eyes turned on Nisha as she walked into the room, except Alok's. He looked up briefly and lowered his gaze. Sarika stared unabashedly at him. At five feet four, he was almost the same height as Nisha, though he looked shorter because of his neck. He watched nervously as Nisha sat on a chair next to him, so that he was between his sister and Nisha. Sweat appeared under his armpits. He turned his head toward his sister and talked to her continuously in a whisper, as Nisha sat uncomfortably in her chair and looked at her long, manicured hands. The grownups tried to keep up a casual chatter, but after a brief exchange, all eyes turned toward the two, unable to converse. The families touched on a range of subjects — the declining political situation in the state, the music college, Alok's training with the State Bank of India, Pradeep brought up socialism — but the discussion was so forced that it kept dying, until someone thought of something else to say. Veena passed out the elaborate snacks and went to each person, offering seconds and thirds in the frequent breaks in the conversation. Poor Nisha, thought Sarika. All witticisms had frozen in her. Alok's sister did ask her hobbies, but that was hardly anything in which she could show her wit. And once Nisha told her that she read almost all the time, Alok's sister had nothing much to add. Nisha kept her beautiful eyes, so much like her mother's, lowered.

It was in one of those long silences that Nisha's stomach let out a loud growl. It wasn't just a growl either, coupled as it was with a higher pitched roll. Sarika and Veena turned at once to Nisha. The others may not have figured the source, except that Nisha involuntarily threw her arms across her belly. Nirmala and Ashwini groped for something to say. Pradeep started to say something about the government, then kept quiet. Alok's mother glanced at Nisha, then at Alok, before fixing her eyes on the rug. Nisha blushed, looked at Sarika and gave the barest nod. Oh dear, thought Sarika. If only someone would restart the conversation. But the room was as quiet as a meditation hall. Nisha shifted slightly in her chair and Sarika understood that her need to escape was immediate. Sarika cleared her throat as if getting ready to sing. Suddenly Veena got up and started passing out the snacks again. But in a hurry to cover up the embarrassing moment, she tripped on her saree. The plate of samosas fell from her hands and she kept her balance by holding on to Nirmala's knee.

'Ramu?' called Nirmala. 'Come on out here.'

Veena picked up the plate, then let Ramu collect everything from the floor. Abashed, she sat down on her chair. Alok's father began to tell a joke about a party in which all the food fell. Sarika whisked Nisha out of the room.

'You'd better hurry,' said Sarika, once they were in her room. 'Don't take off your saree this time.'

'I know.'

'I'll hold the fort, while you're in the bathroom.'

'The trouble is I'll have to tell them I had kababs yesterday if this continues,' Nisha said from the bathroom. 'Then, I'll get scolded not only for eating meat but for creating this crisis at the most important time in my life.'

'The tablet should work. I've had it before and it's fast acting. This is probably it.'

Nisha now felt even more self conscious as she walked into the drawing room.

'I was nervous, too, when my husband's family came to see me,' said Alok's sister, as Nisha slunk back into her chair.

Nisha managed a weak smile. Sarika suppressed a giggle. The conversation picked up and petered out as it had all evening. Nisha sighed when Alok's parents got up to take leave.

'That was some viewing,' said Nisha, as soon as everyone had left the drawing room and the two girls remained. 'How embarrassing. Oh dear.' She slumped on to a couch.

'You'll remember it for this. How does your stomach feel?'

Nisha shrugged. 'I'm sure they'll reject me for my errant stomach, if nothing else. The mother trips, the daughter has the runs, the son thinks all capitalists should be eliminated.'

'How can anyone reject you because your stomach makes a noise?' asked Sarika. 'The more important thing is, do you like him?'

'Not much grounds to feel one way or another.'

'Can he speak English?'

'He better be able to speak English,' said Nisha, 'although how would I know. I didn't say a word to him.'

'Come now, don't sound so despondent,' said Sarika. 'Did he go to an English-medium school?' asked Sarika.

'Yes. Went to a very good college in Delhi,' said Nisha. 'Oh dear, oh dear. One would think we were living in the seventeenth century.'

'You're supposed to make your decision on the basis of this meeting.'

'I've seen him. That should be good enough. That and my stomach.' They sat in silence. 'He's toad-necked,' said Nisha, as soon as the grownups and Pradeep had returned to the drawing room from seeing off Alok and his family.

'That's hardly a reason to reject a boy,' said Nirmala, smiling nevertheless. 'He's a handsome boy. You girls, these days,' she said shaking her head in mock disapproval. 'And what happened to you?'

'Butterflies,' said Nisha.

'Amazing.'

'So, what do you all think?' asked Ashok, walking in as if unaware of Nisha's little crisis.

'He's a good boy,' said Nirmala.

'Good job, decent family, no liabilities,' said Ashok. 'One sister and she, too, is married.'

'Good family,' said Ashwini.

'Let us see what they say,' said Veena.

'What will they say,' said Lakshmi. 'What will they refuse our girl on? They can go around the globe with a torch in their hands and they won't come across a family or a girl like ours.'

Two days later, the Kumars heard from Alok's parents. They liked the girl and were ready to perform a small engagement ceremony, said Alok's father on the phone. What did Nisha think?

Veena rushed into Sarika's room and asked Nisha if she liked Alok. Ashok held the line. Nisha muttered something. Taking Nisha's non refusal as assent, Veena rushed back to her husband and said that Nisha had said 'yes.'

'The girl says "yes," ' Ashok yelled into the phone. 'Yes, yes, we can do the ceremony tomorrow. No, no, it won't be a problem at all. No formality. It is just a small, simple ceremony. Why wait long for the performance of an auspicious deed.'

As soon as Ashok hung up, the grownups laughed, breaking out of a week's worth of escalating anxiety. They congratulated one another — we didn't have to 'show' our girl to anyone; this was it. What if they'd refused? We'd have felt so bad.

Ashok sat with his knees wide apart in Lakshmi's room. 'Amma, this is such a big weight off our shoulders. The first time we show our girl, everything is finalized.'

Lakshmi responded, 'What would they have rejected our girl on? Beautiful, intelligent, good family.'

Preparations began — trips to the *halwai*, first to order, then to pick up laddoos and burfis; trips to the bank to request crisp bank notes in hundreds and ones, carefully put into brand new envelopes with the name of everyone from Alok's family and decorated with a red *satiya* made with *roli*; trips to the saree store for sarees for the boy's mother and sister and, of course, for Nisha; trips to the family jeweler for a diamond ring for Alok. Just a simple ceremony for the two families. The formal engagement would be later. A big ceremony to be followed by the wedding in winter.

And the ceremony happened. The exchange of rings — Alok's mother put a diamond necklace around Nisha's neck and a gorgeous ring on her slender ring finger. Nisha's older brother, Pradeep, slid the brand new diamond ring on Alok's finger, although not before telling his mother during the preparation for the ceremony that diamonds were ostentatious. Alok's mother suggested that Nisha and Alok go out, maybe to 'ganj, but Nirmala said a firm 'no.' The girl and boy would go out together only after marriage. So they sat around — Nisha, uncomfortable in her bright orange organza saree with heavy gold work and lots of jewelry, keeping her head down from the sheer weight of the *palla*; Alok, in his brand new safari suit, sweating large circles under his armpits — until everyone had dinner and the boy and his family left.

Sarika and Nisha came back to their room and Sarika left her cousin alone with her thoughts. Some time later as the two lay quietly in their own beds, Sarika dozed off. Suddenly, she woke up and wondered at the sound that had shaken her out of her slumber. She sat up and heard a loud hiccup.

'Nisha?' she said to the dim shape lying on a cot next to her bed. The sound of weeping grew louder.

Sarika held up her watch to the light that came from the slightly open bathroom door. Midnight. She must have slept around 11.

'Nisha. Aai.'

Sarika got up and opened the bathroom door fully. The room lit up partially with a diffused light. Nisha lay on her stomach, legs crossed at the ankles, arms straight by her side, weeping into the pillow. When Sarika came close to her, Nisha covered her face with one hand, leaving the other stiffly by her side. Sarika sat down next to her and put her hand gently on her waist.

'Nisha,' she said softly. 'Nisha, what's the matter?'

Nisha continued to weep.

'Are you not happy? Do you not like Alok? Nisha, you'll dehydrate if you keep crying like this,' she said, hoping a silly remark would get her cousin to snap out of her tears. 'Aai Nisha.'

Nisha cried harder. Sarika put her arm around her shoulder.

'What is it? Are you crying because Amma wouldn't let you go out with Alok?'

Nisha shook her head.

'Then?'

Silence.

'Stop crying. Tell me what it is,' said Sarika, removing Nisha's hand from her face and taking it in hers.

The sobs subsided. Nisha withdrew her hand from Sarika's and sat up.

'What is it?'

'Nothing.'

'You don't like Alok?'

'I don't feel anything for him and I'm going to be led to him like a cow to spend the rest of my life in a cow stall.'

Sarika sat still. 'Aren't you supposed to feel excited?' she asked very softly.

109

Nisha made a face. 'A couple of my friends in college who got married recently were so excited,' she continued. 'They came to college after the engagement, flaunting their diamond rings, nails painted, eyebrows done. All groomed and everything. New clothes every day. Looking at them I felt it was all so great. Yet here I am, engaged to be married, and I can't seem to get excited. I don't feel anything, except I am scared to death.'

'Scared? Why?'

'I don't know him or his mother. What if she is really mean to me? You know, the sort you see in Hindi movies. And Alok? What if he supports her, instead of defending me, when she is mean? And how do I know he won't be mean? He could take me somewhere and then leave me and run away. Or maybe he has a lecherous boss and he decides to make an offering out of me. What will I do?'

Sarika thought for a minute. 'But chacha and chachi know Alok's family through a friend?' Sarika asked.

'Yes. But how do I know what they are like? Haven't you read novels where people seem so nice but have unbelievable double lives?'

Sarika nodded.

'I don't know,' said Nisha, sighing. 'Maybe I'm letting my imagination run riot.'

'Well, the good thing is that Alok is posted in Lucknow. We'll always be here. And maybe, once you get to know him better, you won't have the same misgivings.'

'And how will I get to know him better?' asked Nisha angrily. 'The grownups in our family are pretty determined that he and I not meet alone until the wedding. Besides, technically I'm only eighteen. What's the big hurry? I don't want to get married just now. Not for another two or three years. Why can't I just enjoy life? But you know how they are. They never listen.'

'Once you're back in Moradabad, maybe chacha and chachi can invite him for a day or so,' said Sarika. 'Are they as strict as Amma? Do you think they'll let you go out alone with him for ice cream or something?'

'I don't know,' said Nisha. 'It's hard to say. I didn't think Taiji would say no, especially when Alok's mother said that we go out to get to know each other a bit. How can you tell what they think? They are so bloody conservative. I'm not asking to go on a pre-wedding honeymoon with him that they're getting so worked up. Just to 'ganj for a cold drink or a coffee. Everyone these days lets the bride- and groom-to-be go on innocent little outings.'

'I know,' said Sarika. 'The women in our family hold the belief that if you go out with him, even though you are engaged, he will take you for a woman of easy morals. I think this has happened in a couple of cases and our families are scared.'

'I know. But it doesn't happen all the time. And we are formally engaged.'

They sat together on the side of the cot, swinging their legs in silence, wide awake. The drone of the fan filled the room. Alley dogs barked violently, then went silent again. After a moment, Nisha stopped swinging her legs. She stiffened and continued, 'I wanted the romance of courtship...'

'Yes, Elizabeth and Mr. Darcy,' said Sarika. 'Doesn't look like...'

'Exactly. Elizabeth and Mr. Darcy. Why can't I have that? Even if I can't have a Mr. Darcy — all of that happened in a novel — this should be the best time in my life, going out with my betrothed and being made to feel special before settling into dull matrimony. They are denying me that. I'm first being forced to enter holy wedlock at eighteen and then being held in seclusion.'

She was quiet again. Sarika let her words sink in.

'I don't know. I am so confused,' Nisha added.

Sarika nodded in sympathy.

21

'Don't sing like an old woman. Keep your voice steady. Start again.' Sarika tried again.

'Steady.' Kirana mimicked her. 'What's happened to your voice?'

She hung her head. Nirmala watched her daughter anxiously from her cane chair.

'Come on, start again,' he said gently. 'Boldly.' He let out a sonorous *sa*.

Sarika blended her voice with his.

111

'Again. Why is your voice tremulous?'

'I am nervous about singing in front of five hundred people.'

'The lights will be so strong that you won't be able to see anyone. You can imagine that you are sitting and singing at home, that I'm giving you a lesson.'

'How can I imagine I'm at home when I'm sitting on stage?'

'It is natural to feel nervous for the first one or two minutes. Everyone feels that way. I do, too. After that you will be fine. Come on, start again. This time do *omkar*. *Om-m-m*. Let your whole being merge with the universe. Our music is very spiritual. No other musical tradition is like ours. Lose yourself in it. If you don't lose yourself in your music, how will your listeners lose themselves in your music? Come on. *Om-m-m*.'

'*Om-m-m*.'

Kirana started the alap, a few notes at a time. Sarika followed.

'Why do you jerk in going from *sa* to *ga*?' He sang like her. 'Sing like this.' He sang again, voice smooth as he connected one note to the next.

'*Bihag* is an evening raga,' he said. 'Your voice has to be soothing. It has to relax the audience. Let them feel they are sitting on the side of a beautiful lake on a moonlit night and your music is smoothly rippling over to them. You don't want your alap to create big waves. Think. Imagine.'

She tried again.

'Good. Again.'

She sang the same note combination again. And again.

'Try new combinations and see what sounds good. Improvise not only with your mind, but with your heart,' he said. 'That which touches the heart is music.'

Nirmala opened her mouth to say something when Lakshmi came shuffling in.

Kirana paused for a moment before continuing, 'When you sing,' he said, 'the *aah* should come spontaneously from deep within the listener's heart. Many artists sing to get a *vah* from the audience. But that's showmanship, acrobatics, showing marvelous vocal feats. It is not music. Music should bring out a sigh from the innermost depths of being.' He sang to illustrate his meaning.

Nirmala listened intently, deeply moved; her lips and chin quivered as she suppressed a sob. A lump rose in Sarika's throat in sympathy. Lakshmi sat mesmerized, still, unmoving. Kirana continued to sing. He went into the lower octave, demonstrating richness, depth, and range as his honey-coated voice connected notes effortlessly, caressingly. His smooth voice wafted to Sarika as if over the calm waters of a lake on a moonlit night. He began the *bandish* and gestured to her. She looked full into his eyes and saw her image on his irises. She joined in, softly, tremulously; gradually, her voice became steady and strong. They sang in unison — his deep, mellifluous voice blending with Sarika's younger, higher pitch. They embraced through their music as they expressed a deep longing for an absent lover.

Sarika forgot her fears of facing an audience. She felt closer to her teacher than she had to anyone, needing no words to feel the bond created through their voices joined together in music, their bodies moving rhythmically. Each note thrilled her body. Each sense came alive. Each emotion echoed through their two beings. It was surreal. For the first time Sarika experienced the sensuality of music.

~

That night, Lakshmi ate a sparse meal and retired to her room with the help of Sarika and Ravi.

Lakshmi's condition was worsening. Her loss of orientation worried Ravi, who monitored her condition closely on his short, weekly — sometimes more frequent — visits home from the medical college. The cancer had invaded his grandma's brain and lungs.

'How sick is she?' asked Sarika.

'Very. I wouldn't give her more than two months, if that,' said Ravi. 'What should we do then?' asked Ashwini.

'Not much. Make her comfortable,' said Ravi.

'Do you think she can come to my concert?' asked Sarika.

Ravi shook his head.

The lights did not go off at the Kumar residence. Ravi was the first to hear it as the family sat in the living room after Sarika's music lesson and dinner. It was a faint sound. Ravi turned his ear in the direction of the sound, but heard nothing. He looked up at the light, alert, ear cocked to hear the sound better if it came again. A gecko, apparently watching carefully the movements of a cockroach, rushed forward and attacked with lightening speed. In one swift movement, it snapped its jaws shut on the hapless insect's body. Too large to be swallowed whole, the cockroach protruded from all sides of the predator's mouth, hairy legs moving violently against the sharp teeth that held it in a deathly grip. The gecko rested calmly on the wall, aware of the largeness of its victim, but seemingly undisturbed. It would wait till its hunt was dead. Ravi watched them with disgusted fascination as they stayed locked in an unequal combat. He shuddered and continued reading his *New England Journal of Medicine*.

This time there was no mistaking the sound. Ravi put down his journal and walked to Lakshmi's room.

'Ravi?' said Nirmala, a hint of panic in her voice, hand and crochet needle suspended midair. 'What is the matter? Is Dadiji alright?'

Ravi didn't answer. Lakshmi's room was dark. In the dim light of the zero watt bulb, Ravi saw that Lakshmi had pulled herself up into a sitting position on the edge of her bed. Her legs hung limply on the side of the bed. She moaned softly.

'Dadiji?' said Ravi, turning on the lowest wattage light in the room.

'What is the matter?'

'Pain,' she said softly.

Ravi sat down next to her. 'Where is the pain?'

Lakshmi indicated her stomach and chest. Ashwini and Nirmala were now in Lakshmi's room. Nirmala sat down on the other side of Lakshmi and rubbed her back.

'Ammaji,' she cooed, 'you will be okay just now. You'll feel fine.' She kept rubbing her back.

'I can't sit,' she said panting; 'I want to lie down.'

Nirmala covered her with her pale yellow silk sheet. Lakshmi lay on her back, a wisp of a figure framed by pillows in white pillowcases, moving her head from side to side, letting out soft moans alternating with little muted cries that contorted her face already cut into furrows. Her dry, cracked lips moved slightly as if she were chanting a mantra to keep her courage alive. She kept her hands on her belly, digging her nails into her skin.

'What's the matter? Why is she in so much pain?' asked Ashwini.

Ravi shrugged. 'The cancer has spread all over her body.'

'I understand. Can't we give her anything to relieve her of the pain?' he asked.

'I've already put a painkiller on her tongue, but I don't think it is helping. I don't think oral painkillers will do much at this point. I gave her two sleeping pills. But nothing seems to be helping.'

Nirmala continued to rub Lakshmi's back. 'Try to sleep,' she said soothingly to her mother-in-law, moving both hands slowly and gently over her back. Sarika watched her mother and wondered about the complexity of adult emotions. She thought about the change in her feelings for her grandma once she had relinquished her hold over Ashwini's family — stopped putting her mother down, ordering the servants, changing the menu for lunch or dinner. Nirmala had always been respectful, even so Sarika sensed that though her mother was responsible for everything, she was granted power only by a domineering mother-in-law. Then the cancer had returned. Life, feelings, expectations, everything had changed after that. Forgiveness had intermingled with the air they breathed in the house.

Nirmala still rubbed Lakshmi's back. She looked at her husband, sitting up in his cane chair, fatigued. She urged him softly to go to sleep; he nodded and kept sitting. A bottomless well of energy, she now changed the motion of her hands on Lakshmi's back, pressing down on each vertebra, then ran her hand up and down the smooth texture of the housecoat. The soft moans were becoming louder. Ravi sat attentively by Lakshmi's side, holding a hot water bottle to her stomach.

'I can't take it any more,' cried Lakshmi.

Nirmala and Ravi looked at each other. Ravi got up and took Lakshmi's painkiller from her nightstand.

It was past midnight and Nirmala had stopped nagging Sarika about going to bed. She lay wide awake next to Lakshmi. Every time her grandmother lay still for a few minutes, the drone of the fan lulled her to sleep. But then Ravi's and Nirmala's activity, occasioned by Lakshmi's moaning, startled her into alert wakefulness. She heard the sounds of the night. The crickets were out in full force, providing a monotonous musical backdrop to the occasional truck that went thundering by on the main road, honking its horn without reason, the lone dog running the length of the street beside the truck, the screeching brakes. A light rain fell on the window, making this sober night even more somber. Rain made Sarika want to sing a *Malhar*, but today it made her grandma's condition seem bleaker.

Sarika had heard her Veena chachi and her Amma talk about Dadiji. Veena chachi had the most complaints, since as a young bride she had lived with Lakshmi. A little before Lakshmi was first diagnosed with cancer, Veena bought a South silk saree for four hundred rupees. That year the business had done exceptionally well and Ashok had taken her out on her birthday to pick a saree. On the way home she debated whether to wear it herself or keep it for Nisha's trousseau, but Ashok had said emphatically it was his birthday gift to her.

Lakshmi perused this purchase, as she did all others. Four hundred rupees, she had exclaimed in disbelief. Did she think money grew on trees? Would a two hundred-rupee saree not have been good enough for her? Veena had burst out crying, ready to return the saree, but Ashok wouldn't hear of it. He didn't say anything to his mother, either.

'I think, at her age, and especially now that she has cancer, she should give up her interest in worldly things and turn her mind to God.' Veena said. 'Why is she so involved in the non spiritual?'

'She's the same here,' Nirmala had said. 'Everytime I have to go somewhere, she kicks up a big fuss. One day I got very angry. I told Ravi's Papa, "Why don't you take your mother instead of me to all the official functions?" '

Now when the two women met, they talked only about Lakshmi's courage in handling her illness. There was something touchingly pathetic about a strong person being brought to her knees by disease: Pity at first, then as the victim's hold on life became more tenuous, pure love arising from involvement in something so much larger than the pettiness of individual life. Sarika was beginning to doze off.

'I can't take it any more.' Lakshmi was writhing in pain. Sarika sat up with a start.

'What should we do?' said Nirmala, turning to her son.

'We can't do anything till the morning. Everything is closed just now. Unless I go to the medical college and see if I can get some morphine.'

'No, not at this time,' said Ashwini. 'It's not safe to be out at this hour.'

Lakshmi tried to get up.

'Ammaji?'

'I want to throw up.'

Ravi sat her up and Nirmala pulled out the plastic basin from under the bed and held it under her chin. Lakshmi brought up her small dinner. She lay down. Her breathing eased. Soon she fell asleep.

The next morning Sarika woke up with a scratchy throat. She said a few words to hear the sound of her voice. With every word she spoke, she cleared her throat. Would her voice become heavy? Panic seized her. With barely a week to go before the concert, she wondered if her throat would give up on her.

That evening, Kirana said to Sarika, 'You have to sing with more emotion.'

Sarika looked down at her tanpura and fingered the birds carved into the deep, polished wood. Nirmala smiled. 'She is very young,' she said. 'Emotion comes with maturity.'

'Oh,' said Sarika remembering her second-year exam. 'Principal sahib said I sang with a lot of emotion for one so young.'

'That is true,' said Kirana. 'But you are older now and your voice and face should express the same feeling. Deep within you, you have to feel what you're singing,' he said. Ravi came into the room and greeted Kirana with a nod. 'For a woman, it's easy to express herself, for expression comes so naturally to women. A beautiful woman expressing words with great feeling. What greater pleasure can there be for the listener!' Kirana cast a quick glance at Ravi to see if he was listening. Sarika fidgeted.

Ravi looked sharply at Kirana, then turned his head toward his mother, enjoying Kirana sahib's romps into sensuous imagery. Kirana had been tutoring Sarika privately for more than a year, but the crazy schedule of a resident's life had never allowed Ravi to meet Kirana until today. And his first impression of the man did not match Sarika's bubbly accounts of this gifted teacher. Somehow Kirana's ease in describing a world fraught with troubles for a girl devoted to the art made him recoil. Swati — he remembered everything about her except her name — her music, her involvement with a man who professed to love her music, her abortion, flashed across his mind and the suddenness of the appearance of the image of the young woman in the context of his sister's musical training made him shudder. Aware of this charming man's power, Ravi sat down next to his mother to observe Kirana.

'Music without emotion is just melodic sound,' Kirana continued. 'It does not touch the heart. It does not transport you into the kingdom of the apsaras. It is like a beautiful but frigid woman, incapable of giving pleasure.'

Nirmala giggled. Sarika, embarrassed, lowered her head and continued tracing the birds on her instrument. Ravi tensed at the references to sex.

'Now sing again,' Kirana said, 'and try to think of what you're singing.'

Sarika started again. And then it happened. Just as she negotiated her first high note, her voice rent asunder. It was as if someone had taken a piece of poplin and torn it down the center. Sarika stopped singing and looked at Kirana sahib. He smiled gently at her. She burst into tears.

'I can't sing next week,' she said sobbing.

'There's still almost a week,' he said soothingly. 'Gargle, take care of your throat. Tell your Ravi Bhaiya to give you some medicine and your throat will be fine.'

'No, I can't sing. What if my voice gives on stage?'

'It won't. Nothing will happen,' he said. 'Practice and leave the rest to God. Our music is so spiritual. It is called *Nada Brahma*, the language of God. Dedicate it to Him.'

22

It was the morning of Sarika's concert. Kirana listened to her in her living room one last time.

'What do you think of her preparation, Kirana sahib?' Nirmala asked.

'My children are lions. They always do well.'

'Sarika is very nervous. She has not eaten a thing since the morning,' Nirmala said.

'If you don't eat, how will you sing? Sarika? You need a lot of energy to sing. Nice and loud. What's there to be afraid of?'

Sarika stared mutely.

118

'Sing,' Kirana said. 'I will time you. Remember, ten minutes for the *vilambit khayal* and five minutes for the *drut*.'

Sarika started the slow-tempo piece. She stopped and cleared her throat. Unsteadily, she started again.

'I can't do it,' she said tearfully.

'Your voice is much better today than it was four-five days ago. Clear your throat, take a deep breath and begin. Start with *Om*. That will help.'

'*Om-m-m*.'

Sarika hung her head.

'Why have you stopped? Don't stop. Come on. You sound fine.'

'*Om-m-m*.'

Kirana listened carefully. A little nervous himself about Sarika's throat, he wondered what indeed would happen if Sarika's voice gave on stage. As he started accompanying her on the tabla, he saw his student struggle with her voice. It didn't soar effortlessly like a bird today, but sounded like a creature caged. He looked at her nervous adolescent face. Her light skin looked even paler. Her big hazel eyes seemed deeper set. They hadn't brightened at the sight of him as they always did; today, they were clouded with worry. He looked at her long, straight nose, the somewhat full mouth with pale pink lips, the prominent chin and jawbone, all the more noticeable because Sarika was so diminutive. She had rolled her thick, brown plait into a bun at the nape of her neck. Kirana looked at the dupatta wrapped around her throat as protection from the harmful breeze of the ceiling fan, the prominent collar bones, the fine skin on the blue-veined hands, one holding the tanpura tight, the other strumming it with its long, sensitive, upward tipping fingers. His heart surged. He was shaping her musical career. His thoughts, his beliefs, his style were becoming hers. All his art would be hers. This concert was a coming-out party for both of them and in her triumph lay his. Sarika's voice was steadier now. It still came to him over a gravel road, but with rest and honey and a little luck that would go away. She had progressed to the medium on her way to the fast tempo. Kirana relaxed his body. Sarika's *Bihag* continued without a hitch.

'Good,' said Kirana. 'Sing like this and you'll be fine.'

'You sang very well,' said Nirmala. 'What should she wear in the evening, master sahib?'

'A cotton saree,' said Kirana. 'It suits your body,' he said to Sarika.

Sarika giggled but Nirmala seemed unabashed by Kirana sahib's comment.

'At what time do you want her in Ravindralaya?' Nirmala asked.

'Six, six-thirty will be fine,' he said. He turned to Sarika. 'Get plenty of rest in the afternoon. Lick lots of honey. And no more singing. Rest your throat. Behanji,' he said to Nirmala, 'you and Bhaisaheb will be there in the evening?' asked Kirana.

'Yes,' said Nirmala.

'Good. We will all meet in the evening then,' said Kirana smiling. He opened the screen door to the verandah and left.

'What a nice man,' said Nirmala, as she heard the sound of his feet over the gravel. 'Most unlike a musician. I noticed his facial expressions when he was talking to you about your dress for the evening. He looked so playful, as one talking to a child.'

~

Kirana held Sarika's tanpura close to his ear to drown out the ambient sound, repeatedly playing the two middle strings to see if they droned in harmony. Sarika answered last-minute questions from the announcer from All India Radio. She barely knew what she said, keeping her eyes on her teacher, who now struggled with the first string of her tanpura. Geeta, sitting behind Sarika to her left, on a wooden platform covered characteristically with a *dhurrie* and a white sheet, provided the drone on her instrument to which Kirana tuned Sarika's. Mrs. Sinha had offered her tanpura-strumming services to Sarika, who had politely declined.

'This air conditioning messes up the instruments,' Kirana complained. 'I can't get the *pa* to hold.'

'We should have electronic instruments,' said the harmonium player merrily, as he held down the tonic, fifth and eighth notes on his instrument.

Sarika wondered at his calm on stage. She felt no laughter or anything in any part of her body, feeling instead, a big, cavernous hole where her stomach should have been. Into this hole her heart had sunk and now pounded maniacally. She wished the sensation would go away, but the harder she tried to push it away, the fiercer it clung. Kirana finished

120

tuning and handed her the tanpura. The tabla player was ready to go. It was curtain time.

'Okay Sarika. Sing very well,' said Kirana, standing up on the platform. He smiled, stepped down onto the stage and put on his sandals.

'My voice?' she whispered, touching his knees, since his feet were out of range.

'It will be fine,' he whispered, holding his hand up in a sign of a blessing. 'Don't think about it. I've told you, my students are lions.'

'Come on, *beta*, let's get started,' said Sitaram Mishra, the harmonium player, who sat on Sarika's right.

'Let's go,' said Gajendra Mishra, the tabla player, who sat to her left.

Sarika gulped.

The AIR announcer peeked from the wings. 'Should I announce?' she asked.

A hush fell on the stage. Sarika looked about nervously. Everyone was in place, ready to start. One word from her and the curtains would part, revealing five hundred listeners. The moment had come; there was no escape. She pulled out her handkerchief from her waist, opened its knot with her cold, sweaty hands and took out a piece of *mishri*, which she popped into her mouth to keep her throat moist, leaving her handkerchief open in front of her. She could hear the mad beating of her heart above the drone of the tanpuras. She held her instrument tighter. The announcer looked at Sarika again.

'Yes,' said the harmonium player.

The microphones crackled into life as the AIR audio technician gave his signal and the announcer said, 'And now you will hear a vocal recital by Kumari Sarika. She will be accompanied on the tabla by Shri Gajendra Mishra and on the harmonium by Shri Sitaram Mishra. Kumari Sarika will sing two compositions in Raga *Bihag*. The *vilambit*....'

Sarika was not listening any more, trying instead to immerse herself in the drone of the tanpura, which rang out over the microphone, filling the now-quiet auditorium with its resonance. The curtains parted and Sarika sang *sa*, but did not look at the audience. Her voice came out steady, but grated a little. She turned her head away from the microphone, cleared her throat, put another piece of *mishri* in her mouth, and began the exposition. Her voice was smoother now. As she began the piece in the

121

slow tempo, her voice grew steadier and soon filled the auditorium with its melodious fluidity. Relief flooded her body. She dared raise her eyes for the first time as she finished the rhythm-bound, non-improvisational part of her composition and prepared to display the improvisational element, feeling more settled now. Kirana sahib had been right. The audience lacked a face behind the strong lights. When she had adjusted to the light, Sarika searched for master sahib. She saw the principal in the first row, sitting with the chief minister of the state, the chief guest for that day, and her parents and brother. She swept the side section of the auditorium. There he was — in the first row, nearest the entrance, his wife and three children two rows behind him. Kirana sahib sat in the position she loved so much — his spine resting against the back of the yellow-brown seat, legs slightly parted at the knees, head tilted to one side, listening raptly. She sang to him, just like he had told her to. She wanted him to be proud. She wanted to proclaim to the universe that she was his *shishya*. She wanted... she didn't know what else she wanted. She didn't care if everyone knew how much she loved him. She didn't want to keep her feelings hidden. After all, isn't that what life was about — loving and being loved. She brought her eyes back to the stage, smiling at her accompanists, who both rocked in enjoyment. Her voice blossomed in the high notes. Feeling stronger, she dared to try a combination that went into very high notes, then took a complicated *tihai* and came perfectly to the first beat of the tabla. It was spectacular. '*Shabash, beta*' murmured Sitaram ji as he echoed her rendition on his harmonium. Sarika grinned and went on to the piece in the fast tempo. The curtain came down amidst deafening applause.

Almost before she had time to set her tanpura down, Kirana was there, smiling broadly.

Sarika jumped off the platform and touched her teacher's feet. Speechless, he put his arm around her shoulders for one quick second. Sarika's heart jumped.

'*Vah*, Sarika *beta, vah*' said Sitaram ji. '*Kya gaya*! You sang beautifully. *Ananda aa gaya*. I enjoyed it. Kirana sahib, your student.'

'Come on, come on, move off the stage,' said the mustachioed college servant, as he and others ran on and off the stage, preparing for the next item — dance — on the program. But teachers, tabla players, the AIR announcer had all congregated on the stage and were hopelessly in the way.

122

'Sarika, *bitiya*, move,' said Ahmed. 'Master sahib, move. You can talk outside.'

Kirana went backstage to look after the guest artist for the evening, who had just arrived. Sarika floated off the stage and out to the steps that led from the wings to the foyer of the auditorium. Her legs felt wobbly and her hands were cold and still tremulous. But her heart had now moved out of her belly and was beating once again in her pericardium.

She stood alone for several minutes in the deserted foyer to compose herself. Her mind was flooded. The concert. That was over, thank heavens. Kirana sahib. His touch. She took a deep breath and headed toward the auditorium door to join her family.

'Congratulations, Sarika ji,' said Naushad, coming up suddenly from behind. 'Sarika ji, you have been blessed with a beautiful voice.'

'Thank you, Naushad ji,' Sarika turned toward him. Naushad had started at the college after the summer break, just as Kirana sahib had said, but she had caught only a few quick glimpses of him in the two months he had been there. In those two months, she had never seen him in the bell-bottomed pants that the teachers swore were the reason he could never be as good as his illustrious father. For how could someone so 'mod' play north Indian classical music well.

He was dressed to perform. A pair of spotless white pajamas, with a crisp crease running down the center, a natural-coloured silk *kurta* — with three gold buttons, each with a tiny diamond in the center, joined to each other by a fine gold chain — with delicate embroidery in white around the button placket, and rough-hewn leather sandals stood well on his medium, slender frame. He left the top button open. A gold ring in his ring finger and a gold HMT men's watch gave his left hand a distinctly ornamental look. Sarika wondered if he was married. 'Thank you for your kind words. You perform today, too?'

'Yes,' said Naushad.

'Are you nervous?' This was to be his first solo performance since coming to the college.

'No. I have been performing on stage since the age of ten, eleven.'

'What raga will you play on your violin?'

'I'm thinking of a couple. *Yaman* or *Pooriya*. I'll see what my mood dictates before I go on stage.'

'You mean you haven't decided yet?' Sarika asked. 'Wow.'

'I will before I sit on stage.'

'Good luck.'

'Okay. Will you stay till the end?'

'I think so, but I'll have to ask my parents. You are right before the intermission, before the guest artist comes on?'

'Yes.'

'I'll listen to your recital then,' she said as he went up the steps and into the wings. Sarika turned to go into the concert hall, when someone came up to her, walking briskly. She squinted in the dim lights to see the face, but saw that it wasn't anyone she knew. She had almost opened the door, when the person softly called out her name. Sarika turned around now and stood facing the woman.

'Very good recital, Sarika.'

Only then Sarika recognized her. 'Swati ji! I didn't recognize you.' Sarika took in Swati's altered appearance even as she tried not to stare too hard at her. Her face looked white with heavy makeup that ended at the jaw line and drew a clear line of demarcation between her face and neck. She wore heavy, black eye makeup that ill suited her, and red lipstick. As Sarika moved closer to her, Swati's heavy Intimate overwhelmed her and she took a small step back. Startled by her appearance, Sarika continued mechanically. 'It must have been the lights that I didn't recognize you. They keep them low when something's going on inside. And I think I'm becoming a little short sighted.'

'I came out right after you finished to congratulate you.'

'Thank you. Your praise means a lot. I didn't know you were here still. It's been so long. So you're still in Lucknow?' Sarika had last seen Swati when her senior had sung her eighth-year practical exam, which was open to an audience. That was several months ago. And just like Sarika had imagined, she remembered Swati's abortion every time she saw her. Sarika knew that lacking the option of returning home, Swati had continued at the college after the unfortunate incident. It had been tough for her, once everyone knew. Swati had responded by becoming extremely withdrawn. She went to the college only for her class and returned to her room as soon as it was over. She spent most of her time in her room. Once the girls at the hostel had recovered from the shock of her news, they had accepted her without reservation. Gradually she began to come out of her room, but still confined herself to the girls' hostel. Swati had apparently recovered from the damage.

'Yes, I'm still in Lucknow,' said Swati.

'I thought you had moved to Assam after eighth year?'

'I had thought, too, I would move to Assam after eighth year, but you know how it is. People are killed every day. My parents want me to stay here. They feel it's safer here.'

'So what are you doing?'

'Tuitions, mainly. Some radio programs, but those are few and far between and they don't pay much. Sometimes I go to people's homes and sing.'

'Do you sometimes meet others from the college? Mrs. Sinha?'

'Only one or two girls from the hostel. Not Mrs. Sinha. I caught a glimpse of her here, though.'

'Yes, I've seen her here, too. She wanted to play the tanpura with me,' Sarika couldn't resist adding.

'Always the same issue,' added Swati. 'It's hard to shake her off.'

'She's good. Okay.'

'Okay.'

~

When she came home from Ravindralaya that night, Sarika sat down next to her grandmother and told her about Swati and her makeup, which she still had trouble accepting, about Naushad's violin and the guest artist who showed exquisite mastery over the sitar. Her grandma's dry, dim, dark eyes shone with love as Sarika took Lakshmi's hand in both her own. Lakshmi held Sarika in her gaze, then turned her face and closed her eyes. Sarika kept her eyes on Lakshmi's face, wondering if she had fallen asleep or was just too weak to leave her eyes open. Her mind began to replay her performance — the announcement, the reverberation of the tanpuras, the lights, the fear, the kudos, the ecstasy of success, master sahib. Kirana sahib. How pleased he was when other teachers came up to him to congratulate. Sarika smiled, glad to make him proud of her. Her mind drifted to her lessons at home taught painstakingly, each note perfect every time, so much patience, so much love for the student. She couldn't understand her feeling for him. It was unlike anything she'd felt before. She became aware of her grandma's eyes on her.

'How is Kirana sahib?' asked Lakshmi.

Had her grandmother read her thoughts? She squirmed. 'He's fine.'

'Was he pleased with your performance?'

'Yes. Very.'

Lakshmi closed her eyes.

'Dadiji,' said Sarika softly. 'Dadiji,' Sarika said again, when she received no response.

Lakshmi's eyes snapped open. 'Hunh?' she said as if shaken out of a dream.

'Were you sleeping?'

'No. I had just closed my eyes.'

'Really? Just closed your eyes,' said Sarika smiling mischievously.

'Okay, I slept a little,' said Lakshmi smiling like a child caught in mischief. 'What are Amma-Papa doing?

'They're having dinner.'

Lakshmi nodded and closed her eyes again.

'Dadiji.' She wanted to ask if it was okay to have a special feeling — the sort that made the heart pump faster — for Kirana sahib.

Lakshmi's eyes snapped open again.

'Should I bring you some milk?' she asked instead.

Swati did not return to her seat after seeking out Sarika, nor did she go home and make an entry in her diary. As soon as the door shut behind Sarika, she left the concert hall — as if her only purpose in coming to the concert, in meeting Sarika, was being seen — and hailed a tempo to Hazratganj, the shopping area in the center of town. Getting off the tempo, she briskly walked two blocks to the petrol pump. She slowed down, stood behind a tree and caught her breath. It was late. A few cars still came in to have their tanks filled and though every thing was winding down for the night, the light was still on in the manager's office. Swati peeked from behind the tree to see if she could catch a glimpse of the person inside, but the air conditioner in the window blocked her view. Her heart raced. With a deliberate step, she marched up to the office, swung the door open and went in.

'Swati ji!' Sinha sank back into his chair. 'What a surprise. It has been a long time.' He looked directly into her eyes.

'Yes.'

'Please sit down, Swati ji. Why are you standing? What brings you here?' He smiled broadly at her, noting her heavy makeup, her artificial-silk saree, the red nail polish, as she sat down with her hands in her lap. His mind worked quickly. It had been roughly six months since she had finished her eighth year from the college. Did she need a place to stay? In the urgency to see him, she had forgotten that he had told her never to come to his office. This once he would let slide.

'I haven't seen you in a long time,' Swati said. 'I thought I would come see you.'

'I am glad you did. I thought you were angry with me.'

'Angry?'

'After your unfortunate visit to Queen Mary's hospital, you just disappeared. I came to Mrs. Yadav's a few times, but you remained distant. I thought you were angry with me and I would never see you again.'

'There's nothing to be angry about,' she mumbled at his reference to her abortion. 'What is past is past.' She paused. 'And I was busy with my eighth year. It was a lot of work. I just didn't have the time.'

'Have you finished your eighth year, then?' He scrutinized her.

'Yes. Last December.'

'So you decided to stay here and not go to Assam?'

'You know how it is in Assam. So much turbulence. Refugees from Bangla Desh have taken over our state. There are no jobs anywhere. My parents want as many of their children to get out of there as possible.'

'Ah, yes. So where are you staying? No longer at the music college?' She probably needed money. That is why she had come to see him. The urge was strong in him to make her rub her nose on the ground. He had been decent, after all, paying completely for her abortion with some money to spare for her own expenses. She had no reason, then, to withdraw from him. He had done what any decent man would do. He could have refused to part with any money and what would she have done then. No, she had no reason to distance herself. She who had always accepted his generosity unflinchingly.

'I have rented a room in Chowk,' she said.

'Chowk? That far!'

'It doesn't matter. I have some tuitions close by.'

'Good. I am glad you have enough tuitions to support yourself.'

'Now that I have a room, maybe you can come and see me. It has been a long time.'

'So you came to invite me?' He smiled. He had known the moment he saw her. She had grown.

'Yes. All these years, I could not call you to my place, because I didn't have one.' She smiled in turn. 'I couldn't possibly ask you to come to my room at the music college. The warden would have thrown a fit.' Swati's journey to her own place had not been an easy one. Just before she finished her eighth year from the music college, one of the teachers offered her a place to stay. His wife was ill and he needed some help at home. Swati could stay rent free in exchange for house work. The arrangement would allow her plenty of time for *riyaz*. Grateful, Swati moved in, only to find the teacher and his wife's demands so unreasonable that she felt enslaved, with little time to practice. A few months into this situation, she realized that she was losing the preparedness of the voice that distinguishes the 'are' from the 'have been.' She searched and found an inexpensive room in the old part of town. Running her own place made money even tighter. 'You must come and see my place,' she said.

'Of course, I'll come,' he said benevolently. 'How can it be that you come all the way to invite me and I don't come. It is an honour, Swati ji, an honour.'

'You embarrass me, Sinha ji.'

'What do you say! Why should it embarrass you. It is truly an honour. I've heard you on radio. You are a radio artist now.'

'It is a small thing. It's not too hard to become B grade. I will soon audition for A grade.'

'An achievement, regardless. I will come, Swati ji. What will you sing for me?'

'Whatever your heart desires.'

He gave her his sweetest smile.

23

In a week, Sarika's post-concert euphoria had subsided and her life settled back into the normalcy of routine and the attendant worry of exams hovering over the horizon. Kirana stopped dropping in after college and came every Sunday morning.

'It is all about love,' he said one Sunday morning as he worked with her on expressing greater feeling, 'for love is the center of life. Without it, there cannot be creation or procreation. Brahma ji created the universe.' He lowered his voice. 'He also decreed that men and women should procreate and for that, there has to be love. Learn to love. Let love flow through your body.'

Sarika squirmed and lowered her eyes.

'Learn to love the notes in your music the way a man loves a woman. After all, music is an expression of love. You love, you are joyful, you burst into song. Isn't that how it is in nature when the flower bursts into joyful bloom, the bird sings unrestrainedly, the buoyant calf bounds in the pasture? Don't animals attract each other through their love songs? Music is nothing but the natural expression of love and joy. There is no place for hatred in music. Learn to love...'

Nirmala walked into the room. Sarika fidgeted. Taken aback, Kirana smiled sheepishly at Nirmala and continued. 'I once went to a concert by an instrumentalist, a very plain-looking artist. But when he started playing, what a transformation came over him! I thought no more of the face, but of the beauty within. His face looked so angelic. His music was the outpouring of love in his heart. So divine. That is how you have to be. Sing with love.'

As Kirana spoke, Sarika scrutinized her mother's face to determine if she had heard the bit about man and woman.

'Hatred and anger have no place in music,' Kirana said, casting a glance at Nirmala. 'I have told you music is *Nada Brahma*. You sing *Om* and you feel your voice reverberating in *Brahmand*, the cosmos. Vocal music, especially, is the highest art form. It does not require anything except your own thoughts and your own voice. What is music, after all? It is like tying knots in the abstract. Like stringing pearls into a beautiful necklace. Giving something intangible an almost tangible form. If the artist can create that form for himself, others can see it, too. But he has to create it for himself. He cannot keep an audience in mind, for if he does, he will show craft not spiritual depth.'

'It's like seeing something that touches you deeply,' said Sarika. 'The moment you think you will share that thought with someone, the depth of feeling goes away. It takes on a sort of superficiality, a sentimentality.'

'Yes,' said Kirana, barely listening. Comfortable now, he was pleased with himself, enjoying few pleasures more than talking philosophically about music. The divinity of the art form gave him a feeling of dwelling in the celestial. 'But how difficult that is! How difficult it is to achieve perfection in music. You sing *sa*. What is *sa*? You are somehow trying to create a perfect sound out of nothing. Some days you achieve that perfection, other days you don't. But you keep trying. And when you do achieve that perfection, you forget everything. The whole material world sinks into nothingness. You find such peace. *Sukoon*. It is a form of yoga, a perfect union, except it is a higher form than the bodily yoga for it draws on a spiritual idea.'

Sarika's mind drifted off. Kirana sahib sat across from her in his sparkling white pajama and kurta, very straight in a cross-legged position, his thick black hair, brushed back and down to his shoulders, held in place by a fragrant hair oil. Kantheridine. Sarika knew the distinctive smell. His forehead played host to two fine horizontal lines. His large, expressive eyes seemed just as involved in explaining the perfection of music as his voice. She noted his smooth, close shave, the neatly trimmed moustache that gave him the appearance of always chuckling, his fine nose, the full lips. What a handsome man. She realized suddenly she had never dwelled on his physical characteristics before.

'...which is why Mrs. Sinha will never make a good musician. She is always angry with those who sing better than her.'

'Almost everyone does,' Sarika said.

'Sarika.' Nirmala shook her head and tried to suppress a smile. She stood up. 'I had better go and see what Amma ji is doing. I was going to her room but sat down here instead. Your conversation was so interesting.'

Kirana laughed. '*Sangeet cheez hi aisi hai*. It is hard not to be completely engrossed in music. How is mataji?'

'Marking time,' said Nirmala. 'What can anyone do at this stage? It is just a question of letting her finish her journey as comfortably as possible.'

'Mrs. Sinha is not a woman of good character,' Kirana continued, as soon as Nirmala had left the room. 'Have you seen how she dresses? Showing so much of her body?'

'Hm,' said Sarika.

'The other day,' Kirana elaborated, 'she asked me to give her a ride home on my scooter.'

'What happened to her car?' Sarika asked reluctantly.

'She said she came on a rickshaw, because she left her car lights on and the battery got drained. Her husband was out of station. It was late and she was afraid because there are so many dark areas between the college and her house.'

'So did you give her a ride on your scooter?'

'Yes. What could I do? What she did while she was on my scooter... What should I say?'

'Okay.'

'You've understood?'

'Yes, it's obvious.'

'I had to tell my wife each and every detail,' he said, sighing deeply. 'She doesn't understand a mere gesture. Everything has to be explained.'

'And was she angry?'

'No, she understands that I don't like Mrs. Sinha,' he said.

'Good.'

'What if someone from the college had seen me and her like that? What would they have said? Do you know a man's reputation can be gone in a second? One second is all it takes. What takes years to build. I want to keep a distance from her, but she's hard to shake off.'

Sarika felt uncomfortable at the meaningless, unintelligent conversation. What if her father heard them? 'Did you like Naushad ji's violin recital?' she asked, trying to change the subject. 'He chose his raga just before getting on stage!' she said, still incredulous.

'That's not so unusual. But he is young and talented. I hope he does well. So, what was I saying when you changed the subject. Ah, Mrs. Sinha. I don't like her,' he said. 'She invites me to her house all the time. Says she has questions about ragas that she never has the time to ask about in class. I avoid her totally, but she doesn't seem to understand.'

'But you do go to her house?' she forced herself to ask.

'Yes, sometimes. What should I do? I keep saying no, but she's so insistent. I go sometimes just to get her off my back. And then her husband is a very successful businessman.' Surprised by his own thought,

131

let alone words, and trying to resume the original argument, he said, 'She hounds me.'

Kirana grew up in a middle-class family with no social rank, which was reserved for the wealthy and the bureaucracy. The upper classes held a fascination for him and he reveled in inclusion. He had caught rare glimpses into those spheres, much as one sometimes passes by an expensive store and looks at the articles on display as belonging to a different realm. The ideal life, of course, was that of the artist — above it all — simply pursuing his passion. *Maya* didn't affect him. But that was the ideal life.

'Why does she insist so much? I think she knows that you come here, to my house...'

'Yes, she does. She even said that to me once. And that's the other reason I have to go to her house when she asks me to.'

'Why? Why should that matter?'

'She puts forth these arguments that I can't refute.'

'Like what?'

'She says for a guru all students should be equal. So, if the guru is going to one *shishya's* house, how can he refuse another?'

'What you do outside of class is not her business.' Now that the conversation had moved out of the forbidden realm of sex, Sarika was enjoying this closeness with Kirana sahib, even as in a far corner of her consciousness, she saw its futility. But it was a way of fostering closeness with a man who was so removed from her in age and background. Kirana sahib's confessions about Mrs. Sinha engendered a strong sense of security in her in the knowledge that Kirana sahib did not like the only other person in her class whom he taught at home. If Mrs. Sinha considered herself a rival, Sarika had no choice but to treat her as one.

'She is a very cunning woman, with lots of money and time on her hands. Her husband is a very good businessman with lots of black money. I have been to her house. What a house! Glass everywhere. The moment you go and sit down, the servant comes out with a trayful of cold drinks. Everything that you can get in the market is there.'

'Then why do you come here if they look after you so well?' Sarika asked.

'I don't come here for cold drinks. Her wealth doesn't impress me...'

132

Doesn't it, Sarika wondered, but then didn't we all get somewhat impressed by big houses and fancy cars?

'... what kind of a person is she? I come here because your family is so nice. Oh, Sarika.' His voice changed. 'Do you realize what you mean to me? You don't know how through your reactions, you have shown me a new way to look at the world, a way to clear the muddiness of my nature. Meeting you is like the confluence of a fresh new brooklet and an old stream. That is why I come here so often,' he concluded in a trembling voice.

Sarika's heart leapt. She looked at Kirana sahib's eloquent face and lowered her eyes.

'That is why I like to teach you music. You understand what is within my soul. Mrs. Sinha never does.'

Sarika let his words seep in.

'Pick up your tanpura. Let us begin,' he said quietly. *Sa.*

~

Later that hot September afternoon, as Lakshmi lay dozing in her room, Sarika sat down next to her on a folding chair and felt a trickle of sweat run down her neck. The ceiling fan was off. As she got up and turned it on, Lakshmi opened her eyes.

'It's cold,' she said. 'Cover me with a blanket.'

Sarika regarded her grandmother sadly as she drifted into sleep. Lakshmi looked so small and pale. Radiation had killed most of the baby white hair that had begun to sprout after the chemotherapy, but at least the pain had gone. After writhing in pain all that terrible night, Ravi had always been armed with morphine, but she hadn't needed it. Her pink scalp was clearly visible through the sparse hair. The lines on her gaunt face looked deeper. Her dry lips, stuck together, flapped open with a little explosion with each exhalation, creating a steam engine effect. Sarika smiled despite her sadness.

She turned her attention to her Hindi book. She read a page and began to doze. Frustrated with herself, she stood up and paced up and down the room. After a few minutes, she sat down again, but found that poetry was no easier after the pacing than before. Her mind drifted to Kirana sahib, as the book lay open on her knees. His talk about Mrs. Sinha had strangely upset her. It was distasteful, low. It was good that he had told his wife. Sarika stood up and paced. Why was her mind in turmoil? She couldn't put her finger on it.

'Is something bothering you? You have been pacing,' said Lakshmi suddenly.

Sarika shook her head.

'Will Kirana sahib come to teach you today?' Lakshmi stared at the ceiling.

'He came this morning.' How was it that Lakshmi asked her about Kirana sahib every time her mind was in a turmoil over him?

'Your music finals are barely two months away.'

'Yes. I am not thinking about them yet.'

'You have your theory exam first, don't you?'

'Yes. I have to study for that, too,' Sarika said dully. 'I hate studying for theory.'

Sarika's mind spiralled again to Mrs. Sinha riding Kirana sahib's scooter. Why did it bother her so?

'Mrs. Sinha asked Kirana sahib for a lift on his scooter,' said Sarika. 'He drove her home from the college one day.'

'He told you?'

'Yes. He said her behaviour was most inappropriate; she sat close to him and put her hand on his shoulder. I don't know what to think.' Lakshmi listened attentively. 'Mrs. Sinha is always criticizing everyone at the college for even looking at another. Then she goes and behaves like this. Putting poor master sahib in a very awkward position. What is a man to do if a woman behaves this way? And the way she dresses!'

Lakshmi smiled at Sarika, then drifted away. Sarika regretted having said anything.

'It seems you are more upset that Kirana sahib gave Mrs. Sinha the lift than that Mrs. Sinha asked for it,' said Lakshmi in a soft, broken voice. Sarika was about to issue a denial, but held back, as her grandmother continued. 'The ways of men and women are very strange. Women have always tested a man's strength. Remember the story of Vishwamitra? He wanted so much to attain salvation, but a beautiful woman sent by a jealous god didn't let him. You are too young to understand all this just now. Just don't get involved...'

'But, Dadiji,' Sarika protested. 'I'm not involved with Kirana sahib.'

'I'm not saying you are. But you have to be careful for the woman always bears the brunt of a relationship gone awry. You have to learn to draw the line — thus far, and no farther — or you could end up terribly hurt. Kirana sahib is a good man, but he is a man and you are fast becoming a woman. Let Mrs. Sinha be. What do you have to do with her? Hers are the ways of a street woman. You are a lovely child. Just keep yourself aloof.' Lakshmi stopped and began to pant for air. After several seconds, Lakshmi extended her open hand. Sarika slipped her hand into her grandma's and squeezed it. Tears filled her eyes. That her grandmother understood her feelings, when no one else did, was unbelievable. Embarrassed, she wondered what else her grandmother understood. Did she understand her feelings for Kirana sahib, which she could barely articulate to herself? Yet, she felt relieved. So it really wasn't Kirana sahib's fault. What could he do if a woman, especially one who was older than him, behaved like this? It was clearly Mrs. Sinha's fault. She was glad her grandmother had understood that she was more disturbed about Kirana sahib than Mrs. Sinha. The load felt lighter now that two people carried it. Sarika settled back into her chair, closed her book and put it on the nightstand.

~

A few days later, Veena and Ashok arrived in Lucknow again, after Nirmala's call informed them that it was any day now. Nirmala was nervous. As long as there had been something immediate to focus on — Lakshmi's meals, massages, baths — her nerves had held on. But now Lakshmi's system was shutting down. Her meals lay untouched, her trips to the bathroom became less frequent, she didn't want a massage. She drifted in and out of an undrugged stupor. At times she dazzled Nirmala with the keenness of her mind with her questions about Ashwini and Ravi and Sarika; at others, she seemed to have entered into a tunnel that separated her from the mortals around her. One of these times, she would float away.

The house was deathly quiet. It was mid afternoon and the servants had left for their break after lunch. Ashok, Veena, Ravi, and Sarika were in Lakshmi's room. Ashwini had gone back to the secretariat for a meeting with the minister, having told Ravi to phone his personal assistant if

Lakshmi's condition changed. Nirmala had barely eaten lunch, but no one noticed. They watched Lakshmi, heard her shallow breathing, sat up as she started, opened her eyes, looked around and went back to sleep. Sarika held her hand and talked to her softly, telling her about lunch, about Nisha and the saree she had already bought for her wedding, about Pradeep's passion for the socialistic way of life. Lakshmi listened without curiosity. It was as if she had withdrawn herself from the world like a tortoise pulls its limbs into its shell as it prepares to enter sleep. Sarika squeezed Lakshmi's hand and closed her eyes over her tears. Sarika felt she was now on the bank of a fastflowing river trying to hold back a boat that would rush away into the unknown. She thought of the little rivulets that swirled swiftly past the gate to their house on a rainy day and the newspaper boats she held in her hand before joyfully releasing them into the swelling streams, watching them float upright for a few seconds before they turned on their side, filled with water and were carried away as mere masses of newsprint into the drain further down the street. Except in her grandma's case, Sarika didn't have control over the release of the boat. That, her mother always said, was predestined. Her chest heaved. She wanted her mother. She let go of her grandmother's hand gently and went searching for Nirmala.

She wasn't in the dining room. Kitchen? No. Sarika peeked into her parents' bedroom. Nirmala was lying on her bed, right hand on her heart. She lay still, eyes closed, breathing deeply. Sarika saw her lips mutter *Om, shanti, shanti, shanti.*

'Amma?' she said walking up to her.

Nirmala opened her eyes and Sarika saw that they were swimming in tears.

'Amma, what's the matter?' asked Sarika, sitting down.

'I don't know.' She put her hand over her heart. 'My heart feels it will burst. I feel feverish.'

'Should I take your temperature?'

Nirmala shook her head again. They sat in silence for awhile.

'She will be gone; she will soon be gone,' said Nirmala, bursting into tears. 'An association of thirty years. Gone. Finished,' she said sobbing. Sarika lay down next to her and put her arm across her belly. Nirmala wept softly. 'At least she didn't suffer again like she did that night. God granted her that. That's really all we could hope for. Oh, how my head hurts. Oh God, oh God, oh God.' Sarika touched her forehead. It was burning.

'Amma, you have fever. I am going to call Ravi Bhaiya. You've been up almost every night.'

'No, don't call anyone. She stayed up most of the night two nights ago. Her mind was amazingly clear. She talked like she did in the old times. About the house, her *tulsi* plant, your grandfather and how he had first brought her as a bride to Moradabad, what a tiny baby your Papa was. She talked about it all as if it were yesterday. The weddings of her sons, the birth of her first grandson and his tragic death until Ravi came along and we all tried to forget. Nisha's wedding would be the first among her grandchildren's.' Nirmala stopped; her jaw quivered. 'She won't be around for Nisha's wedding,' she said haltingly, staring vacantly at the ceiling. Sarika lay on her side, propped up on her elbow and embraced her mother lovingly with her eyes. Nirmala's eyes closed, fluttered open, then closed again. She fell asleep. Sarika sat up, pulled out a silk sheet from under the bedcover and covered her mother. She stood watching for a few seconds, then went back into Lakshmi's room.

~

Veena rested her back on the headboard and drew her feet on the bed. It was 4:55 a.m. and the household was quiet. It was still dark outside, but soon the sun would announce with its red messenger streaks that it was ready to emerge from its abode, and the dim, yellow light that had burned all night in the sick room would be dimmed and forgotten. Veena closed her eyes and a sudden wave of tiredness enveloped her shoulders. It was there right between her shoulder blades. She stretched then released her upper body, wiggled her feet, cradled her head in her arms and put them on her flexed knees.

Ravi, who had sat all night reading, closed his journal, put it near Lakshmi's feet and was about to go to see if his mother's temperature was rising again, when Veena sat up with a start. She shot a glance at Lakshmi, then Ravi, who had also started, then Lakshmi again. Lakshmi took quick, shallow breaths through her mouth. Ravi walked up to her and put his fingers on her pulse. Veena swung her legs off the bed and came quickly over to Ravi's side. Lakshmi hiccupped again. Veena bent over her and called her name softly. Ravi held her wrist a little longer, then lay it down gently by her side. 'She is gone,' he said quietly. Veena walked to the foot of the bed, touched her mother-in-law's feet, brought her hands to her forehead and heart, and wept softly. Then she woke her sleeping husband and told Ravi to go wake up his parents.

PART TWO

1

'It scares me to death,' said Nisha, a couple of months later on an unexpected trip to Lucknow.

'Yes?' said Sarika.

'I mean, just the idea.'

Sarika nodded.

'It's bad enough to be sent off with a stranger, without being required to share your body with him. The idea!'

'It can't be so bad,' said Sarika, thinking of her first kiss with Kirana sahib. In the months that had elapsed she had thought about it every day. Sometimes the longing to recreate the moment left her breathless with desire. 'Alok must be nervous, too.'

'Yes. Yes.'

'You've met him after the engagement, haven't you? He came to Moradabad? What did you think of him then?'

'He seems very nice, but…I don't know.'

'Did you spend some time alone with him?'

'Henh. What do you think? Mummy was there the whole time, fussing over him.'

'Oof.'

'Doesn't she understand that I want to be alone with him?'

Sarika shrugged. They sat side by side on the bed in Sarika's room, swinging their legs, still in their nightclothes, each wrapped in a heavy shawl, against the cold December morning. Sarika's music finals were over and she felt relaxed for the first time in several weeks.

'This trip isn't as unexpected as you think,' said Nisha. 'I thought I might be able to somehow meet him. I'm not even allowed to write to him. After all, I'm supposed to get married to this chap. But the grownups seem to think it's okay if *they* know him!' Nisha paused and swallowed. Her facial muscles relaxed. She continued in a softer voice. 'It was nice of Alok's parents, though, to agree to January instead of December. Mummy and Papa would not have been able to handle it so soon after Dadiji's death. May would have been even better, but the astrologer said for me the best time is December or January. So they've moved it to the last auspicious date in January.'

'I miss Dadiji. I had come quite close to her toward the end. It would have been easier to handle her going away if I hadn't.'

'I do, too. She was wonderful, wasn't she? She lived with us in Moradabad almost the whole of my life. She always took my side. Even the decision to send me to Delhi for college was largely hers. Mummy-Papa would have been quite happy to keep me in some crappy college in Moradabad, if you'll believe it. She was almost more open minded than our mothers.'

Sarika nodded. 'I said things to her that Amma would have scolded me for saying.'

'Like what?' asked Nisha.

'Some things about master sahib.'

'What about Kirana sahib?'

'Oh, generally.' Sarika held her shawl in both hands and folded it into small pleats. 'I told her the way Mrs. Sinha flirts with master sahib bothers me. Mrs. Sinha also seems so jealous of me, always trying to undermine me in master sahib's presence.'

'And what did Dadiji say?'

'She understood my feelings. She said women like Mrs. Sinha are not really interested in music or anything and dabble with different things to occupy their time and feel needed. Her husband probably doesn't care much for her and she looks for a certain satisfaction from other men.'

'Oh, my God,' said Nisha grinning. 'Didn't you die when she said that — "satisfaction from other men"?'

'Nearly,' said Sarika laughing, 'but I was so glad that she understood. I could never say all this to Amma. She'd put an end to my music. Do you think if Dadiji had been around and well, she'd have let Alok and you meet?'

'Probably.'

'She was even a generation older than Amma-Papa, but more liberal. I remember how opposed Amma was to having Kirana sahib come home to teach me. Dadiji put her foot down. And now, Amma's the one who thinks of him as a special family friend.'

'I still can't believe the part about seeking satisfaction from other men,' said Nisha after a pause. 'Although I wish someone would tell us something.'

'Like what?' asked Sarika. 'Facts of life?'

'Not really the facts of life. At some level we know something. But our knowledge has so many gaps that it's downright frightening when you are about to be married. No one has ever told us anything and biology books don't talk about the practicality of relationships. They always have diagrams of the ova making their way down the fallopian tubes and a cross section of a penis. And that is supposed to tell you everything.'

Sarika laughed. 'Your descriptions are always so colourful. Must be all the English literature you've studied. Do you think, though, that if you'd met Alok you might have talked to him about some of this stuff?'

'I don't think so; I'd be somewhat embarrassed at this point. But maybe a certain feeling would have grown in me for him. I like to think about him, but my thoughts seem to be swirling in such a vacuum. If I'd met him I may not have had to create an image of him in my mind that may or may not conform to reality. I would have known the man.'

'True.'

'We might have held hands.'

'That would have been so romantic,' said Sarika.

'I know,' said Nisha wistfully.

'Suggest that to the mothers,' Sarika said facetiously.

'Maybe that's why they don't let us meet. They don't want any physical contact before the wedding. And suddenly, after the wedding, we are supposed to launch into it wholeheartedly. Not only that, every time I feel a little sick, they'll ask me if I am about to give them "good news." I tell you. These grownups.'

'I know.'

2

Nisha's wedding went off perfectly and the last car in the motorcade carrying the bride had disappeared around the bend.

'It is hard to give a daughter away,' said her mother, Veena, taking out a handkerchief from her waist and wiping her nose. 'One has to be ruled by one's intellect at this time, else one cannot give a daughter away in marriage. I hope Nisha will be happy in marriage.'

'Of course she will be,' said Nirmala looping her arm around her sister-in-law's waist through the shawl. 'And we'll be there to keep an eye on her.' She dabbed her eyes with her handkerchief. Sarika followed listlessly. Flowers were everywhere, no longer fresh and fragrant, no longer beckoning, no longer symbols of joy, serving now only as reminders of a daughter gone. Roses and marigolds that had adorned stark poles holding up the large tent had wilted and rose petals formed little circles at the base of these poles, the mandap where the wedding ceremony had taken place was now deserted, the brazier whose coals had burned brightly just the night before with the heat of the wedding vows now cold around a heap of ashes. The tent men were pulling off the large red and yellow tent and folding up the wooden chairs; the caterers were counting plates; the *halwai*, loading large pots and pans into a rickshaw. Everyone was moving on to the next job.

The women walked into the large living room where some of the men of the family had already settled down to tea.

'Come in, come in,' said Bharat, Ashwini's brother-in-law from Calcutta, as Veena stood forlornly in the center of the room. 'The wedding went off very well. Very good arrangement, food, everything,' he said approvingly. 'So, Sarika, you are the next in line to be married.'

Sarika grimaced.

'Your Amma will marry you off before you know it,' he teased.

'That's true,' Nirmala laughed. 'As soon as we find someone good.' She went into the kitchen and came out with two plates of sweets and savouries.

'Another train derailment,' Bharat said, as he scanned the newspaper. 'This has become an every day affair — derailment or dacoity.'

'Where did the derailment take place?' asked Nirmala, offering Bharat the snacks.

'Near Patna,' he said. 'And all trains between Calcutta and New Delhi must have been delayed.'

'Trains often don't reach the day they are supposed to,' said Savitri, Bharat's wife and Ashwini's sister. 'Sometimes they reach the next day. That's inexcusable.'

'There is no government anywhere,' said Bharat. 'The situation in Bihar is so bad. Every day somebody is murdered. No one is ever caught. All political murders. I don't know where our country is headed.'

Ashwini nodded.

'Our train was also delayed when we were coming here because of a derailment on our track,' continued Bharat. 'But help was slow in coming to the people on that train. No one cares. There weren't enough doctors and nurses to take care of the injured. People were stranded for hours with no food or water. It is rather distressing that people can be suffering and the government lacks the will to do anything.'

'Maybe Jai Prakash Narayan will do something,' said Savitri. 'He's had some success in Gujrat.'

'JP can't do anything,' said Bharat, looking around angrily. 'The problems run very deep. We were travelling with someone who had a brother in Bihar. Had a medium-sized farm. Two months ago, some *goondas* entered the house late at night, killed everyone and set the house ablaze.'

'This hooliganism...' started Ashwini.

'Some vendetta?' asked Nirmala.

'No. This passenger said his brother never fought with anyone,' said Bharat. 'He had no enemies. Probably just a case of mistaken identity. The police found no one. They have no suspects.'

'The police never have any suspects,' said Ashwini.

'Maybe the Naxalites?' asked Sarika.

'Who knows? They always blame the Naxalites,' said Savitri.

'They weren't wealthy enough for the Naxalites,' said Bharat.

'What answer do we have to all these problems?' asked Nirmala of no one in particular. 'Things seem to be getting worse every day.'

143

'Socialism,' said Pradeep, who had entered the room with Ravi and was helping himself to a generous portion of sweets.

'Why socialism?' asked Sarika.

'Because socialism accepts equality of all human beings,' said Pradeep. 'There is none of that in our society because of caste and religion. How would you like to belong to a lower caste and have people ill treat you simply because of your birth? We would do very well with socialism.'

'Socialism isn't the only way of teaching respect for others,' said Sarika. 'Education is.'

'Socialism is the only way,' said Pradeep. 'With socialism will come education.'

'At what price?' asked Ravi, popping a sweet into his mouth.

'And what liberties are there in a capitalistic society like that in the United States, where a handful of giant corporations control everything?' countered Pradeep, with a feverish look in his eyes. 'Their chief claim is a free press. What free press? There is no free press. It is all controlled by the bourgeoisie. By a handful of people in the bourgeoisie. It is not an objective press. It promotes the selfish ideas and materialistic interests of the bourgeoisie. Newspapers are the biggest means of bourgeois propaganda.'

'And the Soviet press doesn't spew out socialist propaganda?' Ravi asked casually.

'Not any different from bourgeois propaganda,' Pradeep said hotly.

'And what would you say about the Russia that Solzhenitsyn has depicted so powerfully in his works?' asked Ravi.

'Solzhenitsyn was a monarchist,' Pradeep said. 'He was an antisocialist. He did not even support democracy...'

'Okay, but Stalin. He was not a monarchist. He sent millions to their deaths.'

'Stalin had to do what he did because the West were trying to infiltrate the Soviet Union and overturn that first working-class state. Think about that. A working class state. Rule by the downtrodden. And the West wanted to get rid of it. It was the fear of a counterrevolution that brought about an authoritarian, close fisted government.'

'With all due respect to your revolutionary zeal,' said Ashwini, 'socialism hasn't worked in Bengal. Why would it work elsewhere in India?'

144

'We haven't really given socialism a chance, except in some isolated pockets in the country,' said Pradeep. 'It is the only way.'

'That's a fine thing to say after you've helped carry off very successfully a typically capitalist wedding.'

Everyone looked around for the speaker. It was an old man in a corner, one of those forgotten relatives who always surface in a wedding. He had unobtrusively watched the exchange, then removed his scarf from his mouth, said his bit and covered half his face again. Pradeep looked at him in bewilderment, unsure how to defend his sister's lavish wedding in socialist terms. He thought of a rebuttal, but nothing came to him. Meanwhile, the old man chuckled, took a wool shawl off his knees, folded it and hung it over the arm of the chair, as the sun outside became warmer and threw its rays generously into the room.

3

The small studio audience at All India Radio broke into applause as soon as Ustad Mulayam Hasan played the last, long note, followed by his son, Naushad, who accompanied him on his violin. The ustad bowed his head in acknowledgment and passed on his violin to his son, who put his father's instrument away in its red velvet-lined case before putting away his own. As the artist stood up, so did the tabla and tanpura players, both AIR staff, and Naushad, who quickly touched his father's feet. The door to the recording room swung open and the recording technician came out beaming.

'Hasan sahib,' said Singh appreciatively. '*Kya baat hai.*'

A group formed around the ustad and amid the loud mutual congratulation, Naushad slipped away. One by one, the accompanying artists left the violinist and went out for betel and tea. Members of the audience then went up slowly, less surely, to Hasan sahib and surrounded him.

'Hasan sahib, it was a treat to listen to your *Aheer Bhairav*,' said a middle-aged man in a long, black sherwani coat with a plastic portfolio bag tucked under his arm. 'I haven't heard you play that raga live since 1964, when you performed in Allahabad.'

'Ah,' said Hasan sahib, tucking a wad of betel into his cheek. 'That was a very good function. We don't get to perform at those kind of conferences any more. There are few of those nowadays.'

'Hasan sahib,' said another man. 'I wish you had played *Gurjari*. That raga lends itself so well to the *gayaki* you so masterfully perform.'

'Another time,' said the artist. 'I can't empty my whole bag in one day,' he added laughing.

'I kept hoping you would play *Patdeep*, even though this is not the time of day to do it. I had heard you play that in Delhi a few years ago.'

Sarika tried to locate the speaker from her corner. Her voice sounded familiar. No, it couldn't be. She craned her neck forward to see. Ah, there she was, standing close to the ustad and listening very carefully to every word he spoke. So it *was* Mrs. Sinha. She never missed a concert. A man cleared his throat and as Mrs. Sinha turned to look at him, Sarika caught a glimpse of her face. Her eyelids looked puffy under the thick eyeliner and heavy makeup she had worn today. A garland of pink rosebuds adorned her chignon. Mrs. Sinha touched it. Sarika waited to hear Hasan sahib's response.

Hasan sahib gave her a once over. 'I remember you from that time in Delhi,' he said. Sarika noted the playfulness in his eyes.

'You do?!' she said, obviously flattered.

'How is your little girl?' he asked. 'She was ill that time you were in Delhi.'

'Oh, she is fine now and not a little girl any more. How much you remember from times past!' She giggled.

Hasan sahib smiled again and looked around. The men shifted. More than one smirked. Mrs. Sinha touched her chignon again and tucked in a rosebud.

Sarika watched carefully, embarrassed for Mrs. Sinha. Surely she must know what feelings she generated in people around her. Or did she? Sarika wanted to go up and stand by Mulayam Hasan but the group around him was tight and far older than she, and the artist's world overawed her so that she found comfort in her own corner. Suddenly, she became aware of someone's gaze. She jerked her head and saw Naushad. He came up to her smiling.

'It is a different world, isn't it?' said Naushad. 'The world of the famous artist.'

'It fascinates me,' she said.

He smiled at her earnest face.

'You know that world well,' she said.

'Too well. At times I wish I could go back to a time of innocence.' Together they looked at the group. Mrs. Sinha took a strand of her hair and tucked it under her roll. Unsecured, it soon fell and hung loose on her neck. She smoothed her saree over her chest and shoulder. Hasan sahib noticed her even as he carried on a conversation with someone else. A small sigh escaped Naushad.

Ustad Mulayam Hasan was a miracle child. His mother, Asma, had been married young, like all girls in those days. She had a son — Naushad's Uncle Nafasat — soon after marriage. Mulayam Hasan's father, the famous Ustad Riyasat Hasan, was delighted, seeing an immediate heir to his musical throne. He gave his son a rigorous musical training.

One summer, Asma contracted the typhoid. Her only son was five or six. For several weeks she lay in bed, ravaged by high fevers, shrivelling up. A pall hung over the house. Her husband practised every day, but his soul had left his music. Much older than his wife, he doted on her and prayed every evening at the grave of a famous pir or saint, promising to come back with an offering of a sheet if Asma recovered. After four weeks or so it appeared the pir had granted the wish.

But her health was damaged. And soon it became obvious to Asma and her husband that she could not have another child. Nafasat then, became the center of his mother's world. Emotionally involved as she was with her son and husband, Asma nurtured a feeling of loneliness in her heart that she could bear no more children. She prayed every evening at the gravesite of the same pir who had saved her life.

Fifteen years after her illness, she conceived again. Soon, Mulayam Hasan was born. It was as if a little lamp had been lit in his parents' life after fifteen years of darkness. She sent a servant to deliver a box of sweets to every house in the lane. In fact, every fakir who came by the house for a month after the birth was given food and clothes. For you couldn't forget the poor in your joy.

Nafasat was now accompanying his father on his performances. By the time Mulayam was five, he had started receiving his lessons from both his older brother and his father. Meanwhile, the parents sought a bride for Nafasat, but he did not want one. He had seen his mother on the verge of death; he was afraid to love like his father and suffer for another woman he would grow to love. His rare artistic sensitivity showed itself only through the sadness and pathos of his music.

In a sense, then, Mulayam grew up with two fathers. He had instruction at home and rarely stepped out of the house. His father was spending a great deal of time giving concerts. Mulayam was a hard worker, and though his every whim was satisfied, his father and brother were unrelenting when it came to *riyaz*, making him practice eighteen hours a day as an adolescent. And to make sure he didn't doze off while practising, his father tied a strand of his hair with a string to a nail in the ceiling, a common practice among the great musician households.

With all that *riyaz* and instruction, Mulayam grew into a formidable violinist. Soon both he and his brother accompanied their father to concerts. Mulayam's instruction continued on stage.

Mulayam was married at twenty two to Naushad's mother, then fifteen years old. At eighteen, she delivered a girl; within two years, two other girls were born. As she became engrossed in motherhood, Mulayam shifted his gaze to womanhood. It was not hard to target his lust. He was now performing on a regular basis and drawing rave reviews. Women young and old jostled with one another for a chance to play the tanpura for him on stage. Young, handsome, talented, no hurdles stood in his way.

Not the death of two sons, born at two-year intervals after the third girl. Mulayam mourned, but tried to forget his grief by immersing himself in the new life that waited for him outside the four walls of his house — off stage, in hotel rooms, in the homes of prominent men. He was discovering in adulthood the pleasures of adolescence, the power of fame.

And then Naushad came along. It was a great moment and for some months, Mulayam suspended all extra-marital activities. As Naushad grew, his father went back to his old schedule and his training fell to his uncle and grandfather. Unlike his father, Naushad attended regular school and aware of his father's position in the world took upon himself to be a buttoned-down little chap. His world was comfortable even when his father got into rows with his own father over heavy drinking. Naushad had two other fathers and never fully comprehended his own father's absence.

Naushad's comfortable world began to collapse after the death, first of his uncle and then of his heart-broken grandfather. The only person now who cared for him was his mother. His musical training began to slide. His father brought home a new bride. He also began to bring women home.

And over the years, Naushad watched with lowered eyes as his father flattered, cajoled, and discarded women. When he saw Sarika watching what he had seen so many times, his first reaction was to distract her from what he saw as an ungainly sight.

'When will your sixth-year classes start?' he asked.

'Another week or so. Possibly the end of January,' Sarika said.

'I heard your fifth-year exam. It was very good.'

'Thank you,' she said pleased. He lived in a different world, performed with his father, was the only *gharanedar* in college. Praise from him meant something. 'I enjoyed your concert, too, just now.'

'When good people praise, it means something. Come to my class some time. We will talk about ragas.'

'My intermediate board exams start in two months. I have to study. I will barely make it to my own music class. But after that.'

'Whenever. You take care of the things you need to. The ragas will always be there for us to talk about,' he said.

She took leave and turned to go. Just then principal sahib walked up to them with Kirana. She had not seen them enter the studio. Her body stiffened; instinctively she knew Kirana sahib would object. It was just her luck that he should come in during the one brief exchange she had all morning.

'Hello, Sarika,' principal sahib said. 'Is your *riyaz* coming along well?' As Sarika mumbled something, he turned to Naushad. 'You will join us with your father for lunch at my house?'

'Yes,' said Naushad. 'You are also coming, Kirana sahib?'

'Yes. Principal sahib has been kind enough to ask me,' he said.

'So, the recording went well?' the principal asked generally. 'We tried to come on time, but just couldn't make it.' He pivoted toward the ustad. 'Adab, Hasan sahib,' he said striding up to the artist. Hasan sahib took a step toward the principal and the group around him moved back.

As Mrs. Sinha turned her head toward the newcomer to the group, she caught a glimpse of Sarika's retreating back. Surprised that she hadn't seen her rival during the concert, when she had cast her eyes around the room to pick familiar faces, she sought out Kirana, as if on reflex.

'What ragas are you going to talk to her about?' Kirana asked, unaware of Mrs. Sinha's questioning gaze from across the room. As the group re-formed around the principal and the ustad, Kirana had sidled up to Naushad.

'Oh, just show her some things I've been thinking about,' Naushad said, taken aback.

'She's my student,' he said almost inaudibly, between his teeth, and went to join the group.

Mrs. Sinha swung back toward the artist and tried to hide behind a man's shoulder, unable to repress a smile that broke out through her lips. Though unable to hear the exchange between Kirana and Naushad, she had nevertheless quickly grasped Kirana's feelings. Bit by little bit, she gathered her story.

4

'Can't believe you're back from your honeymoon already,' Sarika said. It was the last week of January and Sarika felt her life in the doldrums would roll on forever. The fear of the board exams had hung like a pall over her head for months. Attendance at her day college was more or less discretionary, since the syllabus had been completed. And the music college had barely returned from the slumber of the winter break. 'So, did the honeymoon allay some of your fears about married life?' Sarika asked.

'Don't know about married life,' said Nisha, 'as I am just going to start on that journey, but about Alok, yes. He's a really nice chap.'

'You look the same.' Sarika fixed her large eyes on her cousin.

'Why would I look different?'

'I don't know. I somehow expected you would after marriage. But you are the same and this is just like before.' The two girls sat huddled side by side on the bed in Sarika's room, wrapped in a large blanket. The brick house was cold after two months of near-zero temperatures at night and mostly cloudy days. Nisha's mind was now divided. Sarika could tell

150

that even as her cousin spoke, her thoughts dwelled in another place. 'How was the first night?'

Nisha grinned in response.

'Was it anything like you imagined?' pressed Sarika.

'Full of surprises. Our ignorance is amazing.'

Sarika raised an eyebrow. 'Was he considerate?'

'Very.'

Sarika let that sink in.

'Marriage is wonderful,' Nisha reflected.

'Elizabeth and Mr. Darcy?'

'I don't know about that,' Nisha said laughing loudly. 'I was very hung up on them, wasn't I? I don't know what they did on their honeymoon, but ours was very romantic.'

There was that 'ours' again. Sarika had noticed the change from the 'I' to the 'we' right after the engagement.

'The strange thing is that I was so afraid of entering marriage with a stranger and sharing the most intimate part of myself with him,' said Nisha seriously. 'But he didn't feel like a stranger. What I can't believe is how close I began to feel to him so quickly. I didn't know one could be so close to another. Nor did I believe that I could come so close to anyone so quickly.'

'Yes?'

'It is unlike anything I have ever felt.'

Each remained absorbed in her own thoughts.

'What have you been up to while I've been busy losing my virginity?' Nisha asked at length.

'Not much,' Sarika said. 'My intermediate exams are around the corner. Sixth year has started officially, but the teachers are busy with the Lucknow festival.'

'You'll have a different teacher this year at the music college?' asked Nisha.

'Yes.'

'And Kirana sahib?'

'He'll continue to teach me at home.'

'Are you still close to him?'

'Hm.'

'Nice chap?'

Sarika nodded. 'Very sensitive.'

'What's his wife like?'

'Don't see her much. But he seems to love her.'

'Of course. Does she come to the college functions?'

'Yes, with all her kids in tow.'

'So you'll see her at the Lucknow festival?'

'Don't know. It starts rather late and its very cold.'

'You don't like her?' asked Nisha.

'Nothing to judge her by, except what master sahib tells me. And she seems to be nice, understanding.'

'She must be nice if someone you like so much loves her,' said Nisha.

Sarika put her head on her knees, smiled at her cousin and closed her eyes. Outside, the vegetable vendors shouted out their wares in hoarse voices. Carrots, peas, tomatoes. A fruit vendor knocked on the front door, announcing the season's best guavas, straight from Allahabad. The girls heard Ramu talking to the man, who had sold his fruit to the Kumars for the past fifteen years.

'Pradeep is becoming more and more involved in university politics, to Mummy-Papa's consternation,' said Nisha. 'He was very active in showing support for the student agitation in Gujrat last month.'

Sarika raised an eyebrow.

'He just got elected secretary of the students' union at the university,' continued Nisha.

'Because of Gujrat?'

'I'll bet that had something to do with it, although I'm not sure. At any rate, Mummy-Papa are very upset about it.'

'Becoming secretary is serious, isn't it?' asked Sarika.

'It shows a much greater commitment to politics than anyone in the family wants,' Nisha sighed.

'He's become a true neta.'

'I know.'

'Except I think he's too nice to be a true politician.'

Nisha sighed.

'Young, hot blood,' said Sarika.

'Perhaps. Could be put to better use.'

~

Nisha rushed through the open front door to the Ashwini Kumar house.

'Where's Nirmala memsahib?' Nisha asked Ramu, lazily dusting the drawing room.

'Inside. In her room,' said Ramu, looking up briefly. 'Sarika bibiji is…' But Nisha had disappeared behind the curtains already.

'Nisha?' asked Nirmala coming out of her room and meeting her niece in the verandah.

'Pradeep has been arrested,' said Nisha, without greeting.

'What?' asked Sarika, joining them.

'When?' asked Nirmala.

'Mummy called me this morning,' said Nisha. 'She said she was going to phone you. She mustn't have been able to get through. We have to help him, Taiji. He's in jail.'

'Tell me what happened,' said Nirmala, sitting down on the settee and gently pulling Nisha with her. 'Don't be so distraught. Ramu,' she called out. 'Bring Nisha bibiji a glass of water.'

'Mummy got word just this morning,' said Nisha. 'She phoned me right away.'

'When was he arrested?' asked Sarika, sitting on the other side of Nisha.

'Yesterday, it seems. After that huge rally they had in Delhi the day before.'

Two days ago in New Delhi, three hundred thousand people had marched in a peaceful procession to Parliament to protest the use of money and power in the government. The procession was a reflection of the discontent simmering in the country. Flush with victory after winning a close election as secretary of the students' union at his university, Pradeep was one of the marchers. In the province of Bihar, students had already shown some success in stopping the workings of the corrupt government. They had come out of classrooms in large numbers and brought the entire administration to its knees. The student agitation in Gujrat was to be a test case for the power of the people. Socialism would work if only one had the vision and a singleminded devotion to the cause. Pradeep watched events like a huntsman, waiting for the right moment to establish the dictatorship of the proletariat.

'But the rally was peaceful,' said Nirmala. 'I read about it in the Delhi papers.'

'They arrested him the next day,' said Nisha. 'They said he was carrying arms. The offense is non-bailable.' Nisha started sobbing quietly.

Nirmala put her arm around Nisha's shoulders. 'I will call Sarika's Papa and talk to him. I am sure he can do something. Did your Mummy talk to Pradeep?'

'No. One of his friends phoned her. Pradeep was already in jail on trumped up charges. He's never carried any arms. He's an idealist,' Nisha sobbed as if her heart would break. 'It's just a way of arresting prominent student leaders and putting them away.'

'I understand,' said Nirmala gently.

'A non-bailable offense,' Nisha said again. 'Imagine that. As if he's murdered somebody. And the real murderers go scot free.'

After a few minutes, Nirmala got up and called Ashwini from her bedroom. Sarika sat with her cousin, her arm around her waist and let her weep.

'Your uncle says he will look into it,' said Nirmala to Nisha's expectant face. 'He will get him released right away.'

Nisha nodded.

'Now don't you worry,' Nirmala said. She wiped Nisha's tears with the *palla* of her saree. 'Pradeep will be alright. If you don't have to hurry back home to your mother-in-law, why don't you and Sarika go to Hazratganj for a *dosa*? It will do your spirits good.'

'And Mummy?' asked Nisha. A hint of a smile appeared through the worried expression on her face.

'I will phone her and tell her the news.'

Nisha stood up.

'Do you want to come to the Lucknow Festival with us?' Nirmala asked.

'I'll ask my mother-in-law. But I think we have other plans.'

'Okay, have fun.'

5

They came thundering onto the stage and began to dance, the women energetic but contained, the men bursting with vitality:

The clouds are dark and ominous and begin to pour. Indra, the god of the heavens, is angry. Rain falls in torrents. The people of Brindaban watch in disbelief, which soon turns to despair. The river rises rapidly; the ponds flood. The loud roar of thunder shakes with fear the simple village folk. Krishna says, 'follow me,' and they do. There is a loud roar again. The villagers huddle together in terror of the unknown. Then they notice that Mount Govardhan is rising. Panic. Is this the end of the world? But wait. What is this? What is the young lad Krishna doing? The village folk watch mesmerized as Krishna lifts the mountain and balances it on his little finger. Little finger! they notice with awe. The people and cattle of Brindaban take shelter under the mountain for seven days and seven nights until Indra's temper cools down and the rain stops.

The audience broke out into a rapturous applause as the curtain fell. Sarika, sitting with her hands clenched tightly together, didn't move for several seconds. Then she, too, joined in the applause. Nirmala and Ashwini shook their heads in appreciation and clapped enthusiastically. Sarika let out a big breath.

'How do they do it, Amma?'

Nirmala laughed.

'Their reproduction of the sound of the rain with their *ghungrus* was brilliant! And the way their feet hit the stage, you actually felt you could hear the rain falling on the ground,' said Sarika, eyes round in disbelief.

'Everyone deals with the same themes,' said Ashwini, 'but you can always tell a master apart. What a marvelous Krishna Leela!'

'And these were just his students,' said Nirmala. 'Pundit Gokul Nath will perform next. I wonder if Ravi will be able to join us to see the master. He said he would try to come,' she said looking toward the one entrance that had been left open as all others had been closed against the cold February winds.

'I wonder how long it will take pundit ji to come onstage,' said Sarika.

'He'll take some time. He has to get himself into the right frame of mind,' said Ashwini, smiling broadly. 'Artists have their temperaments. What's the hurry? Oh, there's Ravi.'

'You made it,' Sarika said, grinning at her brother as he joined their little group. Ravi patted her affectionately on the head.

'I almost didn't,' he said. 'We had a last minute admission in our ward. It was quite complicated. But I wanted to see pundit ji.'

Sarika smiled and huddled close to her brother on the newly upholstered sofa. Ravi put his arm around her shoulders. They waited in a huge red and yellow and green tent, pandala, that housed the stage and two thousand steel chairs, divided by two aisles into three sections. The inside of the pandala was decorated with large palms and coleuses and crotons with their variegated leaves that stood at the foot of the stage in large brass cachepots, edging old, well-trampled red *dhurries*, frayed at the ends and spread unevenly over the grass in the V.I.P. section, where Sarika and her family waited patiently for the next item on the program. The pandala was quite full with watchers, listeners, dreamers and sleepers, for the belief around the music world was that some came to listen and watch, some to sleep, and others to show off their clothes. But all groups shared one thing in common: They came prepared for a long night. An old man lay snoring in his chair under a heavy quilt, a family enjoyed a picnic dinner of paratha rolls and tea, some had strolled out, leaving a friend to guard their blankets, to buy food from the vendors that set up their stoves and giant griddles at the outskirts of the park.

'Sarika,' said Nirmala.

Sarika, who had been looking at people streaming in and out of the entrance hoping to catch a glimpse of Kirana sahib, turned around and saw that the curtain was rising. The tabla, *naal*, sitar, and harmonium players were tuning up, each in front of a microphone, on a raised platform to the left of the stage. The murmur in the tent ceased as Gokul Nath in a white pajama and yellow satin, double-breasted *angarkha*-style kurta and three long strings of pearls came floating out onto the stage, his tread so light that not a dry leaf would have crackled under the weight. His eyes looked big with kohl, face shone with makeup, and lips appeared a ripe bright red.

'How much he has aged in ten years!' remarked Nirmala in a whisper. 'His hair is all grey now. When I saw him ten years ago, he didn't have a single grey hair. They say he drinks a lot.'

Without a word, Gokul Nath started the Saraswati *vandana* in praise of the goddess of music and knowledge. He finished solemnly and walked up to the tall microphone that stood close to the accompanists.

'Brothers and sisters,' he said joining his hands in greeting. 'Your immense love has brought me to Lucknow once again. I was here ten years ago and you brought out qualities in my art that I didn't know I possessed. That is what a good audience like you does to a mere dabbler like me. I do nothing; you bring it all out. I do something once; later, I can't recall what I did or if I ever will be able to repeat it. But your love makes me dance like few audiences do.

'Today, I will take you to the potter's world,' he said, holding up his hands to indicate a vase. 'The clay is the rhythm that pervades all of nature,' he said, gesturing a world of hills and plains, 'and sound is the potter's hand. And you will see the hand that crafts this clay. But first I will start with *tatkar*.'

He walked to the middle of the stage, close to a small floor microphone and looked at his accompanists. The tabla exploded and simultaneously, Gokul Nath started his energetic footwork, startling the audience with his vigour. His feet sounded sharply on the floor; the five hundred bells on each ankle pealed to a climax, foot and bell thundering their way into the goddess Saraswati's favour. Then slowly, the sound diminished, until out of the five hundred only one single bell on each foot created the softest tinkle. Then another bell tinkled and another and another, until all the bells tintinnabulated in unison to a powerful crescendo. Deafening applause followed the silence of appreciation. Gokul Nath joined his hands and bowed his head to the audience as he came to the tall mike near the accompanists' platform. Sweat streaming down his face, he explained in a steady voice that he would display *abhinaya* or drama next:

Krishna, the incorrigible cowherd plays his bamboo flute nonchalantly on the tree, after hiding the clothes of the cowgirls bathing in the pond below. They are upset, naturally. Where has he thrown their clothes? How will they come out of the pond? What will the people of Braj say? They will die of shame. Krishna just grins. Gokul Nath told the story through mudra, gestures, and facial expressions as the accompanists softly followed along. He was soon at the center of the stage, portraying the same story through dance, as the accompanists took over. Then alternating between intricate footwork and *abhinaya* in the next few pieces, he sat down with the accompanists as his troupe came out onto the stage again. This time he explained what his students would do.

'These are this potter's work,' he said fondly. 'Live.'

As the students danced, Gokul Nath's eyes focused sharply on their footwork, the bedrock of dance, much as the purity of the note is for music, and he sang along mechanically with the accompanists. Sarika observed him, moved deeply by what she saw as a powerful manifestation of the relationship between the guru and his students. Gokul Nath's complete involvement with his students made him watch them like a mother does her toddler. At Sarika's own concert the year before in Ravindralaya, Kirana sahib's ears had been only for her: He had sat in the audience, surrounded by five hundred people, but never lost his focus. That surely was a strong proof of his love. Gokul Nath's troupe continued to dance. Had he ever kissed his girl students? Here he looked so paternal that it was hard to imagine him as a lover to these same students. Yet Sarika knew. This was more common in dance than in music for the guru had to continually touch the student's hands to correct the mudra. And touch made the blood rush. After all, wasn't it this fear that had made her mother so reluctant at first to have Kirana sahib teach her privately?

Kirana sahib and she had been alone on a couple of occasions, but the months following the day of her grandma's *shanti path* had been marked by restraint and in Sarika's mind, shame. Nonetheless, she longed for him and wished to talk to someone about her confused emotions. She thought of Nisha but quickly ruled her out for Nisha would be shocked. Nisha had wanted to go out with her betrothed, but had submitted to the family's rules. She would certainly not approve of Sarika's feelings for Kirana sahib. So conforming had Nisha turned out to be that Sarika had arranged a meeting on the sly between Nisha and Alok the last time her cousin had visited Lucknow before her wedding. Sarika had gone to the

State Bank of India with her mother, who had to renew a fixed deposit. Alok had been there. As Nirmala worked with another officer, Sarika quickly told Alok that Nisha was coming to Lucknow that evening.

'We can meet in Hazratganj,' she whispered. 'I will have to come with her to avoid suspicion, but then I'll disappear.'

Alok had looked stunned for a second, then smiled and said, 'What time? Where?'

'Outside Lukhnavi Drinks and Ice Cream.'

'Where will you go?'

Nirmala had finished.

'So, you think life in the bank is quite a lot of fun and Nisha will enjoy it,' said Sarika, glaring at him, hoping he wouldn't let the cat out of the bag.

'What were you and Alok talking about?' Nirmala asked later in the car.

'Nothing. He was asking how Nisha was.'

'Did you tell her that she's coming today?'

'Yes.'

'What did he say?'

' "That's nice." Can't you invite him over so Nisha and he can have some time together?'

'They'll have plenty of time together once they're married.'

Nisha and Alok had loved their rendezvous, however short, and Sarika had dashed to a nearby Chinese beauty salon as the two shyly downed their Cokes.

The curtain was coming down again. Sarika clapped loudly and long.

'Soon we'll be coming to watch you,' said Ravi, as the family stood up to leave well after midnight.

～

Kanti Devi had just finished an impelling rendition of *Basant Bahar*, a seasonal raga that celebrates the burst of tiny new leaves on the branches of trees rendered bare by the winter and Sarika wanted to rush out in the dark to see if the trees had erupted into foliage.

159

'May I go get her autograph?'

'Alone?' asked Nirmala.

'It's just backstage.'

'Go,' said Ashwini.

'Will they let you in?' asked Nirmala.

'Master sahib should be there on duty.'

Sarika walked briskly toward the entrance. All evening she had hoped to catch a glimpse of Kirana sahib, apparently too busy to come out into the audience. One day during the festival, he had sat with the family, discreetly by her father, looking at her only when the artist had finished performing. And then work kept him away. With luck, she would see him now. She stopped at the entrance to the green rooms. Kirana sahib stood nearby, talking to a college servant. Sarika called softly. He paused, turned around, and strode toward her, smiling broadly. The constable guarding the entrance — a little flap in the canvas — let her in.

'Master sahib, can I get her autograph?'

'Yes. Come with me.'

'We'll never get in,' Sarika said, standing on her toes in the long line outside the booth and trying to see above the heads of people much taller than she. 'And I want to be back in my seat for the next item.'

'We'll get there,' he said, walking away. 'Just wait.'

Sarika moved away from the crowd and took a peek into the next room. A violinist and her tabla player tried in vain to tune up.

'The wind won't let us stay in tune,' the violinist said. 'My strings keep going off the note,' she said, rubbing her hands hard to get the blood flowing.

'You can tell there are no musicians in the government,' the tabla player said laughing. He looked at his hands, stiff from the cold. 'Why else would they have a "programh" outdoors in the cold. You can't tune the instruments, can't get the hands warm. The wind is so strong even on the stage that you have to tune constantly.'

The violinist rubbed her hands and tucked them under her shawl. Sarika felt a light tap on her shoulder. She turned around to see Kirana sahib.

'We'll get you the autograph in a minute,' he said.

Sarika followed him and stood near a pole that pegged the tent to the ground. Kirana sahib stood next to her. He wore a steel grey handknitted sweater, a grey/black wool jacket, wool gloves, also hand knitted, a cap and a muffler that went over his cap, down the sides of his head and around his neck. Sarika felt his warmth. He stood on his toes and looked in.

'Let's go,' he said, holding out his arms, so people would move away.

Sarika went in and touched the elderly artist's feet. Kanti Devi patted her on the head. She sat on a thick mattress on the ground, covered with colourful *dhurries*, tanpura on one side and a big, black handbag on the other. Four or five people sat around the booth, indolently chewing betel leaf. Sarika didn't know any of them. They looked at her with great interest. Sarika kept standing.

'Sit down, *beta*. Why are you standing?' said the artist.

Sarika sat down close to her feet. She looked at her idol. Kanti Devi, a portly old lady, wore a shaded purple saree. Her silver grey hair, which she wore in a tiny bun in the back, gave her wheat-brown skin a saintly look. Her diamond earrings, diamond nose stud, the diamond ring in the right ring finger, that sparkled when she played her tanpura, a thick gold chain around the neck, gave her the look of one well grounded in the earthly life. Sarika thought with awe that she was the only one she had ever seen who sang to the drone of four tanpuras.

'Who do you learn from, *beta*?' Kanti Devi asked kindly, her mouth full of betel juice.

Sarika tried to say something, but couldn't form the words. She looked up and nodded at Kirana sahib, who was standing near the entrance.

'Ah, Kirana sahib? Good.'

Sarika looked at the pattern in the *dhurrie* and felt the grass under its thin cover. She sat awkwardly for a few seconds. The men stared at her. Suddenly, she thrust her autograph book at Kanti Devi.

'Do your *riyaz* with sincerity and see how high you will go,' Kanti Devi said, handing back her book.

Outside, Sarika opened her autograph book to see the artist's inscription. Kirana sahib came over and glanced at the page over her shoulder. 'Music is the reflection of the divine in man.' At the bottom, she had signed her name. Sarika did not know if those were the artist's words or some poet's.

The artist's words thrilled Sarika, making her feel that she was in the presence of achievable greatness. Maybe years of *riyaz* and the love of her guru would make her music as divine as Kanti Devi's. The love of the guru was key. Without that the landscape seemed desolate. She gave Kirana sahib a quick hug. He responded immediately, then let her go.

Kirana looked after her as she went out to the front, saw the constable at the flap entrance watching him, turned around quickly and went into an empty green room. Sarika's hug had sent a charge of electricity all over his body. He had felt her slender, firm, young body for a split second through her heavy coat and had not wanted to let her go. After the day of the *shanti path* when he had kissed her, he had become intensely aware of his attraction to her. But a voice nagged him.

That voice. It never let him rest in peace. It made him miserable when his mother picked on his wife constantly, back in the days when they all lived together in Punjab. His father, a freedom fighter, had asked Surya's mother for her daughter's hand for his son, when Surya's father, also a freedom fighter, had died unexpectedly. Years ago, when they had become involved with the freedom movement, they had pledged to always look out for one another. The senior Kirana had felt it his duty to marry his oldest son to his friend's oldest daughter. He had seen the girl growing up and liked her. She would keep his family together.

But Kirana's mother had not been pleased. Surya was average looking and poor. For a son as handsome as hers, Mrs. Kirana would have got a beautiful bride and a good wedding. Her husband's idealism had tied her first born to a woman so much his inferior. From the first day, she made it a point to let Surya know. Kirana knew his mother's feelings, but felt powerless. Yes, a more beautiful wife would have been good, but Surya's good nature gave her face a pleasant look, something some beautiful women with harsher natures lacked. And, after all, his father had taught him, youth would fade, but character wouldn't. Other than Surya, no woman would have put up so good naturedly with his mother, who nagged his wife constantly. And what guarantee was there that a beautiful woman would escape the nagging? At first, it was about her looks. Then, as she took over all the work of the house, it was about her laziness. And finally, when she gave birth to a daughter, she started calling her the mother of a son.

Kirana wanted to somehow get his mother to stop. She was a doting, loving mother and he never could bring himself to say 'Ma, she works all day.' When Surya came into the bedroom and cried every night, he told her his mother didn't mean anything. It was just her way of talking. But he sensed that Surya knew he didn't have the strength to stand up to his mother. Surya didn't say anything and Kirana felt sheepish and weak. Perhaps an outburst from Surya would have been more palatable. This quiet acceptance riddled his mind with guilt. He knew his mother was wrong, was poisoning his relationship with his wife, but felt like a little boy following his mother around. In trying to please both, he pleased neither.

Things improved after Kirana and Surya moved to Lucknow, upon his acceptance of a job at the music school. His name had been of great interest at the college. Kirana's great grandfather had been the owner of a provisions store. Over time, his name had been lost to the profession and his descendants had kept the name that indicated the sort of merchandise they sold. But for Kirana, the name was a happy coincidence for in the music world it denoted a very prominent *gharana*. Kirana and Surya often chuckled at the reverence people had first shown for the name, but now that it was clear that Kirana did not belong to that line of illustrious musicians, he had to struggle like other artists. Once the family began to live on its own, Kirana had to work harder to make ends meet. Teaching at the college plus private tuition for those who wanted it left little time for home. And Surya had started complaining in a good-natured sort of way about his absence, the lack of money, his relationships with his women students. She never threw tantrums, but he understood her anguish.

And now, there was that voice again, upbraiding him about Sarika. He had been wrong in kissing Sarika that day, especially when grief had lowered the family's guard. She was young, and he had no doubt she would accept him as a lover. He saw it in her eyes. As the teacher, it was for him to stay away. So, he deliberately stayed physically distant from her. Since that day when desire clouded reason, he had been alone with her a few times but had not touched her. Yet, his conscience bothered him. And now she had hugged him and thrown his mind out of gear again. Young, beautiful Sarika. She made him feel like an adolescent, in love for the first time. How had it come to be? He who was always so controlled. It was good that she was in the sixth year now learning from Manmohan Prasad at the college. Distance would help him.

That weekend when he came to teach Sarika, Kirana steered clear of emotional conversations, telling Nirmala and Sarika about the artist of divinity instead.

'We had a tough time with her,' he said. 'She believes in astrology, so much that every thing has to be governed by the stars, including when she will or will not go on stage. We had everything scheduled. Hers was to be the last item before the intermission. Around 10 p.m. About seven o' clock, she asked us what time she would be going on stage. We told her. She said she couldn't. Principal sahib and I looked at her in disbelief, saying we couldn't change any plans at the last minute. The concert would start in an hour and we couldn't reschedule. All the artists would come according to the time we had given them.' 'But it can't be,' she said.

'Why?' asked principal sahib.

'Because my astrologer says so. He says I can't go on stage before ten-thirty. The best time is really a quarter to eleven, but that's the earliest.'

'Why didn't you tell us before?'

'Because I consult him every day. I talked to him from the hotel at four o' clock this afternoon.'

'Why didn't you talk to him earlier and tell us?' principal sahib said with obvious frustration.

'Because the auspicious moment keeps changing. So you have to ask as close to the time as possible.'

'We were speechless,' continued Kirana, as Nirmala and Sarika giggled.

'Oh, so that's why the program started late,' said Nirmala.

'Yes, we decided to start late rather than make people wait between two items. That would have made them very restless. We could have started on time and kept the intermission sooner, but she didn't want to be the first one after the break.'

Nirmala laughed.

'And that wasn't all,' continued Kirana animatedly. 'At eight o'clock, when the tabla player came in — he was a guest artist, too — she said the kurta he wore was of the wrong colour.

'What do you mean wrong colour!' cried principal sahib.

'He's wearing a yellow silk kurta,' she said. 'I cannot sing with anyone in yellow today. My astrologer has advised me against it.'

The principal hit his forehead with the palm of his hand. He then sent Kirana to check Sitaram Mishra's clothes, since he would be playing the harmonium with her. Kirana came back and told the principal that Mishra ji was wearing black.'

'That cannot be,' she said. 'I cannot sing with those colours.'

'Then what should they wear?' asked principal sahib, ready to explode, holding back, playing the gracious host.

'They will have to wear red,' she said with determination.

'Red? How can they wear red?' he asked.

'I will not sing if they are dressed in any other colour.'

'I will ask them if they have red,' he said, 'but if they don't?'

'They will just have to buy.'

'It's eight o'clock. All the shops are closed. How do you expect them to go and buy red kurtas at eight o'clock at night in winter?'

Kanti Devi shrugged. Leaving her with the principal, Kirana went running to the two accompanists and told them what 'madam' had ordered. They cursed and spat out oodles of betel juice as they stood in conference. Kirana and the harmonium player would go on his scooter to old Lucknow, where a friend of Kirana's owned a kurta business. It was well past closing time, but if they caught anyone at home the owners would open it for them. They sped through dirty narrow lanes, coughing from smoke from burning tires, until they reached the house of Kirana's friend. His wife invited them in. No, they did not have any red kurtas, because they worked only in cotton and no one wears a red cotton kurta in the heat of summer in Lucknow. Sitaram's lips puckered. His watch unemotionally showed nine o'clock. Kirana asked his friend's wife if someone in the business might have a red kurta. She thought for a moment, then said her brother might, since he had a kurta business, too, and dealt in cotton and terecot. Sitaram chanted as the friend's wife made the call. Her brother might have red kurtas in the shop, said his wife, but he wasn't home. He had eaten a sweet bought from a vendor and had gone to the doctor with diarrhoea. The wife would call as soon as her husband returned. The two men paced. The phone rang. He was back and would meet the men at the showroom. But they'd better hurry for he couldn't stay away from home for too long. Kirana and Sitaram charged. Fortunately, he had two in the desired sizes. It was now nine forty and they were a little less than half an hour away from Begum Hazrat Mahal Park.

'Behanji,' said Kirana to Nirmala, 'I have never driven like I did that day. We got there just after ten o'clock. Principal sahib was close to a nervous breakdown, walking the green-room area so furiously that his sherwani coat flapped like a tent around a pole, but the lady was sitting in meditation. I stood agape. She was sitting in samadhi!'

'She sang really well, after all that,' Sarika said.

'Yes,' Kirana said reluctantly. 'I'm surprised the tabla player could perform at all. His anxiety made him querulous. When he had changed, he came out and said, "I look like a monkey. Does she expect me to go on stage like that?" '

'What did you say?' Nirmala asked, holding her sides with laughter.

'What could I say? Making a man wear red. Principal sahib said to him, "Close your eyes and your mind and play." And that's what he did.'

~

In the four months between her intermediate exams and the beginning of her B.A. classes, Sarika immersed herself in her music, listening attentively to her new teacher at college. Prasad sahib spent a lot of time lecturing and demonstrating the minor differences between ragas. His classes made her think more about what she was singing and why. He made her think of 'proportion' in notes, where heavy usage of one note might change one raga into another. He showed his class different ways of improvising. Unlike Kirana sahib, he treated her like any other student, except when a visitor came to class. That's when he called on her to sing, gratifying by his unspoken pride in her.

Sarika also had time to contemplate the artist of divinity. Kanti Devi, like many in her profession, had descended from a line of courtesans. During British rule, they struggled for survival with the help and patronage of local rajas and nawabs. After the British left, these artists continued in their line of work, often with support from the government of independent India, which swore to uphold art. Within the musical profession, they were regarded as decent women, who did not practice prostitution and remained faithful to one man only — their benefactor. They were also the keepers of court manners and culture. But to those on the outside of the music world, their lives blurred into that of the ordinary whore.

Sarika understood the rigorous training that went into making these artists and bowed her head in reverence. Yet, it was hard for her to comprehend their world, which seemed based on the physical, even when transcending it. That Kanti Devi had told her that music was the reflection of the divine in man suggested the artist's belief in the supercelestial. And she had arrived at that conclusion from deliberations on her own life, which had been so deeply rooted in the earthly. Clearly, her meditation before going on stage and the brilliant performance later showed that her mind had risen above the world. Her brilliance had been different from that of Naushad's father. Her music showed a desire to please only herself and her personal god. Nothing in it could even remotely be construed as playing to an audience. No marvelous feats. Just the purest form of music from the soul. She could not change where society placed her, but within those parameters she had attained as much of the spiritual as she aspired toward. Her soul and her music were one. Sarika knew that though a performer, she lived a hermitic life, with her students providing her only daily contact with the outside world. She was as much a whore as a nun. But she was still the daughter of a courtesan.

Sometimes, when Prasad sahib talked in class about the history of music, Sarika longed to ask him about Kanti Devi and how she straddled the two seemingly irreconcilable worlds. But the overtones of sex in the life of one like the artist of divinity kept Sarika from talking to her teacher. And her lessons continued as before.

After class, she ran upstairs to meet Kirana sahib and tell him every incident, significant or otherwise. These meetings took on the form of strong habit. His interest in her chatter served as a strong endorsement of her impression of the events around her. His approval became a filter through which she viewed the world. The bond with her teacher contributed to the excitement the college held for her. Not just excitement, but a need, both social and emotional, born out of an increasing isolation from the ambient world. He would always be there for her. He had to be. She felt his physical presence every time she was in it, although somehow the physicality became more alluring from under a thick winter coat.

Sometimes as she replayed the kiss, she yearned for more. She waited for his arrival at the house. They talked of her music and after he went away, she wondered if her mind wasn't playing tricks on her. His calmness puzzled her. But though yearning, the concept of teacher as lover never became clear in her mind.

'Keep working on expressing greater emotion,' Kirana said, one morning just before the start of the summer holidays. 'But along with voice culture, you have to think about the image you project.'

Artists must have an aura. That was important for both him and Sarika, for as a teacher-student team, they must appear above the rest. If some of the feeling was dictated by a desire to keep Sarika to himself, he was not consciously aware of it.

Sarika did not quite understanding his meaning at first.

'For one,' he said, 'you have to stop sitting out on the front lawn with the girls from the hostel and those from other classes. What do you have in common with them? You come from such a good family and yet you spend so much time talking to girls who come from very ordinary families.'

'I had never quite thought of them that way,' she said, taken aback. 'What difference does my father's position make?'

'You don't understand what I am saying,' he said in exasperation. 'People have to look at you as a performer, not as one of them. You have to be a little higher than they are. Only then will they respect you.'

Sarika nodded reluctantly.

'I do not want you to talk unnecessarily to anyone at the college,' he continued. 'You are now sixteen. You have to be careful. You talk to that boy from eighth year sometimes.'

'Yes, he is a socialist,' she said, taken aback at his observation of her. 'I love telling him I don't believe in his beliefs.'

'That's unnecessary,' said Kirana disapprovingly.

Sarika's heart sank at his tone. 'I don't do anything wrong.'

'It is not a question of right and wrong; it is a question of image. You go straight to your class. You come to check with me after class, and then you go home. No unnecessary sitting around and chatting.'

'But I enjoy that.'

'Again the same thing. I've just finished explaining why you can't go on this way. You have to change your behaviour. It is the image that counts.'

'Yes, master sahib. I'll try.'

6

Sarika stood some distance from Naushad humming the theme of the thumri in *Khamaj* he had just finished playing at the Holi concert in

Saraswati Hall, and waited for him to finish talking to his admirers who surrounded him on the courtyard outside the theatre. Suddenly, on older woman came up and stood next to Sarika.

'Are you waiting to talk to Naushad sahib?' she asked. She continued as Sarika nodded, 'You should come hear him teach some time.'

'Do you learn from him?' asked Sarika.

'Yes. There is no comparison between him and his predecessor. It is the difference between cream and nonfat milk. You are a good singer. Naushad sahib says all vocalists should learn some instrumental...'

'Oh, I thought it was the other way round.'

'So did I, but he says it's just as important to learn to play an instrument. And because he plays *gayaki*, you will learn something about singing from his playing,' she added warmly, casting a glance at her teacher.

'How long have you been playing the violin?' Sarika asked. Not waiting to respond, the woman left Sarika and marched up to Naushad in the midst of a momentary lull created by his admirers walking away. Feeling foolish, Sarika followed her. 'I enjoyed your concert, Naushad ji,' Sarika said, when the woman had finished complimenting her teacher. The woman looked on. Sarika wanted to ask him something and wished she'd leave.

'I was lucky to have a good audience,' he said.

Sarika gave the woman a sidelong glance. 'You are kind,' she said to Naushad. 'When the artist is good, the audience has no choice but to enjoy. I'd better go. I have to study.'

'Every minute of the day?' asked Naushad.

'Class again from Tuesday?' the woman asked.

'She is a talented lady,' said Naushad, after he had nodded to the lady, who departed. 'She resents the twenty or so years she couldn't practice after marriage. She picked up her violin after a long gap. I admire her for her courage.'

'It is admirable,' said Sarika absently. 'Tell me one thing, Naushad sahib. When you are practising or performing on stage, do you play to someone?' she asked. Her intermediate boards barely a week away, Sarika spent most of her time at home and her aloneness made her think even more of her teacher as she practised daily. 'Do you think of someone? Does the image of someone come before you?'

'No,' said Naushad, smiling at her earnest face. 'The artist plays to please himself only.'

'Only himself?'

'Sing to please yourself and you'll never go wrong.'

The fluorescent lights in the courtyard blinked into alertness, showing with a clarity that was best absent, the dilapidated walls of the courtyard and the dark rooms of the women's hostel beyond.

'Do you like it at the college now?' Sarika asked.

'It is okay. A different life.'

'But one of your own choosing.'

'*Kabhi aiye.* Come to my class some time,' he said in response. 'I'll tell you then about the life of a *gharanedar*.'

'Sounds very glamorous.'

'Haven't seen Kirana sahib. Is he around?'

'He's taken the day off.'

~

Kirana walked up the steps to the Kumar house humming. The front verandah bore some telltale signs of a holiday enjoyed with coloured water. 'Happy Holi,' he said to Nirmala, who opened the front door to let him in.

'Same to you, Kirana sahib. It is so good of you to come.' She turned her head toward Sarika's room and called out her name. 'Please sit down, Kirana sahib.'

'Holi *Mubarak*,' Sarika said, bursting into the room. 'I'm so glad you came.'

'I almost ended up in the hospital, instead of here,' he said lightly.

'Oh?'

'My fault,' he said. 'I left home after doing my *riyaz* and was still humming the composition I had sung in the morning as I drove through town. I got distracted as I tried to sing a complicated *taan* and did not see a buffalo that had stepped in front of me. I crashed into it.'

'Oh, God,' said Nirmala. 'Did you fall? Did you get hurt?'

'My scooter fell. Fortunately, I did not fall. I'm not hurt at all, but could have broken a bone or two. It has happened to other teachers at the college, all because they were humming or drumming something.'

170

'It's quite funny, actually,' Sarika said, 'now that we know you're safe. Did you not see the buffalo coming at you? I mean, they aren't exactly fleet-footed, so it would take them a while to move. And they are huge.'

'Oh, I'm sure it was there; I didn't see it. All because of a buffalo. Unbelievable. I am sure something like this happens only in India.'

'You missed the program yesterday,' Sarika said. 'Naushad ji played very well. I enjoyed his thumri.'

'Sarika says he's a very talented player,' said Nirmala.

'You've heard him, Amma. Remember he played the same day I sang in Ravindralaya?'

'My memory isn't as sharp as yours,' said Nirmala with a laugh. She stood up.

'He's the jackal son of a lion father,' said Kirana, as soon as Nirmala had left to go into the kitchen. Why did Sarika bring up Naushad? He had come to the house full of bright spirits, excited, as usual, about seeing Sarika, and now she had said she enjoyed another's art and turned him off.

In Kirana's book, being the *shishya* of a guru meant keeping oneself away from all influences. Yet, Sarika looked around, too callow to understand that Naushad was a competitor, by virtue simply of being at the college. He was in a different galaxy when he performed with his father, but then the college leveled him. Could she, with all her perspicacity, not see that? 'The jackal son of a lion father,' he repeated.

'Why?' Sarika winced.

'If your father is a lion, you will inherit some of his traits. Yes, he plays well. If you forget whose son he is.'

'What do you mean?'

'He will never attain the musical height of his father.' Couldn't Sarika see Naushad's diminutive stature vis a vis his father? Why, then, did she think him so great? He felt a pang at the thought.

'But...' started Sarika. Nirmala was back with a plateful of sweets. 'The student movement in Gujrat was very successful,' said Kirana, barely looking at Sarika. 'They dissolved the assembly.'

'Yes, that was awhile ago,' said Nirmala. 'Here try this sweet, Kirana sahib, this one's very good,' she said as she put down the plate and sat on her favourite chair. 'Maybe some good will come from this agitation. It is hard to understand how our country will improve otherwise. Something has to happen.'

Sarika couldn't understand why he was angry with her. He had said in the past that Naushad was a good musician. As for being upset at her talking to someone at the college, Naushad was a teacher, not some gossipy girl from the hostel. Certainly talking to him wouldn't mar her image in any way. She liked talking to Naushad. He was, perhaps, the only one of his kind at the college — a pedigreed musician, who knew the world of the practitioners of high art better than anyone, a thinker, and, from the looks of it, sensitive. And he respected her abilities. How did that affect her relationship with her teacher? Naushad, though important, was not worth risking Kirana sahib's sulking.

'I hadn't planned to teach today,' he said to Nirmala, 'but I think I will. Sarika, go get your tanpura.'

With heavy steps, Sarika left the room.

7

Sinha put down the phone and looked absently at the cars pulling in and out of his service station. The young men in his employ went up to each car that came in, dispensed petrol, and collected the payment. His manager at the pump, Pratap Singh, kept a keen eye on each as he gave out a receipt and put the cash in a small leather bag that looked like a train ticket collector's bag.

Sinha had hired Pratap Singh as a young boy of eleven or twelve, when he came to Lucknow from a village near the border of Nepal to earn a living. At that time, Sinha's father had run the service station, while he devoted himself to setting up Champion Tyres. His venture had succeeded beyond the wildest dreams of his family, both as a result of gruelling labour and developing connections with the right people. And with the money he had made handsomely, he had done what calculating businessmen do all the time: He did not report all his income and with the unreported 'black money,' he started another enterprise, a mini steel factory, which was the cause of the phone call that morning. It was in this newest venture that Sinha wanted to involve his son more deeply.

172

After failing to clear the second part of the chartered accountancy exam, Vineet had joined his father's business, but he was still green and Sinha didn't yet trust his business judgment or his ability to perform in an emergency situation. Sinha saw Pratap Singh pull a young boy's ear for some transgression. Over the years, Pratap Singh had shown himself to be a good, honest lad and Sinha trusted him more and more so that now, twenty years later, he was one of his most trusted lieutenants and he had moved him from the tyre shop to the service station since Sinha spent little time there. Deception didn't even flicker through Pratap Singh's mind since every worldly possession of his had its source in Sinha. Pratap Singh had built a tiny house for himself, owned a motorcycle, maintained a bank account, was married, and had a son. Sinha felt expansive as he thought about his role in providing the building blocks for the life of this young man who would otherwise have been pedalling a rickshaw at best and sleeping on it under a tree at night. Pratap Singh, forever conscious of his debt, remained bowed in obsequiousness.

Sinha played with the paperweight on his desk as he thought about what word he should send to his manager, Yadav, at the steel factory. He could phone, of course, but phone lines weren't safe. His cane chair creaked as he let go the paperweight, stood up and went to the office door. Pratap Singh saw him and came up swiftly. They went in the office and shut the door. The air conditioner hummed in the background.

'Pratap Singh.' Sinha slowly sat down.

'Yessir.' Pratap Singh remained standing.

'You came on your motorcycle today?'

'Yessir.'

'Tell Pheru to bring all the cash from the petrol pumps to me while you are away.'

'Yessir.'

'Go quickly on your motorcycle to the factory and tell Yadav,' Sinha lowered his voice, 'to make sure that the factory is clean. I don't want excess goods on the premises. He does it routinely; I just want to make sure.'

'Yessir.'

'Tell Yadav I want everything to be clean. I want him to see that the ledgers are up to date and that there is no cash on the premises of the factory. He has to make an emergency shipment today because we have too many ingots in storage. I want everything cleaned out. And tell him to fix the electrical meter if it isn't already.'

'Yessir.'

'He might have to work all night to ship the *maal* to the godown. Meanwhile, I will try to find out if the new AC (Assistant Commissioner) knows about our secret godown. If she does, we'll quickly have to do something else. Tell Yadav, sahib said that he will be rewarded for his hard work. If he does his job for Sinha sahib, Sinha sahib will take care of him.'

'Yessir.'

'I will come to the factory later today. Tell Yadav.'

'Yessir.'

'Go now. Make haste.'

'Yessir,' said Pratap Singh, leaving as unobtrusively as possible.

Sinha picked up the phone to call Yadav. 'I am sending Pratap Singh. I will come to the factory later in the day.'

'Yes sahib.'

Sinha hung up and sat back. He would leave the service station early to see that everything was taken care of for him. A tipster had told him that the assistant commissioner of excise might raid the factory. The tipster wasn't certain, saying simply that Sinha's businesses fit the profile of those the AC was targeting. Young and idealistic, the AC resolved to make every businessman pay his due. Sinha had inquired about her from a few people and had as yet not sent her a lets-get-acquainted gift. Maybe he should have. Of course, if she was as stinkingly honest as believed, she would have turned it away, politely but firmly. He knew that women were harder to bribe than men, but sometimes the tiniest thing — a particular brand of cosmetic or nylon sarees not available in India but readily so in Nepal — triggered off the greed and then they could be had. People came with a price tag, which sometimes lay hidden and had to be prised out from under the folds of honesty. Then, of course, there was always her boss, if she played hard to get. Sinha kept him well oiled with imported whisky that Yadav arranged for him, so that no matter what this young lady did, he would be safe because her hands would unofficially be tied. He had kept the ministers, especially the industry minister, happy and the generous hamper baskets of fruit and sweets he sent every Holi and Divali to the clerks in the Income Tax and Excise offices seemed to have paid off, for his tip had come from one such. At any rate, the inconvenience of a raid was best avoided. If Yadav could get all the *maal*, the ingots that they made from scrap metal bought from scavengers, out of the premises during the night, they would be safe. The losses they were showing on their books would then match their inventory and the electricity meter, which would be manipulated to show lower consumption. And again, if the excise people did stumble across merchandise, it could always be passed off as a reject by the wholesalers. He had the genuine-looking letter from a buyer, saying the goods did not match up to specified standards, to prove it. It would be a late night at the factory. Earlier, he had told Swati that he would visit her, but that would have to wait. She didn't have a phone, so he wouldn't be able to tell her. As the thought crossed Sinha's mind, he felt like a reasonable, considerate man for at least wanting to inform her. He turned his attention once again to his men outside.

8

'Your son has a very good hand at the tabla,' said Gajendra Mishra, uncrossing his legs and crossing them again in the lotus position.

'He takes after his guru,' said Kirana, patting Gajendra on the back. 'Like teacher, like student.'

'The teacher is the same for everyone, but not all students are the same,' said Gajendra, shifting position again.

Kirana looked proudly at his son and smiled. 'He has a lot to learn still.'

'Takes after his father.'

'Lalit,' said Kirana to his son, 'put your tabla away and bring out mine. I'll practice with Gajendra now.'

The boy stood up obediently and put the tabla away in one corner of the room. He then removed an old, threadbare table cover from another set of drums, brought them out to his father, and stood uncertainly, looking from father to teacher to father again.

'Go, play, study, do your work,' said Kirana. 'I'll practice with Gajendra...' He stopped as he heard a knock at the door. 'Go, see who it is,' he said to his son. Gajendra and Kirana watched. A smile broke over everyone's lips as the boy opened the door revealing a portly middleaged man in pants that covered his big paunch and came down to just above his ankles, a half-sleeved untucked shirt lay open over his chest revealing a growth of thick black hair, and betel juice coloured his lips a bright red.

'Come in, come in,' said Kirana. 'We're blessed to have this visitation.'

'I was passing by and thought I'd stop to see you,' said Sitaram Mishra.

'Gajendra here just finished giving Lalit his lesson and he and I were going to settle down for our own session. If you say, I'll bring out the harmonium.'

Sitaram nodded and went out of the house to spit out his betel juice. He came back wiping the corners of his mouth with a large handkerchief, took off his Bata chappals and sat down on the worn-out wool rug next to Kirana and Gajendra.

'Lalit, pull out the harmonium and go do your work or sit with Mummy,' said Kirana.

The three men settled down. Kirana tuned his tanpura and began to strum. Gajendra tuned his tabla to the drone.

'What's the occasion for this great production?' asked Sitaram.

'I have a house concert,' said Kirana laughing.

'Where?'

'At the district magistrate's house.'

Sitaram looked impressed. 'How did you swing that?'

'The DM's (District Magistrate) wife contacted principal sahib, who suggested my name.'

'Very good. So what will you sing?'

'It's in the morning. I am thinking of *Gurjari Todi*.'

'Good, good. Let us begin.'

'What do you make of the principal?' asked Gajendra, holding the tuning hammer in his hand.

'I don't know him very well, even though he's been around for a couple of years,' said Kirana. 'He keeps his thoughts to himself. He'll always get your views on something, but never gives his own. He seems to be politically very well connected.'

'How do you know?' asked Gajendra.

'He knows the secretary of cultural affairs very well. Years ago, he taught his wife. He was saying, though, that she isn't much of a singer. He taught her only because her husband is a senior government official,' said Kirana. 'Do you know principal sahib's connection to Mrs. Sinha?'

'Mrs. Sinha?' asked Sitaram.

'It was principal sahib who told her to join my class.'

'But her husband is a very rich businessman,' said Gajendra, 'not a senior government official. I don't know how he knows her. Maybe she just licks the soles of his feet.'

'Possibly. She makes it her business to know every teacher in the college. How do you know that her husband is a rich businessman?' asked Kirana.

Gajendra blushed.

'Well?' asked Sitaram.

'You can tell from the way she dresses,' said Gajendra. 'She shows so much of her body. No officer's wife would dress that way.'

Kirana and Sitaram laughed.

'She's mod,' said Kirana. 'She wears hipster sarees and high blouses. Sometimes, when she stands in front of me revealing so much of her body, I don't know where to look. *Aankh nahin uthtee.* What a lady!' He laughed loudly. 'Did you notice that she's just had a haircut?'

'Very mod,' said Sitaram.

'And she has a daughter of marriageable age, so you'd think she'd be more sober.'

'You don't like her?' asked Sitaram.

'No. She's a nuisance.'

'But you teach her.'

'I know. Sometimes a person has to. She's very competitive. She has no decency. She always comes running after me once class is over to whisper something in my ear.'

'And what does she whisper in your ear?' asked Sitaram, obviously enjoying himself.

'She asks me if I'll come to her house. Everyday. As if I have nothing else to do. What kind of a husband does she have that she's always running after me? Strange lady.'

'Her husband is even stranger,' said Gajendra.

'Why?'

'He comes to the *kotha* where I play the tabla sometimes,' said Gajendra.

'What?' asked both men together.

Gajendra grinned. 'That's how I know he's a rich businessman. He gets whichever girl he wants at the vice den by throwing his money around.'

'He takes girls?' asked Kirana.

'Sometimes. Mostly, he just asks someone to sing or dance for him or massage his legs,' said Gajendra.

'Very good,' said Sitaram smiling broadly. 'Massage his legs. My old legs need a massage sometimes. And wouldn't I like a young girl to give me a massage?'

'His daughter must be the age as some of the girls there?' said Kirana.

'That doesn't mean anything. If you go into a garden, won't you pick a bud that is ready to burst into bloom?' said Gajendra. 'Or will you pick a withered flower? Why would a man choose an old woman when a young one is available?'

'That may be true, but a man has to think. Just very recently, his daughter got engaged,' said Kirana.

'Yes?' asked Sitaram.

'Wasn't there some *lafda*, some problem there?' asked Gajendra. 'Mrs. Sinha had mentioned something in passing to me.'

'Yes,' said Kirana. 'Her daughter, Achala, wanted to marry one of her brother's classmates. He seems to be a good boy, was working on finishing or had already finished his chartered accountancy or something like that, but Mr. and Mrs. Sinha were opposed to it — he more than her.'

'Why?' asked Sitaram.

'Social status. So, Sinha gave Achala an ultimatum, saying that if she didn't leave her beau, he would disown her and consider that he had only one child. He calculated that no man, however good, would want to marry a pauper.'

'Disown her?' asked Sitaram. 'What father would give up his daughter?'

'Apparently, he was ready to. Mrs. Sinha was obviously very upset. She told me all about it because she was sure Achala, being so much like her stubborn father, would not leave this boy. Well, she did, much to Mrs. Sinha's surprise. And the rest was very much like a Hindi film. They looked aggressively for someone and forced her into engagement. Mrs. Sinha said Achala cried and didn't eat for days.'

'She told you all this?' asked Gajendra.

'Not only told me, but brought me a big box of sweets from the engagement,' said Kirana. 'We finished eating the last of those just yesterday or day before.'

'So when is the wedding?' asked Sitaram.

'Sinha wanted a quick wedding. But the boy's paternal grandmother died and the family being very orthodox, the father said they would wait a year. Sinha was not very pleased about it, but what could he do. He is the girl's father and doesn't have much control over these events.'

'You never know what might happen in a year,' said Sitaram. 'The boy Achala wants to marry may come back.'

'True,' said Kirana. He turned to Gajendra. 'With all I've heard from Mrs. Sinha, it is hard to believe that the man who visits your vice den is the same. He has a daughter to marry. He would think of her future, wouldn't he? Are you sure that he is our Mrs. Sinha's husband?'

'What you are saying is right,' said Gajendra clearing his throat, 'but I can tell you only what I know. He came to college one day to pick up Mrs. Sinha. She was talking to me, telling me that she was dressed to go to a wedding, that her husband would pick her up shortly.'

'How does she know you so well?' asked Sitaram leaning toward Gajendra.

'Listen to me,' said Gajendra. 'Let me tell my story.'

Sitaram sat still and tried to relax.

'So we were standing in the driveway, when her husband pulled up in his chauffeur-driven Chevrolet. What a car. Bought with lots of black money. The moment he saw me talking to his wife, he stopped in his

179

tracks; his face went white. I looked at him from the corner of my eye, but pretended to not have noticed and kept talking to Mrs. Sinha, until she saw him and broke away. The next day when she came to college she told me that she didn't want me to be her tabla accompanist anymore.'

'You accompany her?' Sitaram was incredulous.

'I used to. Her husband recognized me as the person who plays at the same *kotha*. He asked Mrs. Sinha how she knew me. She told him. He told her never to let me enter their house again.'

'So he didn't know you were the same person who plays at the *kotha*?' asked Sitaram.

'No, he's never been home when I have accompanied Mrs. Sinha.'

'And did he give her a reason for asking her to stop?'

'No. I asked her. She said she didn't know, that maybe he mistrusted music types, though that is not very convincing since she asks you to teach her. I don't think she has much say in her house,' Gajendra said with a sigh.

'So, you're still playing in the vice den, Gajendra?' asked Kirana.

'Yes. It's good income.'

'You'll get yourself into trouble one day. You never know when the district magistrate might decide to order a raid.'

'You know the DM's wife, Kirana sahib,' said Gajendra laughing.

Kirana was not amused. 'Music is such a beautiful thing. Why should you sully it by playing in a whorehouse?'

'You are right Kirana sahib, but I need the money. Also don't forget that music flourished in *kothas* not so long ago. Think of the *kotha* connection in all of our great women artists.'

'True, but those women didn't sell their bodies. They were courtesans, not prostitutes. They were women of good character.'

'Yes, but what to do,' said Gajendra. 'I need the money to support my growing family.'

'Let us begin,' said Sitaram. 'We can discuss this till nightfall.'

Kirana strummed, Gajendra gently tapped the right drum to see if it sounded in tune, Sitaram held down the tonic note on the harmonium. The small room filled with music. Kirana cleared his throat and began. *Sa.*

9

'Doc' sahib,' someone said in a soft, sweet voice.

'Yes?' Ravi inquired, looking blankly into the face of the patient who tugged at the sleeve of his apron.

'Do you remember me?'

He looked intently at her. 'Have I seen you before?' he asked. She sat at the edge of her bed, one slight form among the thirty or so women patients who occupied two neat rows of metal beds in the large, medium-lit hall. It was just past 8 a.m. and the women's general ward in the department of medicine buzzed with the activity of morning staff relieving the night staff of duty, women janitors walking back and forth with bed pans, sweepers mopping the concrete floor with Pheneol-dipped rags, leaving hospital-hardened flies momentarily stunned from the strength of the disinfectant. At this time, most patients had one attendant, all engaged in chasing away audacious flies from ill faces.

'Yes, you have seen me before,' she said. 'In Queen Mary's.'

'You had a baby?'

She shook her head. 'Cleaning,' she said in a barely audible voice.

The interns accompanying Ravi on his rounds through the general wards at the medical college now looked at their senior. One glanced at the case sheet in his hand. 'Her name is Swati, Sir,' he said. 'She is from Assam.'

'Swati?' Ravi squinted at her. 'Oh, music college.'

Swati smiled wanly and nodded.

Suddenly everything came back to Ravi. He remembered clearly her case history now. It always amazed him how he could never recall names and faces until some little trigger brought back the whole history with remarkable clarity. It had been a few years and the hundreds of patients he saw every day blurred faces. He could see her now, weeping in the first stage room, terror stricken in the septic labour room, trying to be brave as they did a D & C on her, humbled, completely humbled by her experience. Hers had been his first encounter with a medical termination of pregnancy. He had thought about her passingly a few times as he went by the music college and then forgotten her as other more serious patients in other departments took up his mental energies and challenged his intellect and medical judgment rather than tug at his emotions. Here she was again.

'Have you finished your eighth year at the music college?' he asked.

'Yes.'

'Where are you living then?'

'In a room. On my own.'

'Okay.' Ravi smiled at her. 'She had come here two years ago for an MTP...' he briefly told her history to the interns. 'What brings her here now?' An intern handed him Swati's chart and Ravi glanced over it quickly. 'Oh,' he said surprised. 'Sleeping pills.' He looked up at her.

'Yes,' she said.

Ravi glanced at the chart again. Maybe this was just a cry for help or an attempt at getting attention. 'Why?'

She lowered her gaze and Ravi remembered from his earlier contact with her that he would get nothing out of her.

'Who brought her to the college?' he asked his team members.

'Don't know, Sir,' said an intern. 'Looks like someone dumped her outside Emergency and left. She's had no one visit her, either.'

'What about your friend? — can't remember her name.' Ravi tried to remember the name of the woman who had stood so emotionlessly at Swati's side the last time.

'Mandira.'

'Okay. Where is she? Did she go back to Assam?'

'No.'

'Do you see her sometimes?'

'Sometimes.'

'Well,' he said, as he got ready to move on to the next bed, 'take care of yourself.' He paused and smiled at her. A shadow of sadness crossed his mind. 'No one is worth ending your own life over.'

'Yes, Doc' sahib.'

'Go home. Go back to your parents. Why live here like this?'

She lowered her eyes.

∼

Sinha knew about Swati's sleeping pills. He had come to see her one night after the expected raid on the business and finding the sleeping pill wrappers in the room, understood what had happened. He told his chauffeur to take him home, then come back and take Swati to Emergency.

What a nuisance women could become, once one became a little involved with them. Swati had asked Sinha to put her up in a nicer place, similar to the one she had lived in that one summer. He explained, and Swati understood, that their little hideaway was not available throughout the year. But then, Swati wanted something like it. A little respectability was what she sought.

Sinha promised her a place in vague terms. Then, last week, when she made her demand in unambiguous terms, he said he couldn't do it. He would be discovered. He had a daughter to marry. Swati did not seem to understand. And that's where Sinha's problem lay.

He believed that the business of sex and money had always to be guided by reason. He failed to understand how women could never be rational, but were ruled by emotion instead. True, he liked to visit Swati, to hear her sing, to let her massage his feet, but that could never be allowed to jeopardize his family's position. The family was sacrosanct. But kept women never understood that, no matter how decent one was with them. They wanted more and more of a man until he became one with them and fought with his family for them. But that was not possible, even though he liked her and didn't want to cast her off. Still, emotion had to come a distant second to reason. Sinha would do his duty and save her life by having her dropped at Emergency. And tomorrow or whenever she came back from the hospital, he would send a small basket of fruit for her recovery. He, then, got back to work.

10

Sarika ran up the portico steps and into Naushad. 'Oh,' she said, stopping short. 'I wasn't looking.'

'How were your summer holidays?' Naushad asked her smiling broadly. It was the first week of college after the summer holidays.

'Uneventful.'

'Did you go anywhere?'

'Yes, we went into the hills for two weeks — Nainital, Ranikhet, Kumayoon. It was good to get away from the heat of Lucknow.'

'And your *riyaz*?' He continued, when she shrugged. 'I have been practising *Shyam Kalyan*. I want to discuss that with you. You learned that earlier this year?'

'Yes.'

'Have you practised it recently?'

'In the holidays.'

'Do you have some time now? I want to show you some new ways I came up with of rendering it. I want to see what Prasad sahib has shown you.'

They walked toward his ground-floor classroom, Sarika a little concerned that Kirana sahib might see her and sulk. She sat at the edge of the wooden platform and looked out of the window.

Naushad took his violin out of its case as soon as he and Sarika were seated. His mind was in a turmoil. Growing up in the shadow of a famous, negligent father, he had become introverted and a serious thinker. He had been in the college for a year and his sense of loss at the hands of his father was still strong. By the age of fourteen, he had lost the two men — his uncle and his grandfather — who were responsible for most of his musical training. After they passed away, he struggled on his own, with scant guidance from his father, Ustad Mulayam Hasan. If his father had given him what sons in most traditional families took as a right, he would have been on his way to becoming a star himself. Instead, he was here at the college, where everyone told him he had done the unimaginable by leaving his tradition. He shrugged off their comments, often laced with derision, figuring they would soon get used to seeing him around. But the truth was that it was easier to be the second-rate son of a first-rate musician than to strike out on one's own. One could be assured of starting at a level that most never achieved after years of labour. Yet, he had deliberately chosen the harder, less glamorous path, for the urge to find himself was strong. There were rewards. His students adored him and the teachers showed a healthy jealousy of his abilities, but was that enough to make up for the loss of his birthright?

And then, he had to understand his relation to women, who constituted the majority of his students. For his father, all women offered

184

just one thing: Sex. He struggled with trying to understand the role of women vis a vis himself. Not so long ago when he was a student in an academic school and college, he had worn the mantle of his father's success, one that bore him to the ground like lead. For the first time now, he could try to establish for himself how he should think of women. Here was Sarika. Young, beautiful, earnest, talented. Interested in and curious about the world he had come from. He enjoyed talking to her, but wondered if it were possible for music alone to bind a man and woman in friendship. Could a man have a relationship with a woman without desiring her physically, as he had seen his father do all his life? He enjoyed Sarika's intelligence, so rare at the college. His own top student was also a woman, although married and much older. Maybe other relationships were possible. He had finished tuning his instrument.

Tense at first, Sarika watched as Naushad played a few notes of *Shyam Kalyan* on the violin. He played some note combinations that made her look up. Yes, they were definitely within the parameters of the raga he played, but so unusual. Experimental but beautiful. She began to hum what he played so deftly on his instrument. Naushad looked up and laughed as he understood her surprise. As he played the raga, he began to show elements of *Yaman*, until for a few seconds he switched completely to the parent raga and then came back to the theme of *Shyam Kalyan* in a masterful finale.

'Wow,' said Sarika in unabashed awe.

'Sometimes experimentation will produce the desired result more than the traditional approach.'

Kirana heard the music from the corridor, well hidden by the drape that hung over the door. He had seen Sarika and Naushad walk into the latter's classroom together and felt the sharp dagger of jealousy pierce his heart. How could Sarika, given her background, stoop to be alone with another man in the college? That was against her upbringing. He would have branded any other woman a slut for the same thing, but he knew her family too well to say that even in extreme anger. And there she was humming along with Naushad's violin, that loser son of a famous father. They had barely spoken to each other as Naushad tuned up, so he couldn't excoriate Sarika for indulging in useless talk. Yet. He listened for a few minutes as Naushad deftly played a few combinations and walked away to his class. That bit of superior pedigree he had shown turned the dagger that Sarika's presence in Naushad's room had first inserted in Kirana's heart.

Kirana had never had to think except in a general sort of way. He would never evaluate his own relationship with his student too seriously to see that rather than her interest in Naushad, if indeed any, was unnatural. Naushad and Sarika were both young, talented, and unmarried. In a world blind to religious and social differences, they stood a better chance of coming together than he and Sarika. What kind of future did he hold for Sarika? Perhaps at the bottom of his refusal to articulate that to himself lay a dim understanding of his desire. Perhaps, too, he understood in a shadowy sort of way that keeping his wife and desiring Sarika would pose a problem. Maybe the thought was too complex for him to chase down. As the oldest son, he had never been denied or thwarted, never been made to see his faults or atone for his mistakes. And yet, he was a decent man of his generation. Loyal to his wife, a good provider to his family, a dutiful son, a conscientious teacher, a man of honour.

'That was beautiful, Naushad sahib,' said Sarika, standing up.

'Yes, I thought that would interest you. The deeper you go into a raga, the more paths you begin to see. I am glad you could find the time to come.' He looked through the space between the curtain and the doorjamb. 'Come in, come in,' he said to the students who peeped in from outside. He looked at his watch. 'Unbelievable. It's already time for class.'

Sarika bowed slightly and left.

11

Nirmala put down the black-and-white photograph on the coffee table in the drawing room and laughed. 'She's good looking.'

'Let's see,' said Nisha, immediately interested. Sarika looked over her shoulder. She was quiet today. The day before, when she had gone to see Kirana sahib after class, he had been distant from her. He wouldn't say why. Had he seen her in Naushad's room? Did she think he was spying on her? His response left no doubt in Sarika's mind that he had seen her. She tried to focus on her family. It was one of those rare occasions when the whole Ashwini Kumar family was home and Nisha had joined

186

them. It was a relaxed afternoon and Ramu had made tea and pakoras, which were also laid out on the coffee table. Ashwini had a file full of photographs and information about 'matches' for his son. Ravi had no intention of marrying just yet, but always took some interest in seeing the pictures of the young women whose fathers sought the perfect groom for their nubile daughters.

Nirmala passed Nisha the photograph gingerly, trying not to touch the image with fingers that were greasy from eating the fritters. 'Too bad she is twenty-seven years old. Our son is only twenty-four.'

'I don't know who could have recommended our son to these people,' said Ashwini.

'Must be someone who thinks the home secretary is old enough to have a mature son,' said Nirmala with a smile. 'She is beautiful, though. Wonder why she is still unmarried at twenty seven.'

'Don't you want to see it?' Nisha asked Ravi in a teasing voice.

'No,' he said, a little too loudly.

'I've seen you stealing glances in this direction,' she said. 'Here, take a look,' she passed him the picture.

Ravi took the picture and put it down after a quick look.

'Like her?' Nisha persisted. Ravi ignored her. 'Taiji, would you say "yes" if Ravi actually had someone in mind?' Nisha asked Nirmala.

'She's got you cornered, Nirmala,' said Ashwini with a laugh.

'Well?' asked Nisha.

'I'd have to think,' said Nirmala. 'It would be harder to accept if Sarika chose someone.'

'Does that mean yes?' asked Nisha.

'She'd have to be the same caste. And from a good family.'

'There,' said Nisha to Ravi with a naughty smile. 'I've done all I can.'

Sarika's jaw dropped. 'Ravi bhaiya...'

'There is somebody?' asked Ashwini. 'A nurse?'

'A nurse!' exclaimed Nirmala.

Ravi blushed. 'You'll pay for this Nisha,' he said in mock anger. 'There's no one. It's hard to get involved with someone if you're always competing. Besides, there's no girl in my batch in medicine, anyway.'

187

'Oh, but there are always juniors,' said Nisha, 'who'll gladly flutter their eyelids at you. "Sir, I don't understand this case," ' she said in a high-pitched voice.

'Nisha, you'll be sorry.' Ravi pretended to glare at his cousin. 'How come your in-laws let you out today? You're better off with them. "Yes, Mummy," ' he said, mimicking her shy response to her mother-in-law.

'You don't know whom you'll have to accept as your daughter-in-law,' said Ashwini, teasing his wife. 'Times are changing.'

'I guess that means I'll have to change, too,' said Nirmala. 'Regardless of Ravi, we'll still marry Sarika at eighteen.'

Sarika groaned.

'Look at Nisha,' said Nirmala. 'Look how happy she is.'

'That doesn't mean I would have been unhappy if I hadn't been married off so young,' Nisha retorted.

'You girls.'

'Besides,' said Nisha, 'You have a different standard for boys. And not just in marriage. Look at Pradeep. If I had been so involved in the politics of my college, I would have been recalled to Moradabad and asked to finish college in some stupid government inter college. All of you complain he's becoming too political, but don't do a thing about his trying to lead the socialistic agitator's life. Even when he went to jail you all didn't say anything.'

'That's life, Nisha,' said Nirmala, smiling benevolently at her niece. 'You just have to accept it.'

'That is your lot in life as a woman,' said Ravi with a big grin. Nisha came after him with a magazine.

12

It was a typical monsoon day in Lucknow. The overcast sky sent out a rumble and a gentle shower from time to time. Then, all at once, the sun peeked out from behind its celestial curtain and, almost before the wet earth had time to bask in the warmth of its rays, it disappeared. A cool breeze rustled through the newly washed dark green leaves on mango and ashok and pipal trees, providing welcome relief from humid heat.

Sarika loved such days, when she could walk out on the street and the breeze would dry the sweat around her neck and softly play with her hair and dupatta, blowing them as she moved, making her feel like a bird ready to take off on its own. She sat on a rattan chair on her front verandah and watched passersby, women carrying umbrellas and holding their sarees up to avoid the puddles; men marching through with rolled-up pants, getting splattered by water and cowdung as cars drove heedlessly by; alley kids in nothing but underpants, or sometimes an undershirt and no underpants, sailing paper boats in inch-deep puddles; and wet, straggly dogs scavenging for food. The weather launched her into singing a *Malhar*, melodious with the soft wet wind on the verandah. She leaned against a round pillar and thrust her face into the rain, feeling the raga on her face and in her body. But today was different and the weather did not bring out the music from within her being.

Telling her mother that she was going to the university to see if the admissions lists for B.A. were posted, she took her cloth bag, walked out to her gate and flagged a rickshaw. Last evening, Kirana sahib had sought her out after her class with her sixth year teacher, Prasad sahib, and told her to come to his house. He didn't say why and she didn't ask, relieved that he had finally shed his reserve, but the hushed urgency of his tone prompted her to keep this a secret from Nirmala.

Soon, Sarika's rickshaw was going through the narrow, crowded roads of Old Lucknow. The houses along the sides of the streets were claustrophobically joined to one another, with no driveways, no boundary walls, no trees separating them. Each had three or four projecting steps that gave an already narrow street an even more confined and jagged appearance. These steps, bridges over the wide, open gutters full of black, stagnant water and swarms of mosquitoes, doubled on sunny days as platforms for drying spices kept in steel platters. Today, though, all the spices were stored carefully in airtight jars. On a rainy day, dogs sat on these steps, under the overhangs of the dingy, airless nineteenth century buildings. The rains had made the open gutters overflow to the sides of the streets, which were flooded with sewage. Sarika's rickshawman pedaled laboriously. The hood he had put up to shield her from the rain filled with the wind and made him work harder to propel the rickshaw. He groaned and coughed as he went up the slight incline toward Kirana sahib's house, khadi kurta and thin dhoti soaked completely, straining to put all his weight first on one pedal and then on the other. Sarika's mind and heart raced.

As they laboured on, Sarika's nervousness increased. Mrs. Kirana had left with the children for Punjab suddenly to see her ailing mother. Sarika hummed a few notes of the raga she'd been learning in class to still her beating heart, but her mind drifted off as did the notes. She took a deep breath, then through her nose let out short, smart breaths. The rickshawman turned to look at her. 'I'm alright; you carry on.' Her heart pounded.

She looked at the unnumbered houses. Kirana sahib had given her a few landmarks, but they were hard to locate in the long, grey façade of windows with iron grills and battered wooden doors. Kirana sahib's house was past 'the house with the dogs.' He had warned her to not go there even by mistake for those dogs did not like strangers. But, he had said, if she asked anyone for the house with the dogs, they'd be able to tell her. Sarika looked for a 'beware of dogs' sign, but saw nothing. The lane was converging into the slightly broader main street and Sarika knew she had gone past the house already. On her instruction, the rickshawman stopped and asked a shopkeeper for directions and both men gesticulated profusely. Coming back, the rickshawman turned the rickshaw around. They soon arrived at the gate of the house with the dogs. Sarika jumped off the rickshaw and looked around. Kirana sahib had told her that his house was up a flight of circular steps in a yellow building. She spotted it, set back from the street. Paying the rickshawman, she picked up her wet bag from the footrest and walked briskly toward the staircase.

Before she could ring the doorbell, Kirana sahib opened the door.

'I've been waiting for you,' he said. He shut the door and gave her a quick hug.

Sarika's legs felt leaden. Her pulse raced. 'Can we sit down?' she asked.

They went into the living room. Sarika sat on one of two couches, her hands clasped tightly in her lap. In the center of the room was a small rug, with a small, bare coffee table. The walls were lined with iron boxes, covered with old, faded bedcovers. An old rusty iron stood on a wood coaster on the corner of one box that served as an ironing table. The others had stacks of old newspapers and magazines, piles of clothes in need of folding and ironing, two sets of tablas, a harmonium covered with an embroidered tablecloth, and in the only spare corner of the room, a tanpura — a dark wood one with intricate carving, a Miraj. Sarika became increasingly aware of Kirana sahib's presence near the sofa. He had remained standing and loomed over her. Longing for fresh air, she stood up and walked to the window that overlooked the street. Like all the others on the street, it had iron grills. She felt Kirana sahib's hands on her shoulders and turned around.

'You are trembling,' he said.

'Could I have a glass of water, please?'

'Yes, yes.'

He went into the kitchen. She turned again. Halfway down the window on a cord tied to two nails on the wood frame hung a sagging, faded curtain made from an old saree. The iron grills, the window frame, and the small window sill showed many months of dust. Sarika took a deep breath and the dust flew up into her throat. She stepped back, followed Kirana sahib into the kitchen, and watched as he filled a glass with water from the filter. His physical presence exerted a strong force on her and the image of their quick embrace at the Lucknow festival where she had felt him through his heavy winter clothes flashed through her mind and goaded her for an encore. She ran her hand awkwardly down his back. He put the glass down, turned around and embraced her.

'No!' she said, pulling away.

'Don't be scared,' he said, stepping back into the counter. 'I could never dream of hurting you.'

She nodded.

'I will do only what you want. Only as much as you want. I want your pleasure, too.' He saw she continued to tremble. 'Sarika,' he said taking her cold hands in his, 'this is nothing unusual. This is how men show their love for women. This is the highest form of communication between a man and a woman. I love you, Sarika.'

She nodded, but withdrew her hands from his.

'There has to be a spiritual communion between the guru and the shishya. How else can learning take place? I have told you that you have to love the notes you sing just like one person loves another. What greater form of love than this? Come, don't be afraid.' He reached for her hand.

She pulled away.

'I think of you day and night, Sarika. One does not feel this way about everyone. It is a rare blessing.' He paused. 'There is no harm in two people loving each other.'

191

Sarika stood still, unable to formulate words in her mind as adolescent stirring, upbringing, and intellect struggled for supremacy. What would Nirmala do if she found out? Sarika shuddered. Kirana sahib gazed at her. He smiled, desire written all over his face. She looked away. Everything that had come before — the kiss, the electricity, the looking into each other's eyes during class — had singled her out as the chosen one, had made her heart swell, had been sweet, but her mind hadn't travelled any farther than just the immediate, despite her chatter with Nisha. Instinct had guided her, and now instinct frightened her. Had she yearned for this? In her most passionate thoughts about Kirana sahib, she had not gone beyond holding him tight and Nisha's references to the first night had not crystallized the concept for her either.

'Only as much as you want,' he murmured. 'That's what true love is about.' There was a time in every man's life when desire could not be controlled. It was hard to not share the physical with her, as she stood before him — young, beautiful, unsullied. She was there before his eyes at all times, wherever he might be. And now that she was with him, all alone, he wasn't angry with her for going to Naushad's classroom to hear his music. She was Kirana's. He was her *guru*. He would launch her. It was with him that she'd have this unique relationship. Her perspicacity made her company so delightful. She understood his meaning almost before the words were out of his mouth. But she was his student; consequently, like a daughter to him. Oh, but he had never thought of her as a daughter, young as she was. She was always his favourite student and when she sang everyone asked who her teacher was. And didn't gurus and *shishyas* often share this communion? Wasn't the teaching of music a remarkable sensual activity? Perhaps if he gave her a choice, it would be okay. It would then be up to her. She would take the first step. He didn't want to force. That would be wrong. 'That's what love means. You never force the other person. If you don't want to, that's fine, too. I would never dream of making you do what you don't want to.' As he leaned back against the counter, he thought he would burst. 'Oh, Sarika,' he sighed.

Sarika hung her head.

'Here, drink your water,' he said gently, after a long pause. She took a couple of sips, put the glass on the counter and stood next to him, with her back against the counter, too. Immediately she felt his arm around her and snuggled closer to him. This was the warmth of closeness she had always dreamt about. She slipped her arm around his waist and he drew her closer. They stood silently for several minutes, sharing a speechless communion, feeling as close as two human beings can. Kirana then led her to the living room and they sat on the couch. Sarika put her head on his shoulder; he wrapped his arms around her. His one thought was to make love to her. Anticipation was unbearable. He had never known waiting. With Surya, there had not been much unexpressed desire; after the wedding, physical relations had followed as naturally as domesticity. There had been no quickening of the pulse, no quiver in the loins, no trembling of the hand. And then a terrible thought flashed through his mind: If instead of Surya, he had married another woman, he would have loved her the same way. It was almost as if that love was a decision. With Sarika, however, it was different. He had never known such longing. As her body relaxed against his, he kissed her on the face and neck, caressing her with his lips. Slowly, she began to thrill under his lips.

Later, as she lay on the large double bed, she could smell Kirana sahib on the other side of the bed, his sweat mixed with Kantheridine hair oil. She turned her head toward Kirana sahib but his eyes were closed. She looked around the room. No matter what she did in her life, she would always remember this room, the permanency of this moment. The only bedroom in the flat, it had a small cot to the left of the double bed. Above the cot was the only window in the room, with a curtain made from the same saree that hung in the living room. Sarika saw Mrs. Kirana's sewing machine, tucked away in a corner, buried under a pile of clothes. A wooden door opened onto a terrace to the right of the double bed. In a corner by the door stood a large steel Godrej wardrobe crowned with a battered leather suitcase, covered with an old, hand embroidered table cloth. Barely three feet from the foot of the bed where she lay was another door. It was shut. She figured it led into the only bathroom. She looked out of the window at two pigeons cooing happily on the window sill, until, as if conscious of her gaze, one of them flew away. Slowly, the implications of the act dawned on her. She sat up. Kirana sahib opened his eyes and smiled at her, but she lowered her gaze. A strange numbness came over her, through which thoughts of herself and her mother played distantly but persistently in her mind. How would she ever tell her mother? Or anyone. She couldn't tell this to anyone.

'There's no harm in loving a person,' said Kirana, as if reading her mind and setting his own at rest. Sarika looked at him, at the same time making sure her body was well covered with the cotton sheet on the bed. 'I know you have loved me for a long time; I have seen it in your eyes.'

She turned away.

'This is the truest expression of a man's love for a woman,' he continued, moving closer and stroking her hair. 'Did you enjoy it?'

She looked at the ceiling; the experience was too large to comprehend.

'Sarika, Sarika, it's alright. This happens all the time.' He kissed her. He felt released. Loving Sarika had been like sipping the freshest drops of dew from a flower. Her young, awkward, virginal body had made love rush through him so strongly that its force could not be contained. She had been his student. Now she was his entirely. He was her teacher, of music and of love. 'It's alright,' he murmured into her hair.

'It doesn't seem that way.' Her mouth felt very dry. 'When I look around, I don't see this.'

'How do you know what people are doing?' He fell back from her and smiled gently. 'How will anyone know what you and I have done? And what have we done except express our love?'

'They will read my shame on my face. What if somebody finds out?'

'How will anyone find out if you don't tell?' he said. But then his mind began to play out scenarios that might give them away — even the littlest touch could sometimes reveal volumes — and that would be disastrous for both. 'We will have to be careful. That is the way of the world. Do what you like, but in the eyes of the world, you should always look good. The image you project should always be perfect.' He gave her a quick hug. 'But you worry unnecessarily. No one will find out if we continue to behave naturally. Come on, get up,' he said gently. When she didn't move, he added, 'It's time to go to the college.' He got up and headed toward the kitchen. 'I'm thirsty. Would you like a glass of water?'

She shook her head and watched his retreating back. He seemed so comfortable with his nakedness; she had so much trouble with hers. As soon as he was out of the room, she dressed quickly. She opened the bathroom door, pushed it in slowly, went in, and shut it behind her. Sunlight came in through a small window high in the wall. Sarika glanced at it and saw a can of Cinthol talcum powder, a bottle of mustard oil, the telltale Kantheridine hair oil, an old rag, a broken red pumice stone. The Indian-style toilet seat was stained yellow inside and around the rim, making Sarika retch all of a sudden. She peered into the hazy mirror suspended on a nail above the sink and looked hard at herself. To her surprise, she looked the same, apart from dishevelled hair. She sighed, turned on the tap and washed her face with the cool water. Bending over, she dried it with her kurta, and came out of the bathroom. Kirana sahib was there, fully dressed, his face relaxed. He ran his eye over her and smiled. She smiled back weakly, took her comb from her bag and plaited her hair. Together, they walked to the front door.

'Sarika,' he said, putting an arm around her as she opened the door to step out. She stiffened and he lowered his arm. 'Sarika,' he said again. She stopped, but did not look at him. 'There is nothing wrong in giving ourselves to each other, for the unfettered artistic spirit has to find its own expression.'

'Is this the only way a man can love a woman? No matter how young?'

'It is the sincerest form of that expression.'

She nodded and hailed a rickshaw as she descended the steps from his house.

How different her feelings were now from a few hours ago when she had ridden a rickshaw to Kirana sahib's house. The unknown was now known, a terrible secret that she'd always have to carry alone — a secret about the adult world, in which she had opened a box that said DO NOT OPEN and not only looked at its contents, but touched them, felt them, partaken of them, and in the process established a relationship with her teacher from which there was no turning back. The line between the acceptable and unacceptable, a little familiarity and too much had been irretrievably crossed. And somehow what remained after crossing this dangerous frontier was not the euphoria that followed the first kiss but rather an emptiness that was fast sinking into paralyzing self doubt. She had felt often, alone at night as she lay thinking of Kirana sahib and longing for the touch of his strong body, that being held by him would be her greatest joy. Her mother's restrictions felt like shackles on such nights, when her mind gave her no rest as it danced agitatedly like a little droplet of water on a hot griddle. Why then did she find no peace now, when he had offered her the highest communion? Why now was she beginning to feel like an apple that has been left too long on the counter — perfect on the outside but brown and unworthy of consumption on the inside? No matter what she thought about her relationship with her teacher, its novelty, the excitement it offered, she felt sullied, certain that the world would be able to tell. The thought of Nirmala left her cold. Over time, her mother had learned to trust Sarika with Kirana sahib and now she had betrayed that trust. True, there had been little pangs of conscience before, but she had with partial success dismissed them with the thought that her pleasures were simple. That a touch and a kiss weren't wrong when two people loved each other. But this last act was the ultimate, not dismissible as innocent groping. She would now have to live with the thought of having betrayed her mother's trust. And then there was Mrs. Kirana. Would she find out when she returned from the Punjab? Would she find her husband changed? If she did, what would she think or do? Sarika thought of her returning from the Punjab and settling into her household routine — making breakfast for Kirana sahib, washing his clothes, stitching the buttons on his shirts, sharing his bed at night. She thought of him, touching her, playing with the children, picking up vegetables for the family on the way home from the college. So close to each other's sounds and smells — a closeness that could be hers only through stealth. Her thoughts about Mrs. Kirana took her by surprise. Did this one single act change feelings forever?

~

As she came home from college that evening, Sarika slunk by her father listening to Mehndi Hasan on tape and went into her room.

Maana ki muhobbat ka chhupana hai muhabbat
Chupke se kisee roz jatane ke liye aa.

(I admit that the hiding of love means love; come quietly one day just to impress it.)

Jaise tujhe aatey hain na aney ke bahane
Aise hi kisee roz na janey ke liye aa.

(It is as if you know excuses to not come; come one day to not go away.)

Sarika set her bag down on her chair and looked out of the window. The words of the ghazal drifted into her room. She couldn't face everyone just yet; she couldn't do her *riyaz* for her feelings were in turmoil and the images of herself and her teacher from the afternoon danced crazily before her. She went into her bathroom and turned on the tap to fill up her bucket for a bath.

'It is a little chilly today,' said Nirmala. 'You could have skipped your bath.'

'Someone splattered me with dirty water when I was coming home from the college and I felt like a pig,' said Sarika, sitting down to dinner with her family.

'So, are the admissions lists out at the university?' Ashwini asked.

Sarika shook her head.

'No idea when the classes will begin, then?' Nirmala said.

'No.'

'Mrs. Gupta, came over this afternoon,' said Nirmala. 'They are organizing a big cultural program on *Teej*. Mrs. Gupta asked me if I would sing, but I said I have trained my representative.' She smiled at Sarika. 'Will you sing, Sarika?'

'I don't know,' mumbled Sarika.

Ravi looked inquiringly at her. 'Are you sick, Sarika?'

'No, I'm fine,' she said. 'Just tired.'

'She must be tired,' said Nirmala. 'She's been out the whole day.'

Sarika shifted in her chair.

Ravi nodded. 'Is Kirana sahib still coming to teach her?' he asked Nirmala.

'Yes.' She added after a pause, 'He is such a *shareef* man. A perfect gem.'

'Time will tell,' said Ravi. 'Maybe I just don't trust musicians. When I was doing my rotation in gynaecology, a very young woman came there for an abortion. She came from the Bengal, Assam area...'

'Yes, you had told me about her,' said Nirmala. 'She was at the music college. Kirana sahib had mentioned her, too.'

'Right. Barely a few years older than Sarika.'

'Anything new with her?'

'She attempted suicide.'

'Why?' asked Nirmala.

'I don't know,' said Ravi. 'Took sleeping pills, though not enough to kill herself.'

'Did you ever find out who made her pregnant?' Nirmala asked, after a long pause, during which the family ate quietly.

'She said it wasn't anyone from the music college.'

Sarika sat very still. Pregnancy had never crossed her mind. It could not happen the first time?

'Girls land themselves in all kinds of situations,' said Nirmala. They finished the meal in silence.

'Have you decided on your speciality?' Ashwini asked his son, as Ramu began clearing the dishes.

'Neurology.'

'Good,' said Ashwini. 'I'm happy you've decided on such a good branch.'

'There are few good neurologists in Lucknow,' said Ravi. 'The field seems to be wide open.'

'You can go into research if you want.'

'More and more, I find myself drawn toward that. There is so much to be done in that area. Right now at the medical college, neurology is just a division under general medicine. I think it needs to be a department in its own right.'

'Maybe they are waiting for a few good minds like yours,' said Ashwini.

'I don't know about that,' smiled Ravi. His parents laughed.

Ravi went back to the medical college after dinner, Ashwini and Nirmala went for a stroll in the neighbourhood, and Sarika retired to her room. She turned off the light and lay in bed. As she thought of the day's events, her body tensed. She had been untrue to everything her family believed in and when she came home, they loved her like always. If they found out, what would they say? How hurt would they be? And the funny thing about having given herself up to her lust and her teacher's was that at this moment she didn't feel as close to him as she had in the past. Somehow the argument about the soul to soul communion did not sound convincing in the dark aloneness of her bed. The physicality of the moment was too overpowering.

She heard footsteps outside her door and knew her parents were back from their short stroll. The door to her room opened and her mother came in. Sarika lay very still and pretended to be asleep, as her mother turned on the low-wattage bulb and checked to see that locks on all the doors in the room and bathroom were secured.

Sarika slept little that night, falling into an exhausted sleep in the early hours of the morning. Still troubled by her thoughts, she spent the major part of the next day in her room, practising her music and reading. However, determined to not spend another sleepless night, she stole into her mother's room and from her medicine cabinet took out a sleeping pill. Calmpose it said in green on the aluminium package. That night as Sarika's parents went for a stroll, she went into the kitchen and swallowed the sleeping pill. She didn't have to tell her mother each and every thing, to have her review what was acceptable at every step. Yet she looked around furtively. When her mother came in to check on her, Sarika was already fast asleep.

13

Sarika and Kirana stood close to the big tape deck as the All India Radio technician rewound the spool and brought it to a screeching halt, without looking at the counter. He pressed the 'play' button. Sarika's voice came on, miraculously right where she had started her recording.

'*Kya baat hai*, Singh sahib!' said Kirana, slapping the technician on the back. 'What a hand. Without looking, you get to the right spot.'

Singh smiled and took his hand to his forehead in a mock adab. He adjusted the sound, balancing the tabla with the voice and the harmonium, so it came out fuller, richer. He looked complacently at Kirana and opened his mouth to say something when his eye caught a movement outside the heavy wooden door. He looked as the head showed once again through the small rectangular glass in the door. Sarika followed Singh's gaze, while her mind dwelt on Kirana sahib as a lover and his ability to look so detached. She stole a quick look at his face. His exterior showed no internal tumultuousness and she wondered if his mind were as unquiet as hers. Once certain that her family hadn't discovered her rendezvous and classmates at the college didn't exchange meaningful glances with one another as soon as she came into the classroom, she let herself freely relive her moments with Kirana sahib. The feeling of closeness returned. Images from their love making flashed repeatedly through her mind and at times she longed to throw herself into his arms and feel the unbelievable closeness again. By herself in her room at night, her body moved of its own in the darkness. Yearning overcame fear. Next time she would be a more active participant. In the weeks that had elapsed since her tryst with Kirana sahib, she had found no opportunity for intimacy. To see him and not be able to touch felt like the worst sort of torture. She suppressed a sigh. The door opened slowly. Sarika studiously avoided looking at Kirana sahib and sensed he felt the same way. She kept her eyes focused pointedly on the door. Despite her thoughts, she broke into a smile.

'Come in, come in, *huzoor*,' said Singh warmly. 'Come and join our *mehfil*.'

Naushad grinned, showing even white teeth in a world of the betelstained. 'What's going on here?'

In response, they listened quietly to Sarika's alap.

'*Kya baat hai*, Sarika ji,' said Naushad. 'You have a beautiful voice.'

'Thank you.'

'Are you auditioning for B-grade?'

'No. If I'm selected, I will automatically become a B-grade artist. But there are so many candidates competing, I don't know my chances.'

'Oh, is this the AIR competition for upcoming artists?'

'Yes.'

'So you were selected from Lucknow zone?'

'Yes.'

'Well, that's very creditable. Think of how many *gharanedars* you are competing with. You are probably one of the few who do not come from a family of musicians.'

Sarika felt suddenly shy.

'What brings you here?' asked Kirana with polite coldness.

Naushad and Singh looked at each other and smiled. 'I have a recording,' said Naushad.

'Yes, *janab* will play for us today,' said Singh sahib, who sprinkled Urdu words generously into his speech. Sarika had heard he loved *shayari* and could actually turn out a good couplet or two. 'After all, he is the *sahibzada* of a very big artist.' Singh continued in Urdu, talking through a mouthful of betel juice, 'He has been in Lucknow for a year and we don't hear too much of him. I asked him to trouble himself with a visit to us.'

'*Haazir hoon.* I have presented myself to you,' said Naushad smiling.

'You called and he has come,' said Kirana.

'Who are we to call, nonentities that we are,' said Singh.

'When will you record?' asked Naushad.

'Is it lunch time already?' asked Singh, looking at the clock. Sarika suppressed a smile as she noted Singh sahib's pronunciation of 'lunch,' which sounded like 'lench.'

'Not quite,' said Naushad, also looking at the clock. 'It's only twelve o' clock.'

'I have done one recording already today,' said Singh. 'I came in early and started recording at ten instead of two. I will now go to lunch. Come at two-thirty, *phir tassalli se baithenge.* We'll sit at leisure.'

Sarika glanced at Kirana sahib. He had been unfaithful to his wife. Did it matter? Did Mrs. Kirana know and accept what she must understand about the lives of artists? But Kirana sahib was not like other artists and Mrs. Kirana had so far seen no reason to fear. And if Mrs. Kirana didn't know, Sarika was fine, too.

'I have to leave soon,' said Kirana. 'I have to meet director sahib.'

'Everything is okay, no?' asked Singh sahib. '*Khairiyat?*'

'Yes, yes. Everything is fine.' They listened to the rest of Sarika's recording.

'You have a good chance of being selected,' said Naushad as the spools wound to the end. Sarika shrugged. 'Are you leaving?' Naushad asked, turning to Singh, who picked up his black plastic portfolio and thrust it into his armpit. Singh nodded. Sarika noticed that betel juice had begun to dribble out of the corners of his mouth. He swung the studio door open and left with Kirana sahib. 'Are you leaving, too?' Naushad asked Sarika.

'I have to wait for my rickshawman,' said Sarika. Kirana sahib had not even looked at her or taken leave. Did he even want her now that she had given herself to him? She had heard that men did not like a stale woman. Even one whom they'd tasted. And interest went down as soon as they had made the conquest. But quickly another thought flashed through her head and she understood his behaviour. He could not openly notice her in public for fear of raising questions in the minds of others. He could not bring attention to their special relationship. It had to be kept quiet, for his reputation and hers. He had said that to her already. Relieved, she turned again to Naushad. 'I had asked my rickshawman to come at one, because master sahib had told me that we'd do several takes. It went faster than we anticipated. Won't you go to lunch?'

'No,' said Naushad. 'Not yet. After the recording. We can go out and wait at the gate,' said Naushad. 'It is very pleasant today.'

'How is your *riyaz*?' Sarika asked, as they settled into two empty chairs on the front lawn of the AIR building.

Naushad shrugged.

Now that they were out in the open by themselves, the ease of conversation that had marked their earlier encounter disappeared. The necessity of keeping up a conversation left Sarika's mind hopelessly blank and paralyzed. The harder she tried, the more tongue-tied she felt. It was somehow different in the more focused environment of the college. She looked around self consciously until she saw the guard at the gate snoozing in his box. The clouds parted for a few seconds and the strong afternoon sun fell on his face, making him look like an illuminated god in the dark inner sanctum of a temple. Sarika marvelled at his ability to sleep on the job. Flies buzzed over him, now settling on his face, now hovering around momentarily, landing on his khaki shirt then taking off, but he dozed unperturbed. A white Ambassador car came to a stop at the gate; the driver honked. Startled, the guard jumped up from his stool, smoothed his big, upturned moustache that ended in two points spiked painstakingly with Brylcreem, and pushed an open book through the window of his box toward the driver. The driver didn't move. The guard peered sleepily through the car window, saw the occupant in the back seat and came hurriedly out of his box with a pass. Saluting smartly, he opened the one shut door of the gate and let the car through. Sarika turned her head toward Naushad. He turned his head at the same time from the gate. Their gaze met for a second.

'You're a regular artist for the AIR, aren't you?' Sarika asked.

'Yes. But that doesn't really mean much — being an A-grade artist.'

'No? Kirana sahib is an A-grade artist.' It felt good to be able to say his name.

'My father is top-grade.'

'Oh. Is that above A-grade?'

'Yes. It is by invitation only.'

'Wow.'

He shot her a sharp look.

'You will be like your father, too,' she said, hating herself for her dishonesty. 'I'd give anything to be A-grade,' she said quickly. 'I'd give anything to be associated with a man as great as your father.'

Naushad let out a short, bitter laugh. 'Is that what you think? I guess you do. So does the world.'

Sarika looked at him in amazement.

'Do you like the college? You've been there over a year?' Sarika asked.

'Yes. I hated it when I came to it last year. But I'm okay now.'

'Hate? Why?'

'I came to get away from the life I'd known. But I had a difficult time adjusting to the decision, not least because there are no great names associated with the college now, like there were at the time of the founder. But the college has given me a good escape from the only life I knew. The life of a *gharanedar* is not easy if one is on one's own.'

'But your father...?'

'My father lives in his own world, one he has never shared with me or anyone. Nothing pleases him; little things make him unhappy, and that unhappiness brings out the pathos in his music. The unhappier he is, the more beautiful the music he makes.'

'He makes such beautiful music, how can he not be happy?'

'Because he has always lived in the senses.'

'But music has to begin with the senses?' asked Sarika. 'Later it transforms us.'

'But transformation is not easy. Few achieve it.'

'Without the senses, there would be no passion and without passion there'd be no music. That has to be the starting point. After all, the love for notes is the same as that between a man and woman. It is a communion.'

Naushad laughed. 'That's a great line to get a woman to give herself.'

Sarika's heart sank. She thought for a few seconds, then said, 'Isn't there a difference between the passion of love and the passion of lust?'

Naushad gave her a sidelong glance.

'I don't know, Sarika ji, at which point one becomes the other.' He thought for a second and continued. 'But flippancy aside, you do have a point, Sarika ji. You know about my father? Despite his philandering, my mother never complained.'

'A perfect saint,' Sarika murmured. She wanted to understand the feelings of a man who took a woman to his bed.

'Yes, she is a perfect saint. In her younger days, she said my father looked to her for stability in domestic life. He was merely living out the passion he had in his blood. After all, it couldn't just end with the notes, could it?'

14

In early January, 1975, the entire country was involved in solving a murder mystery. A very senior member of Prime Minister Indira Gandhi's cabinet was killed in a bomb blast in Samastipur in the state of Bihar. Every newspaper carried the story and the nation was divided over whether Mrs. Gandhi had ordered her once-close lieutenant, Mr. L.N. Mishra, to be killed. The beliefs were divided mainly along party lines — Mrs. Gandhi's Congress party or other.

That in a nutshell was the news. But many versions of the story went around the country. The most popular was that Mr. Mishra was in Samastipur, amid tight security, to inaugurate a new broad gauge railway line. As he sat on the dais talking, the powerful bomb went off. Mr. Mishra fell and lay bleeding but did not get proper medical attention for a long time. A doctor from the Railways did come to see him, but he said his injuries were superficial. A few hours later, he was taken to Patna, the capital of the state of Bihar, by train but it was already too late. When he finally did get to the medical college in Patna, the doctors performed surgery on him, but soon afterward he suffered a cardiac arrest and died. For one hour, the doctors tried to revive him but he was already gone.

Conversations like the following were heard everywhere:

'This is very grave,' said Sarika's uncle Bharat over a whisky, as he entertained in his large, plush drawing room in Calcutta. 'It is very disturbing that a cabinet-level minister, who was so close to Mrs. Gandhi, should have died this way. At one point, L.N. Mishra raised lakhs, if not crores, of rupees for her party. But the opposition was raising too many questions about his dealings, especially from the time when he was minister of foreign affairs and gave out licenses arbitrarily to people, and Mrs. Gandhi became very uncomfortable. With his position in the party, he could afford to ignore her. You see, if you are a member of a gang of thieves, you can't suddenly start playing holy,' he said looking around wisely. 'So as I said, Mishra ji refused to resign. Mrs. Gandhi doesn't brook disobedience from her party men.'

'But why do you think Mrs. Gandhi would have him killed?' asked Veena, putting down the newspaper in Moradabad. 'They were so close.'

'You see, he was a major source of embarrassment for the Congress Party and Mrs. Gandhi,' said her husband Ashok sitting with his legs wide apart.

'How can we assign guilt until a court of law proves that Mrs. Gandhi gave the orders?' said Ashwini Kumar. 'We have to let the judiciary perform its function.'

'I've heard Mrs. L.N. Mishra gave Mrs. Gandhi a cold shoulder at the funeral,' said Nisha's brother Pradeep to his socialist friends in Delhi. 'It wasn't death; it was murder. Certainly seems Mrs. Mishra believes that. Of course, Mrs. Gandhi is blaming the Anand Marg, but I don't believe that for one second; they blame the Naxalites for every violent incident that takes place in Bihar and West Bengal. And even if violence is perpetrated by the Naxalites and the Anand Marg, why is the government so powerless in handling it? If people are being killed, the government needs to bring the killers to book. Problem is governments themselves are involved.'

The incident struck terror in the hearts of some, but the country limped along.

15

As Ravi rushed in through the department door, someone touched his apron lightly. He turned and looked, then smiled in recollection.

'I didn't see you,' he said.

'I've been waiting outside for you for a long time,' Swati said.

'I forget your name but I remember your case well. What brings you here today?'

'Swati. Doc' sahib…' she began. She struggled to say something.

'Are you feeling alright?' Ravi asked. It had been several months since he had last seen her. He wondered what trouble she had let herself into this time.

'Yes. I am feeling alright.'

'What is it, then?' he asked, looking at his watch.

'Can I get another cleaning?'

'This is not good,' he said sternly, unsurprised. 'When you really want a baby, you may not be able to have one, if you go through cleanings like this.'

Swati hung her head.

'Are you sure you want this done?'

She nodded.

'Is it the same man?' he asked, despite himself.

She nodded.

Ravi sighed. 'I wouldn't recommend it. You can't keep getting yourself pregnant and having an MTP. That is not the way to practice family planning. You are so young. If you contract an infection, you'll become infertile. Ask the man to marry you and have the baby.' He turned to go.

Swati's lower lip quivered.

'What is it, Swati?'

Her eyes filled.

'Go home and think about it. You can get an MTP any time, but you can't undo the damage.'

'Doc' sahib…'

'Come back and see me in a week.' He looked at his watch and rushed into the wards. As he stood talking to Swati, he had seen his professor, the head of medicine, drive up in his car. He would be in the building soon, and Ravi did not want to be seen hanging around.

Two days after this incident, Swati's friend Mandira came to see him. Something about Swati seemed amiss, she said. Mandira did not know what it was, but it worried her. Initially, Swati had given up eating and appeared depressed. Now, an eerie cheerfulness had come over her. At first Mandira attributed Swati's emergence from her gloom as an acceptance of her pregnancy, but now she found her friend's cheerfulness disconcerting. Would he please come and see her? — she conveyed the impression of being out of her mind. Ravi's first instinct was to deny the request, but Swati's youth, her history of treatment with him, and her music college connection somehow made her different from his other patients. As he moved on to his next patient, he promised Mandira that he would come within the next week. She left, clearly unsatisfied with his response.

The week was almost over before Ravi hurried up the narrow, dirty lane looking for the house, surprised that it didn't beckon him. He looked hard at each building, distinct yet so similar in its griminess, covered with a sort of black patina born out of years of dust and rain. He leapt over an open drain from the road onto a concrete sidewalk and looked for a hole-in-the-wall paan shop. A soft wind carried the stench of the gutter, staggering him. He took his handkerchief out of his pocket and covered his nose.

At the end of the road, he looked around in perplexity and wondered how he could have missed the betel shop when he had noted each decaying building so carefully. Turning around, he began to retrace his steps. Slowly, irritation welled up in him: He had allowed himself to feel too sorry for a female patient. And now, when he should either have been studying for his M.D. exams or seeing patients, he was searching for some obscure *paan* shop in hopes of finding a yellow house inside which lay a disturbed young woman who badly wanted an MTP. He stopped in his tracks as his eye caught a movement in the wall. He turned to look and saw a young child cutting betel nuts with a sharp instrument.

'You will cut your hand,' he said instinctively to the child through the folded handkerchief that covered his nose and part of his mouth.

The child looked blankly at him. Ravi looked around and saw a flight of steps.

'Does Swati live here?' he asked.

The child nodded.

'Is she in?'

He received another blank look.

'Where's your Amma?'

'She's gone.'

'Where?'

'There,' he said, lifting his chin and pointing toward the west. His hands did not stop for a minute.

'Next time, ask your Amma to cut these nuts for you,' said Ravi, sighing in frustration. 'You will hurt yourself very badly.' He looked at the child, but the child gave back a dazed look as if nothing had registered.

He ran up the steep steps, gingerly touching the dirty wall for support from time to time. Soon he stood in a gloomy hallway with three doors with no numbers. He looked around to see if any door gave a clue to Swati's whereabouts, but all looked old and heavy and grungy with names scratched into them. Softly, Ravi walked up to one door and listened. He heard faint noises inside. He put his ear to the door, taking care not to come too close. He heard the sounds a little louder now. There was no mistaking it: a man and a woman were having sex. Ravi took a step back. Almost instantly, another door opened and a big, heavy-set man with a well-oiled body wrapped in nothing but a checked lungi stepped out and looked appraisingly at Ravi with his big, hard eyes. Fear gripped Ravi's heart.

'Swati around here?' Ravi asked.

The man pointed to the third door and walked toward the staircase, keeping his eyes fixed on Ravi. Ravi backed slowly toward the door and stood still until he heard the man descend the steps. Once again, he wondered why he had come here, how a poor young woman, who, judging from her medical history, did not possess an upright character, could have moved him to the extent that he stood a chance of being compromised. What a fool he was to be so moved by a woman simply because her musical connection reminded him of his sister. He took a deep breath and knocked. Hearing nothing, he knocked again and waited. He looked around, then cautiously pushed the door. To his surprise, it creaked open. Holding it with his right hand, he pushed it further and stood in the doorway. In the faint light that came in through the dirty, shut glass window, Ravi saw a young woman in a nightgown hanging limply from the fan hook with a noose around her neck made from a nylon saree, the head inclined to the opposite side of the knot. A chair, obviously used as a ladder to tether the saree to the hook, lay on its side, possibly pushed away by the victim to suspend herself. He held the door with both hands to steady himself. Despite years of joking about cadavers, Ravi turned white when faced with one. He had seen pictures of victims of hanging in his jurisprudence books, had assisted in the performance of an autopsy or two on suicide victims but this young woman dangling from the fan hook in the center of the room somehow made all those experiences tame. Slowly, Ravi moved forward and felt for the light switch. He turned it on and a mouse scurried under a small steel pot that sat on the ground below a table. Dingy, airless, sparse, the room was furnished with a small table on which sat a kerosene stove and bottles of spice and food crumbs, a pedestal fan with dusty blades that bespoke neglect, and a bed. In one corner, over a small cotton prayer mat, next to a stone statue of the goddess Saraswati, stood a tanpura, carefully covered with a clean, embroidered table cover. A wave of sadness washed over him and he bowed his head to the young woman's Muse. His breath rattled through his body as he turned his gaze to the walls, which were bare except for one peg over the bed on which hung a cotton shawl, obviously northeastern in its artistry. Careful not to disturb anything with his touch, he searched for signs of life. The ceiling of the room was low and the woman's feet came down to his waist. He moved close to the body. Swati's pale, placid face and half open eyes sent a shudder through him. The external jugular vein he remembered so vividly was clearly visible even through the bloody froth that had gathered at the nostrils and mouth and through the saliva that had run out of one side of her mouth and down her chin and neck and chest.

It looked like a suicide; nevertheless, he looked for signs of violence, so he could report his observations to the police as soon as he left this place. Could it be that someone, maybe the man who kept making her pregnant, had hanged her and made the act look like suicide? Would he now come back to remove all evidence and pretend to have discovered her hanging from the ceiling? He looked at the smooth bare arms and neck for bruises, for signs of resistance, but saw nothing. He walked up to the unmade bed and looked closely at the thin quilt rolled up to the end, the dirty sheets, the brownness of the white pillowcase that showed recent use with the indent of a head, a few woman's hair and streaks of red lipstick — he had never seen Swati wearing lipstick — and a broken red glass bangle with gold overlay half hidden under the pillow. And then he saw the note, peeking from under the pillow. He bent down to sweep it up, realized he would create his own fingerprints on the paper and took out his handkerchief. Shaking it open, he picked up the note and looked at it. It said the usual thing that no one should be held responsible for her death. Had someone else written the note? He looked at the note again and carefully put it in his pocket. As he turned to leave, he looked again at the pillow and instinctively lifted it. He saw a diary. The same writing greeted his curious gaze. He swept it into his pocket, then turning off the light, he shut the door carefully and slowly made his way down the stairs to the police station.

16

'Tell the driver to let me know as soon as he is here. I will leave very early today,' Sinha told the guard.

'Yes, sahib,' he said, putting the *Dainik Samachar* and the *India Times* into Sinha's outstretched hand.

Sinha turned to his tea on the elegant creme-and-red rattan table on the verandah whose arches were overhung with the fragrant white queen-of-the-night jasmine, picked up the delicate bone-china cup and took a sip of the sweet cardamom tea.

'Our *bela* jasmine is doing so well this year,' said Mrs. Sinha, looking at the tiny white flowers on little plants in the courtyard. The sun had just come up above the back wall of her house. 'What does the paper say?' she asked, sipping her own tea. 'Show me one.'

Sinha handed her the local Hindi daily and unfolded the *India Times*.

'Gopal Nath is making a name for himself in the Centre. He's been written about in the Delhi paper,' he said, looking at the article in the national English daily with a picture of the leader of the Lok Morcha. 'He is becoming important,' he mumbled.

'*Achcha*. Okay,' said Mrs. Sinha, already engrossed in the front page story of the *Dainik Samachar*. 'They think Swati was involved with some businessman. Then that rumour in college about her pregnancy was true. I always knew it. That girl Geeta and the flour-tin lady said I was indulging in loose talk. As if. Now it comes out in the paper. Oh.' Her voice changed. 'She committed suicide — hanged herself,' she said, but expecting no reaction from her husband, continued to read. 'That was a few weeks ago; no wonder I didn't hear about it. Must have happened after college closed for the summer. But why this story now?' She scanned the lower part of the paper. 'Oh, I didn't know. She used to perform. They've printed excerpts from her diary.' She continued to read.

The first entry concerning her association with the businessman was dated 9 December, 1971.

I met a businessman today at Mrs. Yadav's place. He seems very interested in music. He listens so deeply, as if it were touching his soul. Shivkumar Sinha is his name.

The paper shook in Mrs. Sinha's hand. There were three little pieces from Swati's diary. Mrs. Sinha jerked her head up, but her husband was hidden behind his newspaper. She read on.

Even now I cannot believe that I have become so involved with Sinha ji. How did it happen? How could I have fallen so? What would Ma-Baba say? I cannot blame anyone. If a bird flies down from a tree lured by the grains of rice the bird catcher has spread to trap her in his net, is it the bird catcher's fault? The bird is foolish.

The following was the last entry in Swati's diary before her suicide, said the newspaper's annotation. It was dated 5 May, 1975.

I had come to Lucknow full of hope, full of dreams of becoming a great artist or a radio performer, but all I have now is despair. Where should I go? What should I do? Another abortion? Sinha ji says I should have another abortion. He says he cannot marry me. I knew, but still I hoped. I cannot tell Ma-Baba. They think I am happy here. I cannot go back to them. They have six others.

Mrs. Sinha's lips trembled. She put down the paper and slowly raised her eyes to her husband's. He held her gaze, until she lowered her eyes.

211

'Why didn't you tell me?' she asked, after several seconds. 'To think all this…' she paused and pressed her lips together, 'and I didn't know.'

'What was there to tell you?' Sinha asked. 'Why would you believe the story of a girl like her? She had no moral character. Who knows how many men she had? Can you tell with a girl like her?'

'But you knew her. For many years.'

'I know many people. I may have met her somewhere. There is nothing to discuss.' He stood up. 'I have to go early to work.'

'Will the police…?' she asked, standing up, too. 'Or have they already questioned…?'

'Why police? I didn't kill her. How can I be responsible for every whore who hangs herself?' The police had, in fact, questioned him at his office, as soon as they had received Swati's diary and had also opened a case in court against him. Sinha, on his part, had tried to meet the doctor who performed the autopsy, but had been turned down. Meanwhile, Swati's post-mortem report had revealed the absence of foul play and since no one else had come forward to give any fresh information on the matter, the police had not questioned Sinha further. The press had found out about the diaries in the court hearings. He knew that Swati's parents, given their station in life, were unlikely to come all the way from Assam to challenge him in court. And if they didn't challenge him, the police would have no case against him. Banking heavily on the police dropping the case in the absence of any incriminating evidence, he felt confident. 'There's nothing for you to be so upset about,' he told his wife, as he turned to go into the house.

'But won't the police want to talk to you?' Mrs. Sinha asked in an extremely agitated tone.

'There is nothing to say about her suicide. She hanged herself. There is no evidence of foul play. And, anyway, the police are loyal to anyone who pays them.'

As he went inside, Achala came out in her thin cotton nightdress. Mrs. Sinha tried hurriedly to pick up the Hindi paper, but in her confusion picked up the English and Achala's eye caught the headline. She scanned the top and came directly to the diary excerpts, which she read quickly. Then, putting the paper down, she looked at her mother and noted her wet eyelashes. Mrs. Sinha sank into her chair. Achala lowered her eyes.

'The paper can print what it wants,' Mrs. Sinha said. She studiously avoided her daughter's gaze. 'Papa is innocent.'

17

'Today the people of India have won a big victory,' crowed the editorial in the 12 June, 1975, special edition of the local paper, just out, which Pradeep read, standing close to the stage. He looked up from time to time to see if the park was filling up with supporters. The Allahabad High Court had declared the prime ministership of Mrs. Indira Gandhi illegal and the excitement in Lucknow was fast reaching a feverish pitch. The court had ruled that Mrs. Gandhi manipulated government machinery for her personal ends and forced a government officer to indulge in electioneering. 'She has acted on several occasions in a manner that suggests she thinks she is above the law,' said the editorial columnist. 'The forces of justice have spoken. The court has underscored what we've always known: Mrs. Gandhi is not above the law. In a final act of justice, the Allahabad High Court has ruled that madam will not be allowed to fight an election for six years. Long live democracy. Long live the people.'

Pradeep folded the newspaper, tucked it into his armpit, and looked around. He was waiting for his friend Gopal Nath to come with his entourage to Begum Hazrat Mahal Park and address the people. Gopal Nath was a rising, young politician. Pradeep had met him when he came to the university a few years ago to address the socialists. He had been immensely moved by the man's power and his appeal to the intellect of the university audience. Gopal Nath had graduated with honours years ago and had bucked the prevailing trend of going into industry or government by deciding to oppose both. Pradeep looked up to him and was here to show his support. He had come to Lucknow the day before and instead of staying with his sister, Nisha, or his uncle Ashwini, had roomed with his friends. It was a break with tradition, one he realized would hurt his family's feelings immensely. But in the struggle for the rights of the people, some things had to be sacrificed. Emotional ties with the family fell in that category. He told a man close to him about the court decision and waited.

Word ran through the swelling crowd like an electrical current. After several seconds of shock, heads began to turn toward neighbouring heads as the impact of the news permeated through the collective consciousness.

Gajendra Mishra, standing several feet from the podium that towered above on a platform, had been rooted to his spot since mid afternoon. He gingerly pinched a few leaves of tobacco from a small packet that he took out from the pocket of his mud-white kurta and put them into the palm of the other hand. Folding the packet, he carefully curled his hand to keep the leaves from falling, and then rubbed the leaves into his palm with his thumb. This motion of rubbing the leaves in his left palm with his right thumb absorbed him completely. He would much rather have been at home practising his tabla, but the workers of Gopal Nath's party, Lok Morcha, had come through his alley promising one hundred rupees to anyone who would come to the massive procession and demonstration that afternoon, before the remote possibility had become fact. He had fallen for it, thinking of pocketing the money and not showing up. Perhaps aware of this all too common practice, the workers had said that they would hand out the money only when they reached Begum Hazrat Mahal Park. Gajendra had then thought of saying no, for artists were not political, but the impending arrival of a new baby, their fifth, had made a hundred rupees seem attractive for an afternoon's work. After all, he made that much in a month for accompanying the likes of Mrs. Sinha twice a week. And now the income from Mrs. Sinha had dried up, too. He clambered up the truck with fifty others, squeezing the muscles of his buttocks as the Lok Morcha worker pushed everyone in with a wave of the hatch, then lifted and secured it. They stood close together, jerking forward and backward in unison as if controlled by some invisible thread, every time the maniacal driver drove over a pothole. There was nothing to hold on to, but it didn't matter for the tightness of space kept them in place. Once outside the park, the Lok Morcha workers herded them like milch cows to behind the rope line. Gajendra gave one last rub, patted the tobacco with his free hand and then blew gently to remove all the impurities that he had so painstakingly worried out of the leaves. Tilting his head back, he put the powdered leaves into his mouth and chewed with pleasure.

The crowd stood patiently and as the news spread, a loud murmur rose like the swell of a turbulent sea. It was late afternoon and the sun bore a hole through the thousands of heads of the collected faithful, some hired, some genuinely wishing to be there.

A hush fell over the crowd suddenly. Gajendra spat out a stream of tobacco into the burned, yellow grass in front of him and looked toward the entrance which had suddenly become a hive of activity. A corpulent man dressed in white from his Gandhi cap to his pajamas stepped out of a white Ambassador car. Immediately, everyone at the gate rushed forward to touch his feet. He looked around and surveyed the crowd with pleasure, barely cognizant of the men jostling to touch his dusty feet housed in their Gandhi Ashram chappals. He made a gesture of impatience with his bejewelled hands as one last man lurched toward his feet and moved away. The new arrival then strode forward with five men behind him. Others followed at a respectable distance. Everyone fell behind as he ascended the platform and sat on a chair while another man in a Gandhi cap introduced him. Gopal Nath marched up to and adjusted the microphone to his height and began. He spoke too loudly and the feedback caused Gajendra's hands to go flying up to his ears. Gopal Nath lowered his voice.

'Brothers and sisters. As you have no doubt heard, the courts have strengthened the people's hands today. Our democracy stands strong. Our people are stronger than ever.'

Gopal Nath paused. The crowd let out a loud hurrah. Gopal Nath's pudgy face was wet with sweat. Streams of perspiration ran continuously from his capped head, down his face, to the collar of his kurta, which was now completely soaked. He took a clove out of his pocket and as he put it into his mouth to soothe his hoarse throat, the diamonds on his fingers caught the light of the sun and sent out a sparkle to the crowd. Pradeep noted the speaker's jewelry with disgust. Why did idealism go out the moment power came in? The crowd kept cheering.

'So, brothers and sisters,' continued the politician. The crowd hushed again. 'We now know that the courts are on our side. We now know that Mrs. Indira Gandhi has indulged in corrupt practices that have kept our country from the path of progress. We now know that Mrs. Indira Gandhi has lied to the nation to hide her misdeeds. We cannot accept these conditions any more. We will not accept the lies any more. We will not accept her dictatorship any more.' The crowd joined him:

Tanashahi nahin chalegi.
Indira Gandhi Murdabad
Indira Gandhi Murdabad

'Yes,' Gopal Nath repeated. 'We will not accept Indira Gandhi's dictatorship. Death to dictatorship. Death to Indira Gandhi.' He paused, then continued in a softer tone. 'Brothers and sisters. Our beloved leader Mahatma Gandhi gave his life for the freedom of our country. He faced police brutality for democracy. He spent long months in jail for democracy. He offered his bare back to a baton for democracy. And what has Indira Gandhi done? She has taken away what Gandhiji won for you. She has taken your power from you. She has emasculated you. I ask you to join me today in calling for her resignation as prime minister of India. I ask you today to join me in taking India out of the hands of a dictator. I ask you today to put the country back on the road to democracy. I ask you today to support *jan satta*, the power of the people. Long live democracy.'

Loktantra Zindabad
Loktantra Zindabad

'We will go now to the governor and put forward our demands. We will ask the governor to send a message to the Centre that we will not live under a dictatorship any more. Will you come with me?'

'Ye-e-s-s,' yelled the hysterical crowd. Hot. Sweaty.

'Onward, then. On to the governor's house.'

'Our leader is Gopal Nath. Long live Gopal Nath.'

~

The crowd moved toward the main shopping area of Hazratganj like a giant wave. At the crossroads, another wave of demonstrators carrying banners joined the swell from the Hanuman Bridge. The sea of heads spreading out across the several streets that converged at the circus now streamlined into the one road that led through the city center to the governor's house.

Gajendra was no longer in the front of the crowd. When Gopal Nath had first issued his clarion call to march to the governor's house, Gajendra had thought of escaping and making his way home, but the crowd had moved out of Begum Hazrat Mahal Park too forcefully, and unable to resist the momentum of the crowd, he had been pushed along by the surge. As he marched along slowly, the soles of his feet burning through the chappals from the heat emanating from the tar roads, his head hot from hours of sun, he felt dizzy from hunger and thirst. He looked at the billowing humanity around him and knew there was no escape. He walked desultorily along, letting others shout the slogans, wondering if a hundred rupees were not too little for an afternoon of torture in the heat of politics.

Meanwhile, a few hundred yards away from Begum Hazrat Mahal Park, Kirana turned off his scooter and rolled it along the side of the street near the tomb of Asaf-ud-daulah. He was stuck. He got off his scooter and looked toward the music college for a means of escape. But a throng of people was marching toward the circus. They were passing by the gates of the music college, filling the street completely. The Hanuman Bridge ahead of him was choked with marching democracy seekers and Hazratganj was already off limits for who knew how many hours. Kirana sighed. His only exit was the street that led away from Hazratganj, but even that would take several hours to clear as the last of the stragglers joined the main procession in the front. He pulled his scooter up on its stand and sat on it.

He watched the crowds swirling around him. He would miss giving Sarika her lesson. Sarika would be waiting for he had told her that he would come after the sun had lowered in the sky. Desire welled in him. He had told Surya that he would go to Gajendra's house to practice with the tabla. He would tell her that this rally had prevented him from practising with Gajendra. That was the truth, after all. Surya did not suspect Sarika and there was no reason to make her do so. Indeed, if there was a strong feeling gnawing at him all the time, duelling for supremacy with his passion for Sarika, it was fear of discovery. Yes, Gajendra would make a good stand-in.

The banners billowed in the soft, welcome breeze as the crowd moved forward. Gajendra let out a long breath as the breeze cooled his sweaty body. Not a drop of water had passed his lips since he had left home that afternoon and his mouth felt as parched as the earth waiting for the first showers of the monsoon. The crowd snaked along the garbage-littered streets of Hazratganj, energetic believers in the front followed by mercenaries dragging their unwilling bodies along, leaving gaps in the center of the procession. In the distance, Gajendra noticed mounted police in their khaki uniforms. Surprised, he stood on his toes for a second and saw that some policemen were marching alongside the procession, keeping a safe distance, holding their lathis or batons in readiness should

217

trouble break out. The heads and banners in front of him blocked his view of the head of the procession.

Suddenly, a flash of lightning went through the crowd, so quickly that Gajendra could not understand where it came from and where it went as he looked around dazedly. A flurry of running chappals announced the breaking up of the crowd. Before he knew where to look, Gajendra heard the sound of shattering glass. The crowd had cleared the center of the street. He, too, loped along to the side where he saw the now irate mobsters breaking shop windows with the poles of their banners, seizing anything that came into their hands from the welldecorated windows. In a panic, shopkeepers rushed to shutter their stores and the sound of wood poles beating over iron shutters filled the evening air. With nothing to do and no one to follow, Gajendra looked around for Gopal Nath. There he was, trying to shout to the crowd to march on ahead, that work lay ahead, that violence would get them nothing. But without the microphone, Gopal Nath's voice drifted away and dispersed like so many particles of pollen. No one heard him above the cries of death to Indira Gandhi, death to black marketeers, breaking glass, banging poles, rushing chappals. The mounted police cantered up and halted the progress of the march.

As Pradeep marched close to Gopal Nath and heard his call to shun violence and destruction and focus on the work at hand, he felt once again the dedication and vision of the man that had first drawn him to his side. The power of the people was immense. Two months ago, the Assembly in the western state of Gujrat had been dissolved because of agitation by students. Certainly, a show of force by the people could get Mrs. Gandhi out of office and hand victory squarely to the people. He smiled in anticipation.

From the glass window of his air-conditioned office at the service station, Sinha watched the advancing mounted police, which had been lingering near his business for several hours to keep the procession from reaching the governor's house. But now the men were actually marching ahead. He got up from his leather-backed chair and walked to the door. Pratap Singh saw him and came over. 'The police are advancing, sahib.' Together they looked at the two forces approaching each other. 'These mobsters have begun to break windows and loot shops. Should we close our pump? They are not too far from us.'

'They won't be able to come this far,' Sinha said. 'The police will break up this procession before it reaches us. Go do your work.' He was a good lad, thought Sinha, as Pratap Singh retreated. Outside, the mounted police halted the procession. He had read about Gopal Nath's rapid rise to power out of nowhere and had hoped to catch a glimpse of him today. Sinha had successfully deflected the last attack on his business, but he knew the tax collectors would be back. If Gopal Nath became the force that he was reported becoming, he might be worth cultivating and could well be the anchor he needed. He had to find out Gopal Nath's price tag.

As marchers scattered, Gajendra felt at a loss. There was no form to the procession, now a mob now that attacked everything in its way. Gajendra saw people in the verandahs of the buildings of Hazratganj and thought he would hide behind one of the pillars. He tried to move ahead, but something was pushing the crowd back. The mob was moving from the verandah and toppling into the street. Still he pressed ahead with one shoulder, but the force was strong and he could not move forward. He heard a yelp, then another. He looked up and saw lathis flying. All at once he understood the force that pushed him back was that of the baton-wielding police. Sometime, someone had ordered a lathi charge. Gajendra hung back now and looked around to see if he could find an opening in the crowd from where to escape. More and more people were stepping back as the police that had been marching along the sides turned on them with a vicious ferocity. Someone stepped on Gajendra's chappal and in order to move back, he had to let it go. The hot road met his one bare foot with startling intensity as he took another step back.

Suddenly, a lathi came flying at the back of Gajendra's head. Before his hand could fly up in a reflex, came another. He put his hand up and felt the warmth of fresh blood on his fingers. The lathi-bearing constable who had hit him had moved on to other targets. Gajendra moved his hand from his head and looked at his blood-soaked fingers in horror. He put his hand in his kurta pocket, felt the little packet of tobacco and pulled it out along with an old rag of a handkerchief. He put the tobacco and the cloth on his head and moved around dazedly, dizzy from heat, hunger, thirst, and the loss of blood. Darkness was fast approaching and the crowd around him had thinned. Pressing his hand hard against his wound, he sat down with a thud on the burning hot street.

18

Contrite over his feelings for Sarika as he waited out the procession with a ready body, Kirana went to her house the next morning after telling Surya. His wife knew, of course, that he taught Sarika at home, but some days when he longed for her so, the words froze on his tongue as he left his house. He knew on such days that control would be hard if an opportunity presented itself. He couldn't tell Surya he was going to teach when his mind dwelt on a thought so different. Surya trusted him. And his telling his wife showed that his intentions were honourable.

'I was expecting you yesterday,' said Sarika with her usual energy, as she let her teacher into the living room. 'I have some wonderful news. I received a letter from the AIR saying that I not only won the national competition, but was awarded the B-high grade.'

'B-high? You sure?' Kirana was in disbelief.

'Here's the letter.'

Kirana read quickly and his eyes shone with pride.

'I couldn't understand why you didn't come yesterday,' said Sarika. 'I was dying to show you this. It came yesterday.'

'I wanted to so much. I was stuck in the procession,' he said, taking off his sandals in a corner and sitting down on the cool cotton rug. 'What wonderful news!'

'A glass of water, master sahib?' Sarika moved on. 'I didn't realize you were stuck in that procession,' she said on returning with his water. 'I heard about it.'

'That was some procession,' he said. 'I went to Gajendra's this morning to practice with him and he said he marched.' Sarika churned up his emotions. And then this news about her. Today, he would just teach her and leave.

'Oh.' Sarika wanted the conversation to focus on him and her, on their relationship, which would somehow stay in this state forever. She didn't think of the future and problems to their liaisons; she envisioned a life in which this present would be everlasting.

'He couldn't play with me because he was hurt in the head.'

'Is he okay now?'

'Under the circumstances. His wife will go into labour any day.'

'She seems very fertile.'

'Let us begin. Bring the instruments.' As Sarika went into her room to bring out the instruments, Kirana was seized by a strong longing for her. He wanted to hold her. The funny thing about an emotion was that the harder you tried to control it, the quicker it slipped through your hand. Perhaps it was best to not even try. She fulfilled him not just physically, but through an emotional connection made body, mind, and music come together. So many times, as he thought of her love for him, he felt like bursting into song. She brought out a new emotion in his singing. Male artists always had physical relations with their female students. He dismissed those trysts as bohemian. Now he saw what a difference it made to him. He had never felt so complete before. Through Sarika, he had found his soul.

Yet, how long could this last? Even though he pushed away those thoughts from his head, he knew that in a year and a half she would be done with the music school. Her parents would marry her to some powerful bureaucrat like her father and while she went off into a new world, he would be left with a hole in his heart. And then there was the more immediate problem of keeping two women. He couldn't resist a smile. How wonderful it would be if Surya could always be there for his family life and Sarika for his soul.

'What raga will you sing today?' he asked gently, pensively.

'*Yaman.*'

'*Sa.*'

Sarika sang the tonic note and after a short exposition, started a composition in the slow tempo. Her rendition was different today. She had spent some time over the past few months pondering over Naushad's creative use of notes and combined it with the severity of form that her teacher at the college — Prasad sahib — favoured. Her style still showed Kirana's strong influence with its powerful emotional overtones, but the overall effect of borrowing from different schools of teaching helped her generate a style that was uniquely and impressively her own. During the college year, she had experimented with bits and pieces but stuck to her lesson. She had not had the nerve to sing her creation before Kirana sahib because even her own ears sensed a disconnect between the concept envisioned by the mind and the voice that tried to make it concrete.

Then, last week, as she sang what she had spent time refining over the summer, she felt for the first time she was ready. The result was not as startling as Naushad's or as severe as Prasad sahib's; within the parameters of Kirana's style, she had created her own.

As she sang, Kirana praised her after every alap, every time she came to the first beat of the tabla. She moved from the slow to the fast composition and ended with a few fast notes rendered so effortlessly that Kirana thought his heart would burst with pure joy. He nodded to Nirmala as she came into the room and sat on her favourite chair.

'*Shabash*. Well done,' he said, when she had finished. 'I'm very pleased with your *riyaz*. Keep it up and who knows where you'll end up.'

'I've been experimenting,' said Sarika. Earlier, she had debated whether to tell Kirana sahib that she had been trying out some of Naushad's techniques and had decided against it. His receptiveness now emboldened her. 'I have been experimenting with three styles — yours, Naushad ji's, and Prasad sahib's,' she said. 'I don't want to use them as discrete units but see how I can blend them. I think emotion becomes so much more pronounced when it is juxtaposed with severity. And that's what I have been trying to do.' She thought for a moment and added, 'I love what Naushad ji does with his violin. He may not be the world's greatest violinist, but he comes up with some truly amazing combinations. I try to emulate those.'

'I am glad you learn from so many different gurus.' He did not smile.

'Naushad ji is not my guru,' she said immediately.

'Any one who teaches you is a guru. Even if he teaches you for one day. And by virtue of that, he is deserving of your respect.'

'Well,' she said, flush from the high of a good rendition, 'as far as I'm concerned, I have only one guru and that is you.'

Nirmala laughed. 'Some tea, Kirana sahib?'

Kirana glanced at her and forced a smile. 'No,' he said, as he stood up. 'I will leave. I left the house fairly early this morning and want to get back in time for lunch.' He slipped on his sandals and left the house quickly.

'Do you think he's upset that I told him I'm borrowing from styles in addition to his?' Sarika asked her mother.

'He did leave rather abruptly,' she said. 'But no, I don't see what he could be upset about. Prasad sahib is your teacher and Naushad is also at the college. He must be tired. He said he'd had a long day. Driving around in this heat will wear the best of us down.'

~

As Kirana drove home on his scooter, his feelings were lathered up as usual, though the passion of desire had given way to the tumultuousness of revelation. He had truly enjoyed Sarika's singing today; yet that joy had been marred. This time by an artless comment from his student. It was clear she didn't understand that he saw Naushad as a rival. Even so, did she have to tell him that she had been adapting his techniques to the peculiarities of voice to make them distinctively her own?

And now his reflections earlier in her house about their future together assumed a completely different hue. In two years, maybe slightly longer, he would have given her all he knew. He would then become irrelevant for her — her nursery school teacher — while she went on to bigger things. Marriage, which in the morning had struck him as a sure thing for her, given her mother's views, now didn't seem so. Maybe her parents would send her off to another guru. Maybe they'd find her a good female teacher. And certainly, at some point, young and beautiful as she was, she'd find a man.

Where would Kirana be then?

In a second, Kirana's future without her — stuck in his job at the college with yearly salary increments, at home with his wife with no heart-quickening excitement, the small house, some radio concerts, the same stale jokes with AIR artists, a few private lessons for money, waking up in the morning with no chance liaison to look forward to, a desultory existence — came before his eyes and so disturbed him that he did not see a three-wheeler taxi coming at him. At the last minute, he swerved and avoided a fatal accident as the driver of the vehicle stuck out his head and yelled at him.

Complaining of a headache from the brutal sun, he ate a quiet lunch with his family and went to sleep. It was late afternoon when he woke up, hot and sweaty. The children were still napping and would wake up and go out to play. He was not sure yet what he would do in the evening that stretched before him. The walls of the house emitted heat like a furnace and he longed to escape from the cloister. But the sun was still beating

223

down mercilessly on the steaming roads. Surya, already up, made him a glass of *Rooh Afza* without ice and the cool, sweet, fragranced drink soothed him immensely.

He rose from bed and as he walked into the bathroom, he was momentarily blinded by the strong light of the sun that streamed in through the high window. He averted his eyes, washed his face quickly and came out of the bathroom. Surya told him that she was going out to buy some provisions. Relieved, he plunged into thoughts of Sarika. The longing never left him. How *could* he lose her? She was more talented than he, yet now that her departure to another *guru* or another man seemed only a matter of time, whether or not she was aware of it, he found his pride and joy in her accomplishments dulled by resentment. She was his, yet she observed everything around her and had no qualms about taking what she could from the world at large. How could it be that born into such a traditional family, she didn't understand his views?

He was her guru. His heart was supposed to be as all-encompassing as the divine sound of *Om*. Was the heart of a guru different from the heart of a man? Or did the two become one after the great physical barrier had been crossed?

He went into the living room. Too weary to sit down with his tanpura and launch into *riyaz*, he pulled out his harmonium and hummed a devotional. Today, this is all he would sing.

19

Sarika sat up and covered her body with her silk sheet. 'Did you hear that?' she asked.

'Yes,' said Kirana. 'It sounded like a knock.'

'There it is again,' she said, alarmed. 'It sounds like it's coming from the back door. I wonder who it could be.'

'You go and check. I'll stay here. I'll come out only when you tell me it's okay to.'

She put her hand on her heart to still the pounding. Her body trembled as she looked at Kirana sahib. She licked her dry lips and with shaking hands, put on her clothes and headed toward the door of her bedroom. Remembering something, she came back and whispered to Kirana sahib to go into the living room, then ran to the back door and stood still a minute, tidying her hair with her hands. She opened the door quickly, but saw nothing. Feeling bolder now, she peeped out, saw no one, and shut the door. It must have been the strong afternoon wind. Her tense shoulders relaxed for a few seconds, but soon another thought crossed her mind as she walked back toward the main house. What if, seeing Kirana sahib's scooter, Ramu had decided to check and see if she needed something — a cup of tea, a glass of *Rooh Afza* without ice, or just plain water — for master sahib. And hearing no response had gone back to his quarter. What if he somehow knew? Would he tell the other servants and laugh at her? Would the entire household know? What were they saying about her? She came back to Kirana, now in the living room fully dressed.

Nirmala and Ashwini were at an inauguration ceremony and the servant was taking his afternoon nap in his quarters. As if by a sixth sense, Kirana sahib had come that afternoon while on his way to the radio station to record a concert, surprising Sarika, both by the strength of his urge and his willingness to court exposure. The risk had increased the intensity of the excitement of the tryst to a feverish pitch and they had made love with abandon.

'What if somebody finds out?' she said, shaken and looking for reassurance.

'No one will find out,' he said soothingly. 'There's no one here.'

'But suppose it was Ramu and hearing nothing, he went away.'

'He would have waited a few minutes for you to come to the door, if he thought you needed him,' he said.

'If he takes it upon himself to see that I'm alright, he will go around the house and try to look in through my window to check on me,' she persisted. 'What if he heard something? Oh, God!' She slumped into the sofa.

The colour fled from his face, and as the worst sort of images rose in his mind, terror seized him. Would he lose both his student and his name? What would he tell his wife? What life remained if one's name was gone? He would be a mere shadow of a man. Scenarios of loss of reputation arose in his imagination.

225

Sarika's own fears of discovery made her oblivious to Kirana sahib's mood.

'Oh God,' she cried. 'What will we do?'

'I don't know,' he mumbled.

'What do you mean?' she asked in alarm.

'I don't know,' he said again. A helpless paralysis struck him. What could he do if they were discovered? It was his worst fear, one that sometimes woke him up at night, until finding his wife sleeping peacefully, he fell back into slumber. 'I had better leave,' he said quietly after several moments. 'I still have to go for the AIR recording.'

'You can't leave, master sahib,' she said, clinging to his sleeve. 'I'm so scared; how can you leave?'

'I have the recording,' he said softly. 'If I don't go, people will wonder. They might send someone to my house to look for me. That would be terrible for us.'

'No, stay.'

'I have to go,' he said in a barely audible voice.

'Why did you come here then?'

He stood quietly before her. His silence angered Sarika. Did he not feel anything, that too, after such passionate love making, that he stood so calmly? Suddenly the flour-tin lady's words came to her. Maybe he didn't care now that she had given herself to him. 'You have to help me,' she hissed. 'You are not going to use me and turn away.'

He glanced at her in pain. 'Please understand,' he said softly. She dug her fingers into his arms. 'I have to go.' She let him go. Quietly, he let himself out the front door. Sarika went into her room and lay face down. The fear of discovery had driven out the pleasure of love making so quickly. And master sahib didn't seem to be helping either. She heard footsteps on the verandah outside her room. It was Ravi.

'The front door was open,' he said, when she emerged from her room.

'Oh, was it,' she said listlessly.

'I saw Kirana sahib on the road outside our house,' he said.

'Yeah, he was here.'

'At this time?'

'He had to go to the AIR for a recording, so he decided to stop by.'

Ravi cast a quizzical glance at Sarika. She avoided his gaze.

'Are you feeling alright?' he asked.

'Yes, I'm fine. What could be wrong with me?' she barked.

'Just asked. You look flushed, like you have fever,' he said touching her forehead with his hand. 'No fever,' he said, giving her a sharp look. 'Is everything okay with Kirana?'

She nodded.

'Where is Amma?'

'She and Papa have gone to an inauguration ceremony.'

'And you were alone with Kirana sahib?'

'Yes.'

'Did he say something to you?'

'No. Why?'

'You don't look yourself.'

'Must be the heat.'

'The cooler is on.'

'It just came on. The electricity was out for a couple of hours,' she lied.

'Where's Ramu? I'm hungry.' Ravi eyed his sister suspiciously.

'I will go call him,' she said. She went to the back door and called out Ramu's name. Then, instead of going back into the dining room to talk to her brother, she went into her room and shut the door.

20

Pradeep was arrested again. This time he was in the exalted company of prominent freedom fighters and opposition members, whom Mrs. Gandhi feared.

When the Supreme Court of India refused to overturn the verdict of the Allahabad High Court, Mrs. Gandhi declared a state of Emergency on June 26, 1975. At midnight, June 25, she sent out the police to round up anyone who was deemed a threat to her administration. Pradeep, already a known figure, was quickly arrested as he lay reading in his room. During the midnight sweep, power supply to newspapers was cut off, so they couldn't print until such time as censors took charge.

Within two days, the president of the country had suspended the citizens' fundamental rights and a day later an ordinance called the Maintenance of Internal Security Act was passed that suspended the right of *habeas corpus*, which meant that anyone could be arrested without having to be told why.

Once again, Ashwini was called upon to intervene on Pradeep's behalf. But times being somewhat different, it took Ashwini longer to get him out and not only because for several days no one knew Pradeep's whereabouts.

Meanwhile, the country saw efficiency it had not seen since the time of the British. Trains ran on time, streets were cleaned, and people showed up to work and stayed.

21

'Memsahib,' said Ramu, 'a Sinha memsahib is here to see you.'

'Sinha memsahib?' asked Nirmala, looking up from the letter she was writing.

'Yes, she says she goes to the music college with Sarika bibiji.'

'Oh.' Nirmala raised an eyebrow. 'Tell Sarika bibiji Sinha memsabib is here.' Nirmala finished her sentence, put down her Parker's pen on her polished teak writing table, and remained seated for a few seconds to collect her thoughts.

Mrs. Sinha stood up as Nirmala walked into the room, followed by Sarika. Unlike the clothes Mrs. Sinha wore to Kirana sahib's class, her blouse today was modest, revealing none of the laciness of her bra. Her expensive cotton saree covered both shoulders as a mark of respect toward those she came to visit.

'Please sit down, Mrs. Sinha,' said Nirmala, taking her favourite chair in the living room. 'You left your house very early this morning. Is everything okay?'

'Yes,' said Mrs. Sinha. She sat down and kept her eyes lowered. 'Is Kumar sahib home?' she asked.

Surprised at her question, Nirmala nodded. 'He is getting ready to go to the office. *Koi khas baat?* Anything I can do for you?' she asked.

'No, I don't need to see him,' Mrs. Sinha said quickly. 'It's okay if I talk to you.'

'How can I help you?' Nirmala asked again.

Mrs. Sinha's eyes bounced from Nirmala to Sarika, who stood by her mother's chair, and into her own lap. Understanding, Nirmala said, 'Sarika *beta*, why don't you go take a bath? I've asked the driver to pick up Nisha and bring her here at about 11 o'clock.' Sarika left reluctantly. Her mind went immediately to Swati's demise and she shuddered. Nirmala turned her full attention now to Mrs. Sinha, who wrung her embroidered handkerchief in her hand. 'How can I help you?'

'I need your help very badly,' said Mrs. Sinha, coming immediately to the point. 'My husband is in jail.' As she spoke, her eyes filled with tears.

'For Swati?' asked Nirmala and immediately regretted her words.

'No!' said Mrs. Sinha, turning red. 'My husband is innocent. He was not responsible for her death. After all, he is a married man, with a daughter of marriageable age.' She paused as she spoke of her daughter, and continued to wring her handkerchief. Her eyelids fluttered and her lips moved as she fought tears.

'I'm sorry,' said Nirmala quietly. 'I'm sure you know the truth. Newspapers always sensationalize, especially local newspapers. Was he arrested under MISA then?'

'I don't know under what. You see, Mrs. Kumar, we have many businesses and...'

Nirmala saw her struggle, but couldn't supply the words for decency.

'Well, and lots of black money,' Mrs. Sinha said at last. 'Some time back, a new assistant commissioner of excise had come to Lucknow and conducted a raid on our steel factory. But she didn't find anything. After the declaration of the Emergency, it seems the power of these government officers has surged and they came again.

'The same AC?'

'No. This time it was an income tax officer. It doesn't matter, Mrs. Kumar. Income tax, excise, it's all the same. He didn't go to the factory. He came to our house. They searched everything, Mrs. Kumar, it was horrible.' Mrs. Sinha sobbed. 'They went through all our cupboards, all our steel almiras, the safe, and even tore open our mattresses to see if we'd hidden any cash in those. They touched everything.' Mrs. Sinha tried to compose herself. 'They took everything and also my mister, saying that black marketeers and tax evaders are to be put in jail.'

'When did this happen?'

'Yesterday. He has been sitting in jail since last evening,' said Mrs. Sinha in a fresh burst of tears. 'I don't know where he is, what kind of food he must be eating, who he must be with.' She wiped her nose and continued to weep. 'How must he be sleeping? On the floor with rats? He'll get sick. He's been under so much tension. Mrs. Kumar, please help me.'

'What can we do for you?'

'Get him released. Kumar sahib is the home secretary and he can get it done without any trouble. Can't he?'

'I will have to ask him. These are hard times for everyone. Even government officers.'

'But in his position...'

'I will talk to him.'

'If my mister could get released by some time today...'

'I will talk to him.'

'Sarika is such a lovely girl,' said Mrs. Sinha, as she stood up to leave. 'She is like my own daughter to me.'

'I will talk to my husband,' said Nirmala. She walked Mrs. Sinha to the door.

22

Sarika gently pushed open the door to Kirana sahib's classroom and took in the emptiness. Stepping back, she shut the door gently and skimmed the deserted corridor in perplexity. Where was everyone — Kirana sahib, the accompanists, the students? It was the first day of college after the summer break, usually marked by lots of activity. Sarika walked down the long corridor, peering through the window of every classroom, and to her surprise saw everyone else teaching conscientiously. Unable to locate Kirana sahib, she walked downstairs and sought out Ahmed.

'Ahmed ji, what's happening? *Aise ulloo bol rahe hain*,' she said.

'Yes, *bitiya*. The corridors look deserted, don't they?' said Ahmed, sitting on his haunches on the bench outside the principal's office and chewing betel. 'This is all because of the Emergency. Everyone is in class teaching. They are all too scared to come out and loiter around during class hours.'

'What does the Emergency have to do with the music college?' asked Sarika.

'The Emergency has to do with every college,' he said laughing. 'They are afraid that they will be suspended if they are caught idling away their time. The college is owned by the government, as you know. Director sahib was here a little while ago from the secretariat, making his rounds. I had to get principal sahib four glasses of water while he was here.'

'Principal sahib was that nervous?' she asked.

'Yes. Director sahib can suspend him, without asking any questions. Things are very bad, *bitiya*. Just yesterday, they came and locked up a judge's clerk who lived in our muhalla. He was a good, honest man, but they said he had been accepting bribes. They put him in jail and wouldn't accept bail.'

'So, what's going to happen to him?' asked Sarika in alarm.

'I don't know, *bitiya*. He was a good man, has three little children and won't get full pay until his case is decided. And who knows how long that will take. Say, aren't you having your class today?'

'I will, I suppose, but later. I came in early looking for Kirana sahib. Have you seen him?'

'Kirana sahib. Are you still learning from him, *bitiya*?' He looked at her openly, honestly.

'At home. In college, I am still learning from Prasad sahib.'

'Prasad sahib is a good man. I have heard him teach; he has a good knowledge of ragas.'

Ahmed manipulated the betel juice in his mouth. Walking stiffly to the spittoon outside the principal's office, he shot. The stream went

231

flawlessly in. Assuming his former position on the bench, he took off his muddy-white cap and scratched his sparse, sweaty scalp.

'Yes, *bitiya*, Kirana sahib. Did you read the paper?'

'What paper?'

'It's in the Lucknow Hindi papers. Principal sahib told me. He read it in *Dainik Samachar*.'

'I didn't read.'

'Kirana sahib was caught in a vice den.'

Sarika stared at him, agape.

'Last week,' he said. 'The police raided the den. Kirana sahib was there, singing probably. They even found a government officer there.'

'So, what did they do?'

'They arrested him, but let him go a day later because he is not involved in running the den.'

'Where is he now?'

'He's at home recovering from the shock. He might be back in college tomorrow. It is hard for him to show his face in the college now.'

'But what was he doing in the vice den?' Sarika asked in a distraught voice.

'What do I know, *bitiya*,' he said sighing deeply.

Sarika stared at him in stunned silence.

~

Waiting to talk to no one, Sarika rushed home after class that day, happy to find her parents gone to a wedding. After telling Ramu she didn't want any dinner or snack, she went to her room, shut the door, turned on the low-wattage incandescent bulb, threw off her chappals and dupatta, and fell on her bed, head in hands, not sure where to begin sorting through the confusion in her mind.

How could she have allowed herself to become involved with a man so low that he carried on indiscriminately with so many women — surely that's what he did in the vice den — when all the time he made her believe that their relationship was the sacred bond of the *guru-shishya*. How did he have the nerve to go to a vice den? What if his wife...? She winced at the thought of his wife. Standing up, Sarika kicked the chappals under the bed and walked to the large black dressing table that had once belonged to her mother and stopped, startled at catching her reflection in the mirror. What sort of 17-year-old did the world see? What did Mrs. Kirana see? Light skin, braided long brown hair, hazel eyes. A pretty face, but what did they see behind the face? She looked at her image intently in the mirror for several seconds, then turned around and started pacing.

She had asked Kirana sahib once, in a mood of childlike flirtation, if he liked her or his wife more. His response had been guarded. I love you both. She is in her place and you are in yours. And then he had said something that Sarika had clung to — You are talented and intelligent. Which meant, of course, that she was ahead of his wife in those attributes. But now, almost a year after this exchange, Sarika wondered if he had deliberately equivocated with her or she been too quick to read what she wanted in his messages. Was he playing with her? Had she been too ready to believe? But, she thought, his attention to her indicated the weakness of his marriage and if it hadn't been Sarika, it would have been someone else.

Suddenly, a thought flashed through her mind and she tilted her head as if straining to listen to something. A moan escaped her lips. She sat heavily on her bed and longed to sob, but felt strangely dry. Prostitute, she said softly to herself, prostitute. If he carried on with her and the prostitutes and his wife at the same time, was Sarika no different from a whore in his mind? She brought forth from memory every gesture, look, snippet of conversation that she could remember and parsed it for signs of her own cheapness of character. What misplaced idealism had prompted her to give herself up to him. *Guru-shishya* indeed! His talk about divinity. Divinity, my ass! He who had no qualms about taking anyone.

Caught in a vice den. Was he singing his divine bhajans when the police busted him? How many other girls had there been? Is that how he'd seen her right from the beginning when for her he had been a revered teacher? He had impressed even Nirmala with his genuine fondness for Sarika as a child. Had he plucked her because she was the freshest, sweetest smelling flower in his garden? And now that he had inhaled her fragrance and sucked her nectar, he could fly away like a bumble bee to the next blossom? Who would that be? Maybe the girl in second year that she had heard him listening to at the end of last year? Sarika had heard her practical exam, sitting on the staircase. Kirana sahib had gone in to listen, cutting through the assembled crowds, but he left before she finished. When the girl came out, she saw Sarika, smiled and came up to say hello. But instead of praising her, Sarika had told her that the *ga* in the *Todi* she had sung wasn't quite right — it was a *shruti* too high, since *Todi's ga* is lower than the regular *komal ga*. Sarika recoiled at the thought of her jealous reaction. All for him? She hated herself for her clinginess. Did she really understand him? There was that time when he had sulked for weeks on end and she had flapped helplessly like a fallen autumn leaf. She had gone to him, she had told him that the world didn't seem the same when he was cross.

'Go talk to Naushad,' he had said.

'Naushad!?'

'You sat on the AIR lawn talking to him for an hour. You talk to him in college. What does the world say, a young girl talking to an unknown man? Why are you lonely? Go talk to him.'

'AIR? That was so long ago, I don't even remember when. As for college, I talk to him only about music or musicians and their lives. How can you…?' How could Kirana sahib have said this? He loved her so much, seemed so possessive, in fact — telling her that apart from attending her class with Prasad sahib, she was to come only to his class — that at times she felt crushed by his tentacles. Why did he make that comment about Naushad? Kirana sahib had been smarting the whole time he had been her lover. Naushad! Naushad flattered her by showing respect for her talent and she talked to him obliquely about Kirana sahib. And Kirana sahib did not understand. Was he in reality a narrow-minded conservative who talked to her about the importance of expressing love freely only because it suited his purpose? Why did he make that comment when *she* showed an unfettered spirit? He had no right to assume that she would never talk to anyone but him.

Now that the paper had written about him, she hoped he needed sleeping pills like she did every time she had an amorous meeting with him. For the past two weeks, since the knock on the door in the midst of their love making, she had not been able to sleep at all without the blessed relief of Calmpose.

How we cling to those who hold out a dream. A fond memory. A piece of ourselves that we are loathe to lose. And so she had gone to college that day with excitement in her footstep, a quiver in her heart that two weeks of separation had once again created in her despite the distance at their parting. Time had diminished the fear of revelation that had so defined their latest interaction.

She resumed pacing. If she told her mother now that she wanted to cut off with Kirana sahib, Nirmala would subject her to an inquisition. Why? What had he done? Had he said something? Had he misbehaved with her? If she continued, she would still have to go upstairs to his room and meet him every day and college without him was a drag — she had no friends left. At the university, she had never had the time to invest in making friends and then her grades had fallen, which made her avoid everyone. Always top of her class, she had gone down steadily till she was embarrassed to say how poorly she fared. Nirmala and Ashwini stayed mum about her academic performance, thinking she was on her way to becoming a great artist, but that vision receded ever more into remoteness. They didn't fully understand that the college couldn't turn out artists. It was like mass media, spreading its message horizontally, not vertically. Kirana himself belonged only to the ranks of upper mediocrity. The best the college and Kirana could do was prepare her to be accepted as a student by the truly great.

How would she now deny herself to him? He might take it as a right, knowing she could go nowhere with her story. And she still had more than a year left at the music college. Maybe, just maybe, his brush with the police would leave him shaken long enough for her to finish eighth year. After all, what must he have told his wife? She smiled, despite herself. The neighbours in his alley must have walked by his place many times to catch a glimpse of him. If it was in the Hindi paper, which probably had a wider circulation in his neighbourhood than in hers, they must all know.

Maybe she could use his diminished status to avoid him at the college. She didn't have to go upstairs to meet him. Would he have the nerve to ask her why? He would still come to the house to teach, keeping the situation under wraps vis a vis Nirmala. Sarika felt better. Maybe she could keep her shameful affair with him a secret, after all.

Sarika heard voices in the drawing room. Her parents had returned from the wedding. She opened the door to her room and went out to meet them.

'Hello,' said Ashwini smiling.

'How was the wedding?' asked Sarika.

'Good,' said Ashwini.

'Did you stay for dinner?'

'Yes, of course,' said Nirmala smiling. 'We were the *baratees*.'

'Was the food good?' asked Sarika.

'Yes, but they had to scale down,' said Nirmala. 'The boy's mother was telling me that the girl's parents had to cut down on the number of guests that could stay for dinner because of the Emergency.'

'Why?' asked Sarika, only half interested.

'Because they require permits for everything — sugar, flour, electricity,' said Nirmala. 'They had to simplify the menu, too, lest somebody think they have number two money. We're already hearing of arrests made because a wedding was too lavish.'

Sarika nodded.

'Have you had dinner?' asked Nirmala.

'No, I didn't feel like it,' said Sarika.

'Why? Are you sick?' asked Nirmala, looking carefully at her.

'No, just tired. Sometimes everything gets too much,' she said in a soft, tired voice.

'Did the driver bring the paper out?' said Nirmala, turning to her husband.

'Yes,' said Ashwini. 'It's right here.'

Sarika's heart leapt. 'What paper?' The tiredness was gone from her voice.

'*Dainik Samachar* from last week,' said Ashwini.

'There's a story about the music college in it,' said Nirmala. Sarika sat down on the sofa. 'Apparently, two teachers were arrested in a vice den in Hazratganj,' she said, glancing at the paper again. 'A dance teacher and Gajendra. Isn't Gajendra the one who accompanies you in your performances?'

'Yes. Gajendra? He has five children and is so nice.'

'Gajendra and he's obviously not very nice,' said Nirmala.

'What was he doing in a vice den?' asked Sarika. And, she thought, what was Kirana sahib doing there?

'Playing the tabla, what else,' said Nirmala. 'To think so many young girls go to the music college and learn from these characters.'

'Ahmed told me about it, although he didn't say anything about Gajendra. Are they still in jail?'

'No,' said Nirmala. 'They were released.'

'Oh.'

'Though they shouldn't have been, the bastards.'

Sarika looked up sharply at her mother. Why didn't she mention Kirana sahib?

'If it hadn't been for Kirana sahib, they would still have been sitting in jail.'

'Kirana sahib?' asked Sarika in disbelief.

'Papa met the director of cultural affairs, and asked him about the story. Here read it for yourself,' she said, giving her the paper. Sarika took it from her mother and glanced at it. 'Papa heard the story just today from his P.A., who had saved the paper when he saw the music college staff were involved. The director told Papa that Kirana sahib had helped these men a lot. Because of the Emergency, no one would come out and stand guarantee for them. You see, they can come and get the guarantor if these men do something stupid again.'

Sarika read the story quickly. 'Amma,' she said sighing deeply, 'you know what Ahmed told me? He said that principal sahib had told him that he read in the paper that Kirana sahib had been arrested for singing in that vice den. He said he'd been released on bail but was probably too embarrassed to come to college and face everyone. I have been so upset all day.'

'You believed that?' asked Nirmala, laughing.

'But Ahmed said that principal sahib had read it in the papers' said Sarika, feeling a little foolish now. 'And Kirana sahib has been gone two weeks. Remember he hasn't been here in two weeks and we were wondering what happened to him? I didn't want to believe Ahmed, but it all fit together. So, where has he been these last two weeks?'

'His wife has been very sick,' said Ashwini. 'She's had a bad attack of the flu. For five days, her temperature didn't come down below one hundred and three degrees. Then, when her fever finally broke, Kirana sahib's youngest daughter came down with the fever. They had to put an ice cap to bring her temperature down; it's so much more dangerous in children. Mr. Singh was telling me it was very hard for Kirana sahib to manage. But despite all the trouble at home, he still went out to help his colleagues. Mr. Singh spoke very highly of Kirana sahib. He said, 'Kirana is a very good artist and human being. You are lucky to have your daughter learning from him.'

Sarika sank deep into the sofa. 'So, when will he be back in the college?' she asked at length.

'I'd say another day or two,' said Ashwini. 'Maybe tomorrow.'

23

Kirana sat bent over his attendance register behind his little desk, gave Sarika a wan smile as she walked into the empty classroom, and continued marking his roster.

'Sit down,' he said at length. 'Why are you standing?'

Sarika sat down on the platform. Kirana sahib closed his register and put it inside his desk.

'So,' he said, still hurting from her words from the last meeting. It was not that he didn't care. Didn't she know that? 'So, what can I do for you?'

Sarika hung her head and felt the tears rising. He sounded so formal.

'Master sahib,' she said. 'I am so sorry. I should never have spoken to you that way that time when you came to my house on the way to the AIR. It was wrong. Please forgive me.'

'What is there to forgive?'

'No, but I should never have,' she said.

'You said what you felt.'

Sarika was quiet.

'See, I was right,' he said. 'You said what you felt. You don't need to say you're sorry.'

Sarika looked down and tried to blink back her tears.

'What is there to say sorry about,' he continued. 'I have loved you like I've loved no other. Your feelings are different and that's fine.'

'Master sahib, please,' said Sarika, bursting into tears. 'Please don't talk like that. I love you, master sahib, I love you.'

He lowered his eyes.

'I love you, master sahib,' Sarika sobbed, unable to handle his silence. 'Please forgive me, master sahib.'

'Hush,' he said. 'Not so loud. What if someone were passing by and heard you? What would he think? What would the world think?'

'I don't care.'

'I do. I care so much about your reputation.' He got up slowly and shut and bolted the door. Coming back to her, he held her as she sobbed. 'Sarika, Sarika. It's okay. I will always love you, no matter what you say to me.'

'Promise?'

'Hm. How can love ever change? Your love for me may change as you go out into the world, but mine never will.'

In response, she clung to him and he cooed in her ear. Twenty minutes later, she came out of the room to see Mrs. Sinha standing outside the classroom. For a second Sarika saw on her face the all-knowing look that always pierced through every door and had today seen right into Kirana sahib's classroom. Then, Mrs. Sinha lowered her eyes. Sarika lowered hers and walked toward the staircase.

～

Kirana parked his scooter under the circular staircase to his house and ran up humming *Darbari*. At the top of the stairs, he stopped suddenly and tried to collect himself before ringing the bell. His unexpected tryst with Sarika at the college left him euphoric and amazed at how each union sharpened rather than dulled his appetite. His obsessive desire to become one with her staggered his senses with its force. The meeting earlier that afternoon had left him pleased and relaxed and eased the tension that had followed the last meeting. While the fear of discovery gnawed at his brain constantly, the whole new world that Sarika had opened to him made it impossible to stop. Sarika aroused a desire in him he had never before experienced, provided him an entree into the world of high bureaucracy he could barely envision, and offered him a chance to mold a phenomenal talent that would bring him fame as well. The complexity of his feelings left him flopping. How could he stop when he had caught a glimpse of the other side? His feeling for Surya was so simple by comparison — he was the provider and she offered him the stability of domesticity. But while the tension of the past weeks had been easy to blame on the Emergency, he did not want Surya to see his exhilaration today. She would ask and he would not be able to tell. Taking a deep breath, he rang the bell.

'Anything new at the college?' Surya asked Kirana as he slipped into his chappals and went into the kitchen.

'The most amazing thing. Mrs. Sinha came to see me today.'

'Is her husband out of jail?'

'Yes, thanks to Sarika's papa, who, by the way was telling me that the director of cultural affairs spoke very highly of me. He said that Sarika's family is lucky to be associated with me. Sarika's papa was thanking me and I said what are you saying, you embarrass me, I am the lucky one.'

'He said that?' she asked with a grin.

'Apparently. But Mrs. Sinha. Her husband's release is not what she came to tell me.'

'Let us sit and eat now,' said Surya, carrying the plate of *parathas* into the enclosed verandah that served as a dining room. Kalavati came running out of the bedroom to show her father a new pencil her mother had bought her that day. Kirana picked her up and sat her on his lap as he took a chair at the table.

'She came to tell me that her daughter's engagement is broken,' he said carefully. 'The daughter now has no prospects.'

'What happened?'

'Remember I told you Sinha sahib didn't let Achala marry the boy she wanted to? Finally, Achala caved under pressure and her parents forced an engagement to the son of a wealthy businessman. As luck would have it, when the story about Swati came out in the paper, these people sent word through a messenger saying that they wanted to break off the engagement. That was it. Over just like that.' He snapped his fingers.

'Couldn't Mr. or Mrs. Sinha do anything about it?'

'What could they do? The story was out in the paper. Everyone read it. Apparently, Sinha sahib tried to meet the boy's father to work something out, but he refused to even see him. How do you argue with a dead girl's diary?'

'To think that all this was happening to one of the girls at the college. They are all so young when they come to learn. You had a feeling years ago about it. I remember you wondered how she came to have such an expensive saree.'

'I had my doubts about her. She had an abortion and then principal sahib asked me to coach her for her AIR audition. I wanted to wriggle out of it, but I did teach her a couple of times. After that, thankfully, she stopped coming. I didn't have to face principal sahib either.'

'I remember. But how sad for Mrs. Sinha's Achala.'

'Mrs. Sinha said to me she would never forgive herself for opposing Achala's marriage to the boy she loved. The girl would have been happily married.'

'Mrs. Sinha has all her life to repent,' said Surya.

24

In Sarika's mind, the events of the past two months twirled round and round but she kept coming back to the starting point. If she was pregnant — when could it have happened? The day he came to her house? Or in his classroom all those weeks ago? And did it really matter when since she was all set to bring shame on her herself and her family?

Not knowing to whom she should turn, she decided to tell Kirana sahib. She peeked into his classroom and saw that he was in with two other teachers. Kirana saw her and smiled.

'Did you see today's paper? The *Lucknow Times*,' he asked.

'No. Someone else caught in a vice den?' she asked seriously.

The teachers laughed.

'No, no,' said Prasad sahib. 'Your name is in it. They covered founder's day and there are two lines about your performance. The critic speaks very highly of you. Congratulations.'

'Your blessings,' Sarika said, quickly going around the room and touching everyone's feet.

Prasad sahib held the paper out to her. She read it quickly.

'And now it's time to put our satin robes back in the box and go listen to principal sahib lecturing us on the declining state of Hindustani music,' said Sitaram Mishra with a mock sigh. He and Prasad sahib rose. Together, they left the room.

'Sit down, Sarika,' said Kirana. 'I'm very proud.'

Sarika remained standing.

'What's the matter?' What could make you so sad on such a happy day?

'I think I might be pregnant,' she said.

'How do you know?' he said. The smile fled his face.

She remained motionless.

'So what will you do?' he asked.

'I don't know what I'm supposed to do. What should I do? Maybe you can tell me,' she said simply.

'What can I tell you? Shut the door,' he said.

She came back and stood in the same spot.

'When did it happen?'

'I don't know.'

'Are you sure there's no mistake?'

She nodded.

'Then you must know when it happened.'

'It doesn't matter. I know I am. What should I do?' she asked.

'I don't know.' Kirana knew only one emotion at this time: Fear. Fear of losing his reputation. His dearly nurtured reputation would be gone. After all the praise that had come to him from the director of cultural affairs. To think that he should find himself in this mess in the only affair he had ever had. That too with the daughter of the home secretary. One word from him to the cultural secretary and Kirana would be finished. The teachers at the college, his wife, his associates at AIR flashed through his mind. No! His wife would be devastated. And then, there was Sarika. He had never intended to hurt her. 'I don't know what to tell you.'

'What do you mean?' she said. Her voice rose in alarm. 'There has to be something we can do about it.'

Petrified, Kirana's imagination presented him only with loss. In his pained state, heightened by fear, the world seemed like a giant trap put out to snare him. Loss of family, reputation, career, tuitions in respectable homes. How could he have been so rash, thinking the whole time he was

242

furthering his career through that of his student while at the same time discovering his soul? Men had always lost their fortunes over women they loved. He shuddered.

Another thought came to him: Would Sarika's father really say something to anyone given that his daughter's reputation was at stake? Wouldn't he try to hide this shame from the world? That, at least, would spare them both. It had been so easy to go through the affair with the belief that their mutual love made them come together. It was harder to carry that idea into the future. Everything assumed an inscrutable complexity. How was he to help Sarika? He couldn't marry her, nor could he take care of the child she carried. And how welcome would a bastard child be in the world? His child born of the woman he loved. As a government servant, it would be suicide for him to take her for an abortion to a government clinic, and he lacked the financial wherewithal to look for a secret, safe place. What was he to tell Sarika? At this moment, she sought him as a pillar of support that she could wrap herself around. But on him rested many other vines that Sarika would cause to wither away. A pained groan escaped his lips.

Sarika turned her head to say something, but stopped. His face had turned ashen, his lips were dry, as if the news had sucked the sap from his body. Leaning against the wall he let his shoulders slump, and faced with the prospect of losing his all, he looked like a cornered animal. She saw in a flash that his wife would never leave him, no matter what his crime. He had said over and over again, Do what you like, but in the eyes of the world you should look good. He would live by that credo. He had never loved her; he merely lusted after her. His eyes told her the state of his soul. She stared at him in revulsion.

'Coward,' she said out aloud. He bent lower into his desk. Another wave of revulsion came over her as she saw him cringe. She laughed a low, bitter, guttural laugh. 'Bloody coward.'

Outside the college gates, she paused before hopping onto a rickshaw to consider what directions to give to her rickshawman. She could go to the medical college and look for her brother, who would be either in his room or in the ward. What would she tell Ravi? She told the rickshawman to take her home.

'Back so early?' asked Nirmala cheerily. 'Look, Nisha is here.'

Sarika smiled at seeing her cousin.

'When did you come back from Moradabad?' she asked Nisha.

'Just this morning.'

'She's come here with good news,' said Nirmala smiling benevolently.

'Are you expecting?' asked Sarika.

'Yes. I'm two months pregnant. I just found out.'

A stone rolled over Sarika's heart. She sat down. 'Delivery? Here in Lucknow?'

'Yes. Better doctors here. Ravi,' Nisha said.

'So ready for motherhood?' asked Sarika, pretending to be herself, as her mother went into the kitchen to give instructions for dinner to the servant.

'Yes. Alok was saying it will mean a change in our love life,' Nisha said with a giggle.

'I guess.'

'What are you girls whispering?' asked Nirmala, as she came into the room.

'Nothing,' said Nisha giggling. 'I have to go now. My mother-in-law wants to take me somewhere.'

The three women walked to the gate. Nirmala hailed a rickshaw. She and Sarika waved to Nisha as she rode slowly off.

'That was a very short visit,' said Nirmala. They walked back inside. 'I'm so happy for her. I'll ring Veena and congratulate her.'

Sarika only half listened. Her heart pounded. She was probably two months pregnant, too, just like Nisha. How would she do it? How would she tell her mother? And then, once she had told her mother, what would happen? Would her mother put an end to her training in music? Would she be married off in a hurry? It didn't matter at this time, when every minute the baby was growing bigger. She sat down on the living room sofa.

'You're not attending class today?' asked Nirmala.

Sarika shook her head.

'Why?'

'Just like that.'

'Why, what's happened?'

244

Sarika shook her head. Was there a way to find out if she was pregnant, without first telling her mother? She didn't know where to go, what to do. A lady doctor would ask for her mother's permission. 'Amma?'

'Yes.'

'Nothing.'

Nirmala picked up her crochet needle and wound the wool on her finger.

'Amma, I think I might be pregnant,' she said quickly, softly.

Nirmala unwound the wool from her finger and put down the antimacassar she was so diligently creating.

'What makes you think that?'

'I think so.'

Nirmala picked up her crotchet and worked furiously. Too scared to move, Sarika dug her nails into her hands. She wished her mother would say something. Anything. This silence was pulverizing her. Where was Ramu? From the silence in the kitchen, she gathered he was running an errand.

'Who is the ...?' Nirmala started to ask, without looking up, then stopped as if the question were irrelevant, the answer too obvious. 'I should never have trusted him. How could I have been so blind?' To Sarika's dismay, long, silent tears rolled down her mother's cheeks as she crocheted, occasionally stopping to blow her nose into her handkerchief. After working frenetically for several minutes, she put down her knitting and sank deep into the sofa. Mother and daughter sat in silence.

'We will have to take you for an abortion. I will ring Papa and tell him to come home immediately. I will then send the driver to the medical college to ask Ravi to come home.'

'Can we not tell Papa?'

'How can we not tell Papa about such a big thing? We have to keep this a complete secret. I'm sure Papa will want to go and talk to the principal to have Kirana sahib suspended.'

'No!' said Sarika in a panic.

'Papa's anger will only hurt you. Nothing will happen to Kirana sahib. That is the way of the world. The men go scot-free.'

Her mother's anguished face drove a stake through Sarika.

'That is why girls have to be protected. I failed miserably.' She burst into tears again. After a few minutes, Nirmala stood up and left the room with slow heavy steps. Sarika heard her dialling her father's number.

25

Just as Sarika hurried down the stairs from Kirana's room, Naushad emerged from the male teachers' bathroom snuggled under the staircase. Sarika did not notice or care who lurked in the corridors at the college. Absorbed in her own terrifying thoughts, her one aim was to somehow wriggle out of her predicament.

But Naushad understood the betrayal that marked Sarika's face. He had seen that expression on innumerable women who visited his father's house after his grandfather passed away.

Naushad's father's routine included an afternoon nap. When Naushad came home from school, Mulayam Hasan would be asleep, waking up about 4 p.m. to a large group of people waiting for him in the living room. They would ask him to teach them, or their sons or daughters. Sometimes he would teach and then the production would assume the grandeur of a performance.

Naushad remembered once a young woman his father liked. He asked her to come for lessons. Naushad watched from behind the curtain. Noting the lust in his father's eyes, his head drooped in shame. The lessons started and Naushad watched his father's desire grow. His hand brushed past hers accidentally. Startled, she moved her hand away quickly. He did nothing for a few days. One day, as she played her violin, her saree fell from her shoulder, revealing her tight cotton blouse. Mulayam Hasan stopped teaching and stared unabashedly at her, until she stopped, too. Embarrassed, she flung her saree back over her shoulder with one quick movement. Over the weeks, as Naushad watched from behind the curtain, he saw a change had come in the woman. Her saree fell repeatedly from her shoulder and she let it lie on her lap for several seconds before restoring it to its rightful place. He noticed the change in her eyes, coquettishness supplanting bashfulness. Naushad knew then that the teacher-student relationship was over, to be replaced first by lust, then possessiveness, and finally, betrayal.

And now he saw that look etched on Sarika's face. As she made a beeline to the main entrance, Naushad hid behind one of the pillars in the corridor. Her questions to him from past conversations flashed through his mind and acquired a clarity that had so far been muddied with some doubt. He had partially understood the source of her questions, but had been unwilling to ascribe any act to her. Kirana's avoidance of him, too, took on a different meaning. It was not merely professional rivalry; Naushad threatened his masculinity. Unlike the common reaction to a divination such as this, Naushad did not gloat over the knowledge of Sarika's unfortunate secret. He knew Sarika would disappear from the college and he would never have a chance to tell her he understood.

Slowly, he took the few steps that separated him from his classroom. His students would not be coming for another half hour or so. Good. He always needed time to think. He shut the door and sat down again.

Somehow, Sarika's fate took him back to his own struggles, the blame for which he put squarely on his father's shoulders. If he had taken some time from his womanizing — true, his father's childhood had been warped due to endless hours of practice and little exposure to the real world, which made him capable of only physical relationships, but still he was a father — and if he had cared enough to raise his son in the musical tradition of the family, Naushad's story would have been different. His father never interfered with him, but did not demand excellence from him either. Naushad took a deep breath. Outside, the teachers and students came and went through the college gates. The teachers — Kirana, for instance — were no match for his father, yet they had their women. It wasn't the proportion of hours spent in the seclusion of practice to time spent in the real world that led to thinking of women in physical terms. One's ranking on the scale of musical ability mattered only in the amount of exposure one had to women. Kirana, with his great reputation as a thoroughly respectable family man had shown that beyond doubt. All human. Too human. He paced up and down his classroom. If he could somehow distance himself from the pain associated with his father...but how?

He felt better about being at the college, although even now he regarded it as a move to a reduced life. But college gave him a chance to be on stage by himself, away from his father, an artist in his own right, rather than as an accompanist to the great man. They still always judged him as his father's son, but maybe over time as he performed increasingly on his own they would look at his merits, his way of rendering a raga and base their judgments on his work alone without reference to his father. The students accepted him readily and loved both his work and the quality of his teaching.

In fact, he was revered as a teacher. That older lady in his class, who had picked up her violin three years ago after twenty years of marriage had put a stop to all music, soaked in every word he spoke. Under Naushad, she progressed rapidly. And then, just yesterday, she had brought a box of sweets for him because she had made the B-grade at All India Radio. She had done the unthinkable.

And he had been true to the family's tradition of teaching, of producing students who went out into the world and produced others. His grandfather, Riyasat, had students whom he taught for twenty, thirty years, who came back for more. In his later life, he took no more students. But there was one youth, who wanted to learn from him so much that he came and sat by the door to his house every day. Riyasat had told the boy's father that he would not take the boy, but his older son, Nafasat, would teach him. The father of the adolescent agreed, but the boy kept coming to the house. He sat patiently for hours on the two-foot wide verandah that kept out neither heat nor rain, listening to Riyasat doing his riyaz. Riyasat sent Nafasat out to explain to him; the boy stood up, nodded, and then sat down again, when Nafasat had gone into the house. For two months he came daily to the house, until one day during the monsoons, as he sat drenched and shivering on the ground, Riyasat could bear it no longer. He went out, brought him in, gave him a rag to dry himself, and began his lessons. Baiju Kingre was a well known violinist.

And maybe Naushad could keep up that tradition. Within the four walls of his classroom, he could be the ideal teacher — devoted, yet unattached. If that older lady could pass the AIR audition after just one year of learning from him, surely others would follow. His father's fame would elude him. That he knew. That had been one reason for coming to the college. But there was still a world outside of alcohol and women that could be his. He just had to bridge the gulf between emotional and intellectual understanding.

His father's use of alcohol was a contentious issue in the family. Riyasat hated it and as a child Naushad heard hot words exchanged between father and son. Mulayam justified alcohol by saying it was his second escape from the world, the first being music. But that statement assumed a nature so sensitive as to be incapable of coping with the harshness of the world. Certainly his father didn't possess that sensitivity. How could he, if he cast women aside without a thought, lashed out at competing artists, didn't think twice before trampling over someone? Alcohol was simply an escape from himself.

Kirana passed by his window and gave the faintest nod and Naushad found himself thinking once more of the event that had first triggered these thoughts in him. Whatever Kirana's involvement with Sarika, Naushad had shown himself in the year or so he had been at the college that he could face women without desiring them. Sarika, the prettiest, most talented, and intelligent girl at the college had sat and chatted with him many a time. He had been able to accept her and not revel in or gossip about her relationship. Would his cynicism about his father help him heal or simply take away his ability to view the world through innocent eyes?. As his wounds filled with positive experiences, maybe he would once again be able to give musicians a higher place in the romantic world. His own life would prove the presence of romance. He heard a knock at the door. 'Come in,' he said. It was time for class.

26

Sarika was home and in her bed. She remembered vaguely walking into her room on her brother's arm. As soon as her eyes fluttered open, her mother peered anxiously into them. Sarika tried to smile, but the drug forced her to close her eyes again. Through the thinning haze of Valium, she went over in her mind the humiliation of the procedure. Over and over again. The hurried meeting among Ashwini, Nirmala, and Ravi the day before; Ravi's and Nirmala's trip to the gynaecologist; the plan to take Sarika there at the break of day so no one would see her enter or leave; the promise of complete secrecy by the doctor who would not even use an assistant; then today, the frightening procedure itself — Sarika alone with the doctor in the operating room. Big bright lights. Local anaesthesia. The frightening instruments. The doctor's cool manner. No reassurance. No kind words. She had wished for someone by her side. In vain. Every detail of the past day was already etched in her memory; the haze merely made her drift in and out.

She turned to her mother. She had been crying again. Ravi stood by her side. Sarika raised her eyes to his angry face. He stepped forward and bent over her.

'Are you still cramping?' he asked gently.

She nodded and closed her eyes.

'The scoundrel,' he said. 'I'm going to skin him alive.'

'Hush, *beta*,' said Nirmala. 'Not now. You'll upset her more.'

'I told you I never trusted him. How dare he do this to her? How dare he!'

Nirmala put her hand on his arm.

'Amma,' he continued, 'you were always so strict about letting Sarika even talk to the neighbour's son across the wall. How did you let the blackguard enter the house? I told you I didn't like him the first time I set eyes upon him.'

Sarika opened her eyes. Her mother was crying again.

'Where's Papa?' asked Sarika.

'In the living room,' said Nirmala softly.

'He didn't go to the office today?'

'No. He wanted to stay home in case we needed him. We gave the driver and Ramu the day off because we didn't want any servants around. We don't want to arouse any suspicions.'

'Is Papa very mad, Amma?' asked Sarika.

'Hush.'

Sarika turned her head away from her mother. The ceiling fan whirred slowly and she counted the blades. He must be. Papa must be mad. He hadn't said anything to Sarika when Nirmala had told him the evening before, but she had let him down.

'Is the fan making you cold?' asked Ravi.

Sarika nodded. Ravi pulled a cotton blanket over her.

'I will come back in the evening after my rounds,' he said, patting her head. 'I will try to ring you in the afternoon.'

Sarika managed a weak smile as he left the room.

'How are you, *beta*?' asked Nirmala.

Sarika licked her dry lips.

'A sip of water?'

Sarika shook her head and closed her eyes.

'Papa...' began Sarika.

'Hush, don't worry about anything just now.'

Tears streamed down Sarika's face because Nirmala hadn't screamed at her. As if reading her mind, her mother took her hand in both of hers and gently stroked it.

'Do you know why I got married at sixteen?'

Sarika shook her head.

'Because my music teacher was trying to lock eyes with me. My aunt, remember the old spinster who used to sit in on the lessons, saw and immediately reported the matter to my parents. All the elders of the family convened, shamed me, and told me I'd be married right away to the first man who came by the house. Fortunately for me, your Papa's father happened to visit at the time. Within a week we were engaged. Of course, once I was married, everyone forgot the unfortunate incident.'

Through her tears, Sarika looked at her mother in disbelief.

'Does Papa know?'

'No.'

'Why? You didn't do anything wrong or anything at all, for that matter.'

'At first I felt ashamed and couldn't tell him. Sometimes shame has little to do with the commission of an act. Other people's perceptions, your own thoughts can make you feel a certain way. Years of keeping it to myself made it hard for me to come out and say it. Then, after a few years, it became irrelevant and too much time had passed for me to bring it up.'

Sarika nodded. As she listened to her mother's words, she debated whether to ask her if Kirana sahib might feel guilty. She felt somehow that the guilt was all hers. Maybe later. It was too soon; the wound was too raw.

'Is that why you didn't yell at me?' Sarika asked instead.

Nirmala nodded.

'Did you love your music teacher?' Sarika asked, surprised at her own boldness.

'No, now that I think of it. But at that time, never exposed to a man not from the family, I didn't know how I felt.'

'But you were always so strict with me, so conservative.'

'Yes, because I knew better than anyone what could go wrong. I had to protect you in every way. A hurt woman makes an overprotective mother. Yet look where it landed you. All that old-fashioned upbringing didn't save you.'

Sarika winced.

'There seems to be no way around it,' said Nirmala. 'As long as men teach young, ambitious girls, this will happen, no matter how close a watch you keep. To think this was happening under my nose...'

Sarika's breathing quickened.

'Yet it is not incomprehensible that this should happen,' continued Nirmala. 'When the artist arouses your senses through his work, why not the desire for the carnal? It is also a sense tied in with the others. And we say an artist is good in proportion to the amount of emotion he arouses in us by playing with our senses. This is the ultimate arousal.'

'This and not the spiritual?'

'Rare.'

For several seconds, the only sound in the room was the whirring of the fan.

'But Swati died as a result of the carnal,' Sarika said. 'She never had a chance to let the world judge her talents. The only difference between her situation and mine was that there was no one to protect her. She died because she was alone and poor.'

Nirmala listened attentively. Sarika fell silent and closed her eyes. Both she and Swati had fallen for the easier path of carnality. Whatever Swati's motivation, Sarika had allowed herself to be lulled into believing that she was on the path to the spiritual. Spirituality could be achieved, though, as the artist of divinity, with all her quirks, had shown all too clearly. Sarika had seen the earthly; she now had to find her own divinity.

'Are you going to marry me off, too, like you were?' she asked Nirmala.

'Your situation is different. You won't get someone like your Papa.'

'I know,' Sarika said.

Nirmala peered into her eyes. 'But don't worry about all that just now. Recover first.'

The room fell into silence. After several minutes, Nirmala rose and drew the curtains from the window. 'I am going to make myself a cup of tea,' she told Sarika. 'Would you like one?'

Epilogue

The sun filtered through the papaya leaves and onto Sarika's listless hands resting on her writing table. The Valium haze had long lifted, the cramping ceased, and the season was moving toward change. Sarika looked out the window into the clear day and saw a rerun of images.

Her life as she knew it had ended — her fall would eventually become known. Young, ambitious, independent, she found herself in a milieu that none in her family knew or understood. The future challenged her, the past pained her, the present left her numb. Kirana sahib's love proved mutable; he had betrayed her.

The answer lay in looking ahead. It was at her grandma's funeral that her parents had told her that after every death comes rebirth, after decay, regeneration. If that was true, could she be reborn after her downfall?

It would not be easy. There would be no path, save what she tread. None in her circle had gone there. None had left the known for the uncharted, the love for the searching, the respectable for the dubious. But therein lay her salvation — the consummation of her desire to become a musician. And so she would do it.

The sun burned stronger. She moved away from her desk and gazed at her tanpura. Yes, she would urge her parents to find a famous musician to be her teacher. Man, woman, it didn't matter now. Nothing remained to protect. Her career, at least, would be brilliant.

And maybe one day she'd find a man who saw her fall as the other side of accomplishment.

Glossary

abhinaya	:	in dance, showing emotion through acting
bandish	:	a composition set to a beat
baratees	:	members of bridegroom's party
bela	:	a type of flower
charitraheen	:	characterless
choti	:	braid
dhurrie	:	a heavy cotton rug
drut	:	a composition rendered in fast tempo
gayaki	:	a form of singing. In instrumental music, it means the mimicking of the vocal style and is considered superior to the instrumental style
gayatri mantra	:	a prayer asking for light
geet	:	a song, usually in Hindi
gharanedar	:	one who comes from a family of performers
ghungrus	:	ankle bells, usually worn while performing Indian dances
guru shishya	:	teacher-student
haazir hoon	:	I am present
halwai	:	a sweet-meat maker
harshringar	:	a small white flower with a vermilion stalk
havan	:	a Hindu purifying (yajna) ritual/prayer to propitiate deities using fire as a sacred medium.
huzoor	:	gentleman
janab	:	gentleman
kand	:	incident
khayal	:	a genre of North Indian classical singing. The word comes from Persian/Arabic language meaning imagination
khairiyat	:	well-being/welfare
kotha	:	A place where courtesans danced and sang usually to entertain the aristocracy

maal	:	goods
maya	:	a temporal world
mehfil	:	assembly
mishri	:	sugar-candy
mubarak	:	congratulations
nankhatai	:	puffed cookie
raga	:	(in Indian-music) a pattern of notes having characteristic intervals, rhythms and embellishments used as a basis for improvisation
riyaz	:	practice
roli	:	sacred red powder
samagri	:	a mixture of herbs, and root bark offered as oblation in havan
satiya	:	a sacred mark
shanti path	:	a prayer ceremony for peace, usually for the departed
shareef	:	noble/honourable
shringar	:	in dance, dressing up
sukoon	:	peace
svaha	:	let this oblation be for our happiness
taar saptak	:	higher octave
tihai	:	one-third
teej	:	a Hindu festival
vandana	:	salutation
vilambit	:	a composition rendered in slow temp

❑❑❑